Introducing Stylistic Analysis

In loving memory of my dad

INTRODUCING STYLISTIC ANALYSIS
Practising the Basics

Gibreel Sadeq Alaghbary

EDINBURGH
University Press

Edinburgh University Press is one of the leading university presses in the UK. We publish academic books and journals in our selected subject areas across the humanities and social sciences, combining cutting-edge scholarship with high editorial and production values to produce academic works of lasting importance. For more information visit our website: edinburghuniversitypress.com

© Gibreel Sadeq Alaghbary, 2022

Edinburgh University Press Ltd
The Tun – Holyrood Road
12(2f) Jackson's Entry
Edinburgh EH8 8PJ

Grateful acknowledgement is made for permission to reproduce material previously published elsewhere. Every effort has been made to trace the copyright holders, but if any have been inadvertently overlooked, the publisher will be pleased to make the necessary arrangements at the first opportunity.

Typeset in 11/13pt Baskerville by
Cheshire Typesetting Ltd, Cuddington, Cheshire

A CIP record for this book is available from the British Library

ISBN 978 1 4744 7716 1 (hardback)
ISBN 978 1 4744 7717 8 (paperback)
ISBN 978 1 4744 7718 5 (webready PDF)
ISBN 978 1 4744 7719 2 (epub)

The right of Gibreel Sadeq Alaghbary to be identified as the author of this work has been asserted in accordance with the Copyright, Designs and Patents Act 1988, and the Copyright and Related Rights Regulations 2003 (SI No. 2498).

CONTENTS

List of Figures and Tables	vi
Preface	viii
Acknowledgements	xvi
Transcription Conventions	xviii

Part I From the Study of Style

1	Style and Stylistics	3

Part II Into the Practice of Stylistics

2	Formalist Analysis of Poetry	25
3	Functionalist Analysis of Poetry	35
4	Critical Linguistic Analysis of Fiction	42
5	Feminist Analysis of Fiction	53
6	Pragmatic Analysis of Drama	63
7	Cognitive Analysis of Linguistic Humour	76
8	Multimodal Analysis of Advertisements	87
9	Critical Stylistic Analysis of Political Discourse	100
10	Corpus Analysis of Online Journalism	111

Part III Extension

11	The Story of Stylistics	125
	Conclusion	147

Answer Key	153
Glossary	178
References	188
Index	197

FIGURES AND TABLES

Figures

1.1	The way language can change the effect of a text	5
8.1	Dettol advertisement	90
8.2	United Way Movement advertisement (danger)	93
8.3	Advil advertisement	96
8.4	United Way Movement advertisement (homeless)	97
10.1	Collocational behaviour of *Islamic* (range −3 to 3) in English Web 2018 (enTenTen18)	116
10.2	Collocational behaviour of اسلامي (*Islamic*) (range −3 to 3) in Arabic Web 2012 (arTenTen12)	117
10AK.1	Collocational behaviour of *Islamic* (range −1 to 1) in English Web 2018 (enTenTen18)	173
10AK.2	Word Sketch of *terrorist* in English Web 2018 (enTen Ten18)	174
10AK.3	Comparison of the collocational behaviour of *good* in the written academic and spoken transcripts subcorpora of the British National Corpus (BNC)	175

Tables

1.1	Regional dialects	6
1.2	Social class dialects	6
1.3	Ethnic dialects	7
1.4	Temporal dialects	7
1.5	Language variation according to tenor	8
1.6	Differences between informal and formal writing styles	9
1.7	Differences between speech and writing	9
1.8	Deviation from language and register norms	13
1.9	Repetition and parallelism	14
1.10	Morphological deviation	15

1.11	Syntactic deviation	16
1.12	Semantic deviation	16
1.13	Graphological deviation	17
1.14	Discoursal deviation	18
4.1	Categorisation of expressions of modality in the extract	47
5.1	Verbal processes involving Offred	57
5.2	Verbal processes involving Nick	58
5.3	Reference to Nick's body parts	59
6.1	Analysis of turn-taking in the extract from *King Lear*	69
6.2	Analysis of speech acts in the extract from *King Lear*	69
9.1	Transitivity and agency in Obama's statement on Tunisia	105

PREFACE

Introducing stylistics

If you are an English learner meeting stylistics for the first time, this textbook will familiarise you with the basic terms and key concepts in this fast-developing field. And if you are taking a stylistics course and you need help on analysing texts, you will find here a step-by-step guide to making stylistic analyses of different text types using different stylistic frameworks. In writing this textbook, I assumed that you have little familiarity with stylistic terminology and little experience with stylistic analysis.

Stylistics is defined as 'a method of textual interpretation in which primacy of place is given to *language*' (Simpson [2004] 2014: 3; original emphasis). There are four constituents of this definition that merit attention. These are: language, textual, interpretation, and method. When we use language, we consciously, and unconsciously, make linguistic choices. We select certain words or expressions from a pool of available options, and we favour certain grammatical structures over others in structuring our messages. These lexical selections and grammatical patterns constituting the linguistic form of our texts serve to index the 'meaning' as well as functional significance of the texts. In other words, our linguistic choices act as a point of entry to the interpretation of our texts.

For stylisticians, interpretation starts with the words on the page. It is essentially a text-based process. Stylistics has traditionally, and conventionally, been concerned with analysis of language. Recent developments in stylistics, including some trends in cognitive stylistics and the growing sub-field of multimodal stylistics, suggest that the discipline has continued to develop by focusing upon the cognitive processes underlying reading and interpretation and upon semiotic modes other than words. However, the text remains an essential component in these frameworks, and remains, as it has always been, at the heart of most other trends in stylistic research. This explains Simpson's choice of the words 'textual interpretation' in the definition of stylistics ([2004] 2014: 3).

The last significant constituent of the definition is 'method'. Since its early days in the first half of the twentieth century, stylistics has developed analytical frameworks by drawing on concepts, insights, and theories from modern linguistics in particular and from other fields such as literary criticism and psychology in general. Advances in systemic functional linguistics (SFL), for example, have informed functionalist stylistics, theories of pragmatics have inspired pragmatic stylistics, and insights from cognitive sciences have led to the development of cognitive stylistics. The result of this point of confluence has been a plethora of stylistics trends and research avenues, each with its own theoretical underpinnings, methodological frameworks, and analytical objectives.

Stylistics today is not only a coherent sub-discipline of linguistics but a well-established field of research. Its object of study is style, which includes authorial styles and text styles (Short [1996] 2014: 326–53). Analysis of authorial style includes, for example, identifying distinguishing linguistic features characteristic of the writings of a particular author. This involves identification of the effect of non-linguistic variables, such as age, gender, education, and so on, on authorial style, and this sort of analysis may be carried out for the purpose of attributing a text or group of texts to their original author (e.g. Evans 2018) or in order to enable us to 'write pastiches and parodies' (Short [1996] 2014: 327).

While analysis of authorial style is an established research track in stylistics (e.g. see Love and Burrows 1998; Hoover 2007; Craig 2004; Evans 2018), the more immediate concern of mainstream stylistics and this textbook is analysis of text style. This refers to the study of the way textual choices index a text's overall meaning and effect by accounting for why a particular word or expression has been selected from among a range of possible options and why a particular structure has been chosen. The bulk of stylistics research and publications in the past seventy or so years is concerned with analysis of text style (e.g. see Halliday 1971; Widdowson 1992; Simpson 1993; Mills 1995; Short [1996] 2014; Ross 1998; Wilson and Sperber 2004; Black 2006; Leech 2008; Jeffries 2010; Mahlberg 2014; Gibbons and Whiteley 2018).

Aims of the textbook

Stylistics is a vibrant and diverse discipline. Early work in the field in the 1960s and 70s developed 'from interdisciplinary contact between linguistics and literary criticism' (Gibbons and Whiteley 2018: 4). This interdisciplinarity has always been at the heart of the discipline, with existing analytical frameworks continually tested and new ones constantly emerging from the contact with modern linguistics and other related disciplines, such as cognitive science and cognitive psychology. Stylistics has diversified considerably since its inception and will surely continue to evolve. This makes it difficult, almost impossible, to offer comprehensive coverage of all the stylistic trends within the narrow confines of a single book.

The aims of this textbook are therefore inevitably limited. It aims to introduce foundation terms and concepts in a progressively developing field and to guide you through making stylistic analyses of different text types using nine stylistic frameworks with an overall functional and pragmatic orientation. These limitations are unavoidable, given the ever-expanding scope of the discipline, and the characteristics of the target readership. This distinctive outlook makes the textbook different from existing introductions to stylistics.

Jeffries and McIntyre's *Stylistics* introduces 'theoretical questions about the nature and scope of the subject via some of the questions that [they] thought *new researchers* might ask' (2010: xiii; my emphasis). It also introduces methodological issues in functionalist, pragmatic, and cognitive stylistic research. The authors' aim is that the book offers 'a statement of a field reaching maturity in the early part of the twenty-first century' and they hope that it will 'encourage *future researchers* to continue developing a rich field which has come so far since the Russian formalist school of early last century' (2010: xiii; my emphasis).

Another important introduction to the field is Paul Simpson's *Stylistics: A Resource Book for Students* ([2004] 2014). The book introduces key concepts and methodological approaches in stylistics, provides activities for students to apply the concepts and analytical tools to the analysis of mainly literary texts, and offers 'a wide-ranging selection of readings by some of the best known stylisticians in the world' ([2004] 2014: viii).

The third textbook to consider is a more recent publication. Gibbons and Whiteley's *Contemporary Stylistics: Language, Cognition, Interpretation* (2018) discusses choice at the different levels of language in considerable detail before making stylistic analyses using different analytical frameworks. In seeking to deliver 'a state-of-the-art picture of what stylistics looks like in the early twenty-first century', the book 'brings together both traditional and well-established ideas in stylistics and relatively newer cognitively informed ideas' (2018: 6). The volume includes functionalist, pragmatic, cognitive, multimodal and corpus stylistic frameworks. Throughout the book, the authors focus 'predominantly on *literary texts written in the modern and contemporary period* – from the twentieth century to the present day' (2018: 6; my emphasis).

Jeffries and McIntyre (2010) speaks to 'new researchers' and targets a more advanced readership than do the other two textbooks. Simpson ([2004] 2014) is a 'resource book for students' that covers key concepts and includes key readings in the area. Its description of stylistic frameworks, however, is less comprehensive than that in Gibbons and Whiteley (2018). While covering many of the prominent frameworks in the stylistics landscape, Gibbons and Whiteley (2018) focuses only on literary texts.

This textbook is different from these publications in terms of aims and scope. It speaks to less advanced students and is more practice-oriented than research-based. The intended audience is first year undergraduates of language and literature who are new to stylistics. It is also intended for more advanced undergraduates for whom English is a second or foreign language and who are coming to stylistics from different backgrounds. In these contexts, students are not well served by the existing textbooks, which they find hard to digest for three reasons. First, the prescribed textbooks make assumptions of previous linguistic knowledge instead of offering it. Second, textbook authors present interesting stylistic analyses but do little to guide students through the process and foster students' independence. Third, some textbooks focus, and rightly so, on the more recent cognitively informed stylistic trends, which require familiarity of cognitive concepts and models. This has the effect of doubling the demands on those students who are still learning language and coping with the demands of language analysis.

The present textbook has been designed to support students' engagement with stylistic concepts and enable independent stylistic analysis. It does not assume previous linguistic knowledge; it offers it wherever needed. In the course of the chapters, when a concept emerges that requires defining in non-technical English, it is highlighted in **BOLD SMALL CAPS** and defined in the Glossary. The book also has a reassuring approach in the presentation of the stylistic frameworks. It suggests checklists of analysis and offers sample analyses before asking students to carry out their own analyses. The activities for practice also offer hints for analysis that are meant to offer guided practice while allowing students to work independently and take responsibility for their own learning. Finally, the selection of stylistic trends with an overall functionalist and pragmatic focus is appropriate for the target students. These trends are more directly language-based than, say, text worlds and blending theory, thereby capitalising on students' interest in language and familiarity with language analysis, especially in foreign language contexts.

This textbook is also different in terms of scope. It offers a wider coverage, covering traditional and text-based as well as more recent and multimodal trends of stylistics. This wide perspective is also a feature of Gibbons and Whiteley (2018) but I add to this wide coverage a range in variety of text-types to analyse. I include for discussion and stylistic analysis extracts from canonical literary texts, such as 'Wants' by Philip Larkin, Margaret Atwood's *The Handmaid's Tale*, and William Shakespeare's *King Lear*. I also use non-canonical literary texts, such as 'Half an Hour After' by the Australian poet Mark O'Connor, and 'Indian Women' by the Indian writer Shiv K. Kumar. In addition, you will find non-literary texts such as short political statements on the Arab Spring by Barack Obama, multimodal advertisements, and corpora, in two languages, made of texts collected from the internet.

Structure

The book is structured in three parts. Part I includes one chapter that focuses on style (in language) and stylistics. This chapter sets out the foundational concepts in the area, such as style as choice, aspects of language variation (dialect and register), deviation from norms at the different levels of language organisation, and the concept of foregrounding – the psychological effect of linguistic deviation, repetition, or parallelism. The chapter also introduces key concepts in language analysis, such as morphemes, phrases, and clauses, and relates them to the relevant branches of linguistics, such as morphology, syntax, and semantics.

Having outlined the key terms and ideas in the field, Part II presents stylistic analyses of different text types. In Chapter 2, I present a 'traditional' formalist stylistic analysis of a non-canonical poem by the Australian poet Mark

O'Connor. I consider the way the foregrounded textual choices, at different levels of language, together produce a coherent interpretation of the poem. Chapter 3 offers a functionalist stylistic analysis of another non-canonical poem by an Indian writer. I analyse the way patterns of transitivity and other textual choices serve to textually construct Indian women as powerless and lacking agency. In Chapters 4 and 5, I turn to fiction. Chapter 4 examines the way ideology and perspective are carried by modality and the modes of narration in an extract from the epistolary novel *Salmon Fishing in the Yemen*. In this chapter, I use analytical concepts from critical linguistics. In Chapter 5, I use a feminist stylistic framework to analyse an extract from Margaret Atwood's *The Handmaid's Tale*. I concentrate particularly on how naming strategies, sex-specific pronouns, transitivity options, and the fragmentation of the body parts are used to textually construct females in the world of the novel. Chapter 6 focuses on drama. Using the pragmatic stylistic framework, I illustrate how power relations between characters are played out in dramatic conversations. The chapter selects for analysis an extract from Shakespeare's *King Lear*.

In the other four chapters, I analyse non-literary texts. Chapter 7 is on linguistic humour. In this chapter, I offer a cognitive theoretical account of communication in a number of jokes by examining the way the joke teller, using linguistic choice at different levels of language, exploits the recipient's cognitive tendency to maximise relevance in order to create humour. In Chapter 8, I move on to multimodal advertising texts. I use pragmatic stylistic categories to analyse the verbal aspects of the adverts, and Kress and van Leeuwen's 'grammar of visual design' ([1996] 2006) to analyse the way visuals contribute to the overall message and effect of the adverts. Chapter 9 takes us back to mode of wording. In this chapter, I analyse political discourse for the way it naturalises ideologies and ideological evaluations. For this purpose, I make use of the ten conceptual functions making up the toolkit of critical stylistics. In the last chapter in this part, Chapter 10, I draw on corpus methods to compare the representation of religion in international and regional online journalism.

Chapter 11 in Part III is the final chapter. It tells the century-long story of stylistics since the formalist days in the early decades of the twentieth century. The aim of this presentation is to extend students' knowledge in the area by positioning the concepts and frameworks introduced in the previous two parts along a timeline of developments in the field since its early days. The chapter relates these concepts and frameworks to the relevant trends in stylistics, and demonstrates the relationship between stylistics and allied fields, such as literary criticism. My choice of the noun 'story', rather than, say, 'history', to represent the development of stylistics is driven by two main considerations. First, the presentation does not, indeed cannot, cover all turns in the history of the discipline. Second, and more importantly, early trends in stylistics, such as formalist stylistics, have not been at all superseded by more recent developments. The formalist concept of foregrounding, for example, has, ever since its introduction, always been central to most stylistic frameworks across the landscape.

The book ends with a brief Conclusion that revisits some of the classic debates about the usefulness of stylistics, especially in relation to the study of literature.

The Conclusion offers a short account of the way stylistics has reinvented itself in response to these attacks and to theoretical and methodological advances in the study of language and language use. The limitations of coverage in the book are also explained and justified. I conclude by redirecting you to further references you can use in exploring the interests that I hope you will have developed after reading the book.

Features

A major concern throughout the textbook is to provide support, or scaffolding, in order to ensure that you have acquired key stylistic concepts and the textual analytical skills that are transferable to unseen texts. When you are ready to carry out stylistic analyses on your own, the support is gradually withdrawn and you are left to engage with the texts independently of the teacher.

In order to achieve this target, the book is divided into small and manageable chapters. Chapter layouts have also been designed carefully in order to guide you through the new terrain. Each chapter in the book begins with an overview and introduction to the chapter that tell you what to expect. This is followed by an outline of the nature of communication in the genre selected for analysis and an outline of the stylistic framework to be used in analysing the text(s). Prior to the presentation of the text and analysis, I offer a checklist of categories to enable you to replicate the analysis on the texts suggested for further practice at the end of each chapter. The checklists are made up of questions that offer a step-by-step guide through the different stages. The text is presented first (for ease of reference) and the analysis follows.

Each chapter contains, or closes with, a number of *Do it yourself* boxes that offer a set of small, manageable tasks to allow you, ideally in discussion with others, to reflect upon the ideas in the chapter, and to allow the teacher to check understanding before proceeding to the next topic. Each activity is followed by *Hints* to guide you through the task and enable you to stand on your own. The activities are presented in boxes that are numbered serially in each chapter. I also suggest answers to these activities in the *Answer Key*, which I would encourage you to consult only after you have responded to the tasks on your own. It is expected that your responses vary from the author's. Each chapter also recommends a list of key publications to further your knowledge of the theory and practice of stylistics. In the course of the chapters, when a new concept is introduced, it will be highlighted and defined in the Glossary. The book closes with an index of key stylistic concepts.

Scope

Part I of the textbook covers basic concepts in stylistics, namely, style, choice, dialect, register, deviation, repetition, parallelism, and foregrounding. This stylistic terminology is needed to come to grips with the hands-on stylistic analyses offered in the second part of the textbook. Part II uses nine stylistic frameworks, with an overall functional and pragmatic orientation, in the analysis of language choice in seven different genres, namely, poetry, fiction, drama, linguistic humour, advertising, political discourse, and online journalism.

The stylistic frameworks selected are listed below with a brief, and certainly not comprehensive, explanation of the nature of each framework, with a special focus on its application to the genre selected for analysis. The nine frameworks are:

- formalist, which focuses on the way deviations, parallelisms, and more conventional choices foreground meanings and contribute to a coherent interpretation (in poetry)
- functionalist, which examines the use of patterns of transitivity and agency to represent human experience (in poetry)
- critical linguistic, which investigates the expression of ideological position using modality and narration (in narrative fiction)
- feminist, which explores the way lexical, clausal, and discourse patterns encode gender differences and power relations (in narrative fiction)
- pragmatic, which reflects on the role of turn management, the maxims of conversation, speech acts, and politeness strategies in representing characters and constructing relations (in drama)
- cognitive, which involves an account of optimal relevance in communication and its exploitation for humorous effect (in jokes)
- multimodal, which combines pragmatic analysis of verbal texts with analysis of the visual material, including the construction of meaning, the positioning of viewer and the placement of visual (in print advertisements)
- critical stylistic, which uses established textual-conceptual tools to problematise the naturalisation of contested ideologies (in political texts)
- corpus stylistic, which draws on corpus linguistics tools to expose ideological representation and attitudes in electronically stored collections of texts (in online journalism).

As evident from the list above, the nine stylistic trends selected have an overall functional and pragmatic outlook. The exclusion of other, more recent, frameworks, possibly more popular with researchers, detracts from the coverage, but it is a welcome trade-off, given the target readership, the introductory nature of the textbook, and, of course, the ever-expanding scope of the discipline.

Part III of the textbook maps the terrain by taking the reader through the journey of stylistics from the days of Russian formalism at the start of the twentieth century to recent twenty-first-century developments such as multimodal stylistics and corpus stylistics.

How to use the textbook

This textbook, as the title suggests, aims at sensitising students to textual analysis. It adopts a practical approach and has been designed to give you a hands-on experience of stylistic analysis. I have designed it primarily for use in the classroom. The structure and the sequencing of material make it possible to use it in two ways. It may be viewed as a 'traditional' textbook, and used in class sequentially straight through from beginning to end. The presentation of stylistic frameworks to reflect the historical development of the field is in line with this approach. Alternatively, and given that each chapter is self-contained, the textbook offers teachers the flexibility of presenting chapters in the order that suits the structure of the course they are teaching, and of selecting chapters to integrate them with other material in the context in which it is used. Accordingly, it may be used as a textbook for an undergraduate stylistics course, or as a recommended reading either for practice in stylistic analysis during class or at home (Chapters 2 to 10), to offer an introduction to style and stylistics (Chapter 1), or to offer an overview of the 'story' of stylistics (Chapter 11).

Origins

This book has its origins in the stylistics courses I have taught and co-taught over the past twelve years in undergraduate and graduate contexts in Yemen, India, and Saudi Arabia. During these years, the prescribed textbooks for my stylistics courses have been interesting to me, but less interesting to my students. 'The analysis is good but how do I do it myself?', 'We need more practice exercises', and 'Isn't there a user-friendlier textbook?' are some of the students' reactions to the prescribed textbooks. The present book is my answer to students' concerns in my classes, and beyond. It is a 'how-to-do' textbook, offering appropriately worded analyses and carefully structured practice activities so the students can see how the findings have been arrived at, and replicate the analytical procedure on previously unseen texts.

Gibreel Sadeq Alaghbary
March 2021

ACKNOWLEDGEMENTS

The process of writing this book has considerably changed the way I teach stylistics. I am more aware now that students would love to see through the process as much as they enjoy the final product. For this reason, I would like to acknowledge the important role of my students in the production of this textbook. I have trialled earlier versions of the analyses and practice activities with successive classes, and their feedback has been substantial in giving the book its current shape. In particular, I would like to thank the students on different stylistics courses at Taiz University and the students on the 'ENG 462 Stylistics' module at Qassim University for their stimulating discussions on earlier drafts of the analyses and activities.

The book has been long in the making due to several reasons. Changing jobs, moving house, and resettling in a new country have not been as disruptive as has been the Covid-19 pandemic. Because of the lockdown, and the subsequent restrictions on movement and social activity, I had to work from home and so did everyone else in the family. It was very difficult to meet deadlines when children needed extra attention and support to avoid the damaging effects of the pandemic on academic performance and mental health.

During this uncertain time, the editorial team at Edinburgh University Press helped me stay focused and on track. Laura Williamson, in particular, showed increasing interest in the book over the course of its development. I am especially grateful for her patience, enthusiasm, and unwavering support. I also owe a deep sense of gratitude to Sam Johnson whose keen interest and dynamism enabled me to stay on schedule and navigate my way through the challenge of copyright clearance. Thanks also to Richard Strachan for his assistance at earlier stages of the manuscript preparation. The anonymous reviewers of the book have provided invaluable feedback on the many versions leading up to the current one. Their constructive criticisms of earlier drafts and their comments on the manuscript as it was being prepared and revised have fed directly into the final version and inspired the present layout and coverage. Thank you.

I am obviously in debt to all the researchers in stylistics who have enriched the profile of the discipline over the years and contributed to our understanding of style in relation to textual choices and extra-textual processes. Informal conversations with colleagues and fellow researchers have also been eye openers. I am grateful to my friends and colleagues Prof Abdelfattah Mofath and Dr Ahmad Alsamawi for their generous support and advice, and to my student, now colleague, Dr Ohood Alnakeeb for proofreading an earlier draft of the book and for the perceptive comments on the analysis of fiction.

My family deserves special words of thanks. My wife, and colleague, Dr Thikra K. Ghalib, has had to proofread the many draft chapters. I would like to thank her for believing in me and for the valuable chapter-by-chapter feedback and comments. Thanks also to my children, Malak, Noor, Ahmad, and Sama, who gave up their rights to recreational trips and to dining out on many weekends so that I might make progress and meet deadlines.

While some extracts in the book are included in accordance with fair use, the author and the publisher are grateful to the following individuals and publishers for permission to reproduce copyright material:

The Australian poet Mark O'Connor for permission to publish his poem 'Half an Hour After'.

Harvard University Press for permission to publish extracts from 'The Brain is Wider than the Sky' by Emily Dickinson from THE POEMS OF EMILY DICKINSON: VARIORUM EDITION, edited by Ralph W. Franklin, Cambridge, Mass.: The Belknap Press of Harvard University Press, Copyright © 1998 by the President and Fellows of Harvard College. Copyright © 1951, 1955 by the President and Fellows of Harvard College. Copyright © renewed 1979, 1983 by the President and Fellows of Harvard College. Copyright © 1914, 1918, 1919, 1924, 1929, 1930, 1932, 1935, 1937, 1942 by Martha Dickinson Bianchi. Copyright © 1952, 1957, 1958, 1963, 1965 by Mary L. Hampson.

Faber and Faber Ltd for permission to publish extracts from 'Wants' by Philip Larkin.

The Orion Publishing Group for permission to publish extracts from *Salmon Fishing in the Yemen* by Paul Torday.

While every effort has been made to contact the copyright holders, it has not always been possible to identify or trace them. The publisher will be pleased to address any other copyright queries or omissions and include those on reprinting.

TRANSCRIPTION CONVENTIONS

The International Phonetic Association (IPA) symbols in the following two charts are used in the textbook, where necessary, to identify consonant and vowel sounds. Any other conventions used in the textbook are explained locally.

Consonants

[p] **p**en
[b] **b**ook
[k] **c**at
[g] **g**oat
[t] **t**ree
[d] **d**oor
[θ] **th**ink
[ð] **th**is
[f] **f**lower
[v] **v**an
[ʃ] **sh**oe
[tʃ] **ch**eese
[ʒ] gara**ge**
[dʒ] **J**une
[m] **m**an
[n] **n**ose
[ŋ] si**ng**
[s] **s**un
[z] **z**oo
[l] **l**eg
[w] **w**ing
[h] **h**at
[j] **y**es
[r] **r**ed

Vowels

[iː] sh**ee**p
[ɪ] sh**i**p
[uː] sh**oo**t
[ʊ] g**oo**d
[e] b**e**d
[ə] teach**er**
[æ] h**a**t
[ʌ] s**u**n
[ɑː] f**a**r
[ɒ] **o**n
[ɜː] b**i**rd
[ɔː] d**oo**r
[eɪ] d**ay**
[aɪ] **eye**
[əʊ] sh**ow**
[aʊ] h**ou**se
[ɪə] d**ear**
[eə] h**air**
[ɔɪ] b**oy**
[ʊə] t**ou**rist

Part I
From the Study of Style

1

STYLE AND STYLISTICS

Chapter Overview

- the concept of style
- stylistics
- dialect and register
- style as choice
- levels of language and branches of linguistics
- style as deviation
- foregrounding

Introduction

This chapter opens by introducing the concept of style in general and goes on to examine style in language. This leads us to stylistics, which is defined in terms of language variation in response to characteristics associated with the user (e.g. dialect) and characteristics associated with the use of language (e.g. field, tenor, and mode). We also learn about the concepts of style as choice and style as deviation and substantiate the discussion with examples of repetition, parallelism, and deviation at different levels of language such as the formation of words, patterns of grammar, and patterns of meaning. Finally, we discuss the concept of foregrounding, which is the psychological effect of unconventional textual choices. The chapter includes six *Do it yourself* activities to check understanding of the concepts introduced.

What is style?

The most common definition of **STYLE** is that it is a way of doing something. Think of yourself shopping for clothes, for example. Do you buy the first jeans you see in the first shop you visit? Probably not. You visit shops looking for a particular brand, a particular fabric, or a particular colour. You might even go online or travel overseas to buy the jeans of your 'style'. Think of the way you choose friends in your first year of college, to take another example. At times this happens naturally, but often we decide who, of all the people we talk to on campus, become our close friends. We observe what campus events they regularly attend, what clubs they join, what physical or artistic activities they prefer, what parties they go to, and what classes they attend. It is these decisions, along with personality traits of course, that help us decide whether or not our interests and personality types, or styles if you like, intersect.

In light of these two examples, let us refine our definition of style. We could now safely contend that style is a matter of choice made from a set of possible options or from a range of possibilities. It is not a random choice. In fact, it is a calculated choice that reflects our background and expresses our character.

Style in language

How about style in language? Will this definition work if we take it beyond clothes and making friends into language use in speech and writing? The simple answer is yes. Let us take an example. Say you are working on an assignment and a group of teenagers playing outside your house are making a lot of noise. 'Shut up, you morons', is one likely reaction. Now if the source of that noise is a conversation between your elderly, sick neighbours next door, your selection of words and structures to express your dissatisfaction will be different. A more likely request for quiet will be, 'I am in the middle of important work that I have to finish tonight. I'd love to have some silence, if you don't mind.' You have selected the direct order 'shut up' when addressing the unfamiliar teenagers, but in addressing the neighbours you have chosen to explain why you need silence. You have opted for the imperative in addressing the unfamiliar teenagers, but selected the declarative mood with the neighbours, which softens the imposition of the request. Finally, you have mitigated the request for silence to the neighbours with the **POLITENESS** marker 'if you don't mind', whereas your direct order to the unfamiliar teenagers is unmitigated with any markers of politeness.

As with clothes and furnishing, so with language. Style in language is a matter of selecting language items from a pre-existing stock of words and structures in response to the specific characteristics of the context of interaction. The study of style in language is known as **STYLISTICS**.

1.1 Do it yourself

You received the following text message from a friend. Edit it so you can re-text it to your teacher. What changes have you made and why?

having a gr8 time r u coming love u m8

What is stylistics?

Stylistics, as you will have rightly guessed, is the study of style in language. We have established so far that the study of style in language is the study of the choices writers or speakers make from a pre-existing stock of words and structures to match the characteristics of the **SPEECH COMMUNITY** or **SPEECH SITUATION**.

Let us now enrich our definition. Stylistics is the study of variation in language that is motivated by contextual factors. A stylistician (a person who carries out stylistic analyses) is interested in why one type of structure is selected from possibly several ways of representing an idea, and in the effect of the choice on the 'meaning' and overall effect. Not that stylistics is not concerned with what a text means, but rather it is first concerned with how it has come to mean what it means and how a text achieves its effect.

Consider this example on how the effect of a text changes when its language changes. Figure 1.1 is an advertisement titled 'change your words, change your world' produced in 2010 by the UK freelance company Purple Feather. The company offers online (and offline) content writing consultation for websites, books, (marketing) companies, and so on. The advertisement we are looking

FIGURE1.1 The way language can change the effect of a text

at promotes the services of the company by highlighting the power of words. It features a poor blind man begging for money, with a cardboard sign right next to him that reads, 'I'M BLIND. PLEASE HELP.' The poor man is ignored by most passers-by and gets a few coins until a lady walks up to him, grabs the sign, writes something on it and then walks away. Money begins to pour into the old man's lap. The woman returns later, and he asks, 'What did you do to my sign?' She answers, 'I wrote the same thing in different words.' The new sign reads, 'IT'S A BEAUTIFUL DAY AND I **CAN'T** SEE IT.'

Speakers and writers make language choices to create an effect as well as reflect their interests, concerns, education, status, and so on. They also adapt their linguistic choices in response to such contextual factors as the topic, knowledge of the audience, formality of the situation, and the medium of communication. A speaker or writer, for example, may use the technical vocabulary of a particular **REGISTER** along with complex grammatical structures with an unfamiliar audience in a formal written situation. Alternatively, they may use more commonplace vocabulary and the speech features of a regional **DIALECT** with a familiar audience in a casual speech situation. Stylisticians seek to describe how contextual factors influence authorial linguistic choice, and also explain the effect a spoken or written text generates with reference to the textual choices made by the author. In achieving these aims, stylisticians are aided by two main aspects of language variation, namely, dialect and register.

Dialect

A dialect may narrowly be defined as a language variety distinguished from other varieties by a set of phonological, morphological, syntactic, and semantic linguistic features that signal their users' belonging to a specific geographical area, social class, ethnicity, or time period. Take British English and American English as examples of regional dialects. These are two dialects of the English language used by people in different parts of the world. Each of these dialects is distinguished from the other by way of its spelling, vocabulary, pronunciation, and grammar. Check out Table 1.1 for illustrative examples of the differences between the two dialects.

TABLE 1.1 Regional dialects

	American English	*British English*
Spelling	color	colour
Vocabulary	soccer	football
Pronunciation	vitamin /vaɪtəmɪn/	vitamin /vɪtəmɪn/
Grammar	I already saw it.	I have already seen it.

A dialect is also defined in terms of features that are 'distinctive of a particular social group or class' (Wales [1990] 2011: 387). This is called a social dialect, also known as a **SOCIOLECT**, which is more difficult to define, especially as modern societies are getting less hierarchical. The Cockney accent associated with working-class people in the East End of London is an example of a 'traditional' sociolect (Accent Bias Britain n.d.), compared with British Standard English (BrSE). In hierarchical societies, people may decide to learn to speak differently in order to increase their chances of hiring or socialising. An interesting film to watch in this connection is *My Fair Lady*, based on George Bernard Shaw's play *Pygmalion*, which features a young lady from a low class who is trained to speak a sociolect associated with a higher class in order to give more social mobility. Check out Table 1.2 for a few examples of differences between Cockney and British Standard English (BrSE).

TABLE 1.2 Social class dialects

	BrSE	*Cockney*
Vocabulary	Do you *believe* it?	You *Adam and Eve* it?
Pronunciation	house /haʊs/	'ouse /aʊs/
Grammar	She does not have any home.	She ain't got no 'ome. (*Sergeant Joe*, p. 37)

The third type of dialect is defined ethnically. The classic example of an ethnic dialect is the African American Vernacular English (AAVE). It is a variety of English associated with a particular ethnicity, namely, Americans of African descent. Table 1.3 compares examples of language use from AAVE with their equivalents in General American English (GAE).

TABLE 1.3 Ethnic dialects

	AAVE	*GAE*
Vocabulary	That's a *bad* car, man!	That's a *very good* car, man!
Pronunciation	It's my /maː/ life.	It's my /maɪ/ life.
Grammar	He done eat his lunch.	He has eaten his lunch.

The fourth, and last, type of dialect is the temporal dialect. Temporal dialects are varieties of a language distinguished by language features defined by time-related factors. In the English language, there have been varieties with well-defined characteristics at different periods in the history of the language. Take Early Modern English (late fifteenth to mid-eighteenth centuries) and Modern English by way of example, as shown in Table 1.4.

TABLE 1.4 Temporal dialects

	Early Modern English	*Modern English*
Vocabulary	My teares will choake me if I *ope* my mouth.	My tears will choke me if I *open* my mouth.
Pronunciation	Come live with me and be my Love /lʊv/	'love' is pronounced as /lʌv/
	And we will all the pleasures prove /prɒv/	'prove' is pronounced as /pruːv/
Grammar	But goes they heart with this?	But does your heart go with this? (Do you mean it?)

Register

Whereas a dialect is a variety of language defined according to the characteristics of its users (such as verities of English spoken by users coming from different regions), a register is a variety of language used for a particular purpose or in a particular communicative situation (such as the English used in neuroscience vs the English used in sports commentary). In other words, dialectal variation is constrained by variables associated with the language user, while register variation is constrained by variables associated with language use. One approach to describing the variables that constrain registers is based on the **FIELD**, **TENOR**, and **MODE**.

Field

The field is essentially the topic you are talking or writing about. The topic may be generalised, such as daily routines and activities at home or at work, or may be highly specialised, such as a research paper on developing customised nanoparticles that can deliver drugs directly to diseased cells in the human body. The style, or the choice of words and structures, varies as does the field. When talking about daily activities at home or work, the chances are that the vocabulary will be general (e.g. *coffee*), the verbs physical (e.g. *drive*), and the sentences short (e.g. *I'll check my emails in a minute*). The nanotechnology research paper, however, will use highly specialised vocabulary (e.g. *gene sequencing*), more passive structures (e.g. *cancer has been extensively researched*), and more complex sentences (e.g. *Nano materials have been proved to increase nano scale effects, hence used as a tool for drug delivery and the advancement of cancer therapy*). A more relevant example would be this chapter you are reading. It contains style-specific technical terms such as dialect, register, field, tenor, and domain, which you would not expect to find in, say, a chemistry textbook.

Tenor

Tenor is the general tone of what you are saying or writing. Language users choose to use officialese, official, formal, neutral, informal, colloquial, **SLANG** or taboo styles (Newmark 1988), depending on (a) the relationship between the participants in the speech situation (for example, your style when you are talking to a close friend over coffee will be less formal than your style when you are talking to your English teacher in class), and (b) the social situation these participants find themselves in (for example, a husband whose wife is a co-worker will talk to her more formally at work than he does at home). Table 1.5 gives examples of the way our choice of vocabulary and syntax changes in response to the general tone of our communication, from officialese to taboo.

TABLE 1.5 Language variation according to tenor (Newmark 1988: 14)

Tenor	*Example sentence*
Officialese	The consumption of any nutriments whatsoever is categorically prohibited in this establishment.
Official	The consumption of nutriments is prohibited.
Formal	You are requested not to consume food in this establishment.
Neutral	Eating is not allowed here.
Informal	Please don't eat here.
Colloquial	You can't feed your face here.
Slang	Lay off the nosh!
Taboo	Lay off the fucking nosh!

Table 1.6 focuses on the two most common points on this tenor scale, namely, the formal and informal tones. The table lists some of the differences between them. The list is inclusive but not exhaustive.

Mode

The last constraint on register is mode, which is the method or medium of communication. A text may use one mode of communication or it may use more than one mode. A text that uses more than one mode is described as multimodal. The New London Group, a group of researchers that met in New London in the United States in 1994, developed a pedagogical approach to accommodate the effect of technology on education. They identified five possible modes of

TABLE 1.6 Differences between informal and formal writing styles

Informal	*Formal*
May use contractions (e.g. *It's in.*)	Avoids contractions (e.g. *It is in.*)
May use abbreviations (e.g. *TV*)	Uses full forms (e.g. *television*)
May use colloquial words (e.g. *This guy is cool.*)	Avoids colloquial words (e.g. *This man is good.*)
May use clichés (e.g. *We had loads of fun.*)	Avoids clichés (e.g. *We had much fun.*)
May drop relative pronouns (e.g. *She knew he was there.*)	Uses relative pronouns (e.g. *She knew that he was there.*)
May use active voice (e.g. *We have noticed that it's expensive.*)	Prefers passive voice (e.g. *It has been noticed that it is expensive.*)
May use imperatives, first and second person pronouns (e.g. *Read the book if you want to know more.*)	Avoids imperatives, first and second person pronouns (e.g. *The reader should refer to the book for more information.*)
May use simple or even incomplete sentences (e.g. *He kind of like [pause] he failed.*)	Prefers complete and more complex sentences (e.g. *His brother failed the test.*)

communication: linguistic (spoken and written), visual (such as images, videos, symbols, and graphs), aural (such as sound and music), gestural (such as body language and facial expressions), and spatial (such as position, direction, and distance). We would like to focus in this chapter on the linguistic mode and we will deal with multimodal texts later in Chapter 8. Our language choices when we speak will be different from the choices we make when we write, as illustrated in Table 1.7.

TABLE 1.7 Differences between speech and writing

Speech	*Writing*
Is spontaneous and unplanned	Is planned
Is often used for immediate interaction (here and now)	Communicates across time and space
Has pauses, repetition and incomplete sentences	Is scripted, edited and often free from performance errors
Uses intonation	Uses punctuation
Is informal (see Table 1.6)	Is formal (see Table 1.6)

The last row in the table suggests that style markers for the two modes of communication correspond with the tenor of discourse, with speech being conventionally informal and writing formal. The boundaries, however, are not as clear-cut. For example, the khutbahs, the Islamic sermons delivered at Friday prayers, are spoken but often delivered in formal language, while text messaging in English is written using features of informal language, such as informal openings *Hi Liz*, abbreviations *4 u* (for you), or the use of stickers and emojis to communicate emotions such as ☺ to suggest a smile. Written books, to take another example, conventionally use formal language, but this textbook employs features of neutral style (which is neither formal nor informal and sticks to the presentation of facts) and, at times, informal style (the use of contractions, the inclusive pronoun 'we, us', and a conversational tone) to suggest both proximity to and familiarity with the readers.

1.2 Do it yourself

Identify the tenor in the following statements. Write *formal* or *informal* against each statement and identify the linguistic choices that lead you to that category.

a) I'll finish the job next month.
b) The project will be completed next month.
c) As the price of five dollars was reasonable, I decided to make the purchase.
d) It was, like, five bucks, so I was like 'okay'.
e) I used random sampling in my study.
f) The study employed the random sampling technique.
g) Dear Mrs Richards, I apologise for not getting in contact with you before now.
h) Hi Mary, Sorry I haven't written for ages.
i) If you lose this paper, contact us ASAP.
j) Any loss of this document should be reported immediately.

1.3 Do it yourself

The following conversation between a professor (A) and students of stylistics (B & C) has been made up by the author. Identify the field, tenor, and mode in the conversation. Rewrite B's turns in the conversation using a different tenor. What changes have you made?

A: Does anyone know what today's discussion is about?
B: It is about style in language.
A: Right. Now style in its most general sense is a specific characteristic of human activity arising as a result of choice, within the accepted norms, of a definite mode or manner of conducting this activity.
B: Can we conclude that natural objects like trees do not have style?
A: You could say that because their shape and colour are not the result of deliberate choice. But it does not take away from their beauty, of course.
C: What does a person's language choice or style tell us about that person?
B: Well, style is indicative of a speaker's social or ethnic group, and their locatedness in region or time period.
A: Well said. Let us move on to our next topic.

1.4 Do it yourself

What dialects are the following conversations in? Rewrite them into British Standard English (BrSE). What changes have you made?

a) 'Someone's been up 'ere,' she said. – 'Yes, it was Mr Cousins,' said Linda. 'I fink 'e was after pinchin' somefing from yer bag, Sergeant Joe, only I come up an' caught him openin' it.' – 'He mentioned he was a friend of yours,' said Dolly. 'I wouldn't want 'im as a friend of mine.' – 'Yes, we fought we'd better see if 'e'd pinched anyfing,' said Linda. (*Sergeant Joe*, p. 61)
b) Now, we're gonna be stopping 20 miles outside of the preserve to gas up and get drinks and stuff. Keep that in mind, guys. (*Hell's Belle*, 2019, horror movie)
c) He ain't finna do nothing. What's happening? – You trying to poach my girls? – Your girls? – Yeah. – What you think, you still running $20 tricks on Stewart Avenue or something? You ain't answered my question, man. You a clown. (*Star*, 2016–19, musical series)
d) Cassius: Will you sup with me tonight, Casca?
   Casca: No, I am promised forth. (*Julius Caesar*, Act 1, Scene 2)

Style and social meaning

We have argued so far that style has a social meaning. It indexes our belonging to social, regional or ethnic groups in different periods of time. This categorisation is based on the presence (or absence) of sufficient similarity between the style markers of the members of these groups. You could pass yourself off as belonging to a particular speech community if your style of speaking, or texting, exhibits sufficient similarity at the phonological, lexical and syntactic levels to the styles of members of the community. In other words, you need to be making language choices that are sufficiently similar to those made by fellow members of the group.

Membership in a group is also defined contrastively. In order to demonstrate belonging to the African American community, for example, you need to depart from the linguistic choices made by Americans outside the African American community. You would depart from conventional choices and choose instead stylistic features specific to the African American Vernacular dialect (see Table 1.3). By breaking away from the stylistic features of General American English and making a different set of linguistic choices, you identify with African Americans in terms of linguistic style.

Style as choice and deviation

Enkvist (1964) considers six different approaches to defining style in language, two of which have gained currency in the stylistics literature. The first approach views style as 'the choice between alternative expressions' and the second one views it as '**DEVIATION** from a norm' (1964: 12).

Style as choice

The first approach to the definition of style in language views style as the tendency of a speaker or writer to consistently choose certain words and structures over others available in the language. In this view of style, the choices that a language user makes are seen as a subset of choices from a network of interrelated choices that can be represented in the form of a system network (Halliday 2003). For Halliday, a 'system network has a horizontal and a vertical dimension' (2003: 8). The vertical dimension represents possibilities of combination. If I am to make a statement, for example, then I have a choice of combining polarity (making it positive or negative), mood (using a declarative, interrogative or imperative statement), tense (situating the activity in the past, present or future), and transitivity (representing the activity as an action, state or process). The horizontal dimension, on the other hand, represents constraints on choice, whereby each choice made limits the number of options available in the next slot on the horizontal axis. For example, if I start my statement with *The boy ate*, the range of options available for the next slot is typically limited to objects that are edible. In this sense, meaning is a function of interrelated choices along the vertical and horizontal dimensions of the language system.

The distinctive style markers that every language user makes are motivated by user-specific factors (such as age, gender, and education) and the situation-specific factors mentioned above, namely, field, tenor, and mode. This view of style involves a degree of careful selection, and this explains the connotations of the word 'style' in such popular expressions in English as *That car has got real style* and *They dine in style*. Indeed, it is this view of style that we have been discussing since the beginning of this chapter.

An important ingredient of this view of style is consistency. Not every textual choice is a marker of style. Some choices are unintentional and not motivated. In order for a linguistic feature to be considered a marker of an author's style, it needs to be selected fairly regularly at the expense of other potential options.

1.5 Do it yourself

Comment on the linguistic choices in the following texts in relation to the variable below each set.

    a) When one is cooking, washing one's hands is important.
    b) When you're cooking, you have to wash your hands.
        (the mode)

c) Use the big knife to break the bones and the small one to separate the meat from the bones.
d) Use the cleaver to break the bones and the boning knife to separate the meat from the bones.
   (the context in which the statement is made)
e) That silver metallic 1970 Cadillac de Ville convertible over there is beautiful.
f) I like that old white car over there.
   (the job of the speaker/writer)
g) Three freedom fighters have been martyred in Gaza.
h) Three terrorists have been killed in Gaza.
   (the ideological point of view of the speaker/writer)
i) Birds of a feather flock together.
j) Ornithological species of identical plumage tend to congregate in closer proximity.
   (the tenor)

Style as deviation

While the first approach to style is associated with variation, the second views style as deviation. The defining feature of the first approach is consistent choice from the resources of language available to language users, whereas the defining feature of the second approach is deviation from the expected norms and selection of less expected language features. The speaker or writer chooses to either deviate from the norms of the language or the norms of the specific register (deviation), repeat the same lexical item or items over and over again (repetition), or repeat the same structure (parallelism). Let us take a look at examples of these operations.

TABLE 1.8 Deviation from language and register norms

Example 1 *Breaking language norms*	*Example 2* *Breaking register norms*
A grief ago This is the title of a poem by the Welsh poet Dylan Thomas. This line deviates from conventional language usage. Before *ago*, we normally use units of time, such as *a year* as in *a year ago* or *a month* as in *a month ago*, because that is how we measure time. A *grief* is not a unit of time and is not expected in this context. It constitutes a deviation from the norms of the English language.	**anyone lived in a pretty how town (with up so floating many bells down) spring summer autumn winter he sang his didn't he danced his did** The convention in poetry is that lines begin with capital letters, regardless of sentence beginnings, and are punctuated at the end of lines and/or STANZAS. All the lines in this stanza from e. e. cummings's poem 'anyone lived in a pretty how town' begin with lower-case letters, and the stanza has no punctuation. These choices constitute a deviation from the norms of the register of poetry.

TABLE 1.9 Repetition and parallelism

Example 3 *Repetition*	*Example 4* *Parallelism*
I have a dream	**Have a break** **Have a KitKat**
In a famous speech on 28 August 1963, the American civil rights activist Martin Luther King, Jr. made a speech (which is available at https://www.americanrhetoric.com/speeches/mlkihaveadream.htm) in which he called for an end to racism in America. The phrase *I have a dream* from the speech is remembered because it was repeated in eight successive sentences.	This is the advertisement for the Nestlé-owned chocolate brand KitKat. In this advertisement, we have two phrases with the same structure and words except for the word in the last slot. We call these structures parallel structures.

While repetition and parallelism are relatively easier to understand, deviation merits further discussion and exemplification. It can operate at any, and all, of the different levels of the language system: the level of words and word formation, the level at which words combine to form larger structures, the meaning and interpretation of words and structures, the written representation of language on the page, and the larger level of spoken and written communication. Let us now examine the way deviation operates at each of these levels, in the same order mentioned above.

Morphological deviation

Words such as *tree, sleep*, and *tall* contain a single unit of meaning. They can stand as meaningful units on their own. The same words may be expanded by attaching another unit of meaning or grammatical function to them, as in *trees, sleeping*, and *taller*. The plural suffix *-s* in *trees*, the progressive marker suffix *-ing* in *sleeping*, and the comparative suffix *-er* in *taller* are not meaningful units on their own but acquire meaning when attached to other units of meaning. The minimal units of meaning which combine to form words are called **MORPHEMES**. A word, therefore, may be composed of one morpheme *heart*, two morphemes *heart-en*, three morphemes *dis-heart-en*, four morphemes *dis-heart-en-ed*, or even more. The study of the rules governing word formation is known as **MORPHOLOGY**.

Morphological deviation occurs when a speaker or writer applies an existing rule of word formation beyond its conventional range of operation. For example, the suffix *-ful* attaches to nouns in English to create an adjective meaning 'having the quality of something' as in *beautiful* or 'causing something' as in *painful*. If an author adds the suffix to another part of speech, the newly coined word, formed by extension of existing rules of morphology beyond their normal range of application, is called a **NEOLOGISM**. Consider the example of neologism from e. e. cummings's poetry in Table 1.10, created via morphological deviation.

TABLE 1.10 Morphological deviation

Example 5
Morphological deviation

over time space doom dream while floats the whole
perhapsless mystery of paradise

(e. e. cummings, 'from spiralling ecstatically this')

English word formation rules allow language users to create new adjectives by adding the suffix *-less* to existing nouns, thereby creating such adjectives as *ageless, priceless, endless, foodless* and even *questionless*. Cummings has added the suffix *-less* to the adverb *perhaps*, not to a noun. This is not attested in English morphology, and so it constitutes a deviation from English word-formation rules. The word *perhapsless* is a neologism, and it is an example of morphological deviation.

Syntactic deviation

Words are grouped and ordered into larger units of structure. They may be patterned into phrases. A **PHRASE** is a group of words whose syntactic category is determined by the main word in the group – the 'head' of the group. The phrase is named after its head. Accordingly, a group of words that is headed by a noun is a noun phrase *the blue car*, a group of words that is headed by an adjective is an adjective phrase *extremely useful*, a group of words that is headed by a verb is a verb phrase *might be coming*, a group of words that is headed by an adverb is an adverb phrase *very carefully*, and a group of words that is headed by a preposition is a prepositional phrase *in the house*.

Words also pattern into clauses. A **CLAUSE** is a meaningful combination of words that contains a subject and a verb. A clause can make a **SIMPLE SENTENCE** *It is raining*, and can be part of a **COMPOUND SENTENCE** *I invited him, but he didn't come*, and can be part of a **COMPLEX SENTENCE** *He did not come because it was raining*. In terms of function, a clause can act as a noun *I know where he is going*, an adjective *The man who lives next door has died*, and an adverb *He came after the doors closed*. These clauses are called noun, adjective, and adverbial clauses, respectively. The study of the rules that govern the patterning of words into phrases and clauses is known as **SYNTAX**.

At the syntactic level, the constituents of the sentence, or clause, may be rearranged in ways that are not frequent in the grammar of the language, resulting in syntactic deviation. An example is given in Table 1.11.

Semantic deviation

Words have meanings. The meanings that we associate with words may be defined in reference to actual objects in the real world, such as is the case with the nouns *dog* and *chair*. They may also be defined in relation to a set of semantic features that make up the meaning of the words, as in *man* [+human, +male, +adult] and *boy* [+human, +male, -adult]. Words may also be defined contrastively, by categorising the relationships that exist between them and other words,

TABLE 1.11 Syntactic deviation

Example 6
Syntactic deviation

No motion has she now, no force;
She neither hears nor sees;
                    (William Wordsworth, 'A Slumber did my Spirit Seal')

In the structure of the English clause, the verb *have* requires a complement that is placed immediately after the verb. In the above lines from Wordsworth, the complement *no motion* is fronted and precedes the verb. The expected word order is *She has no motion now*. Therefore, we speak of the first line above as syntactically deviant, that is, it violates the conventional order of words in the English clause.

---

as in *fast* when defined as the opposite of *slow*. The meanings of words are not always fixed. Words can change their meanings over time and can take on new meanings in different contexts. The study of the linguistic meanings of words, and sentences, is **SEMANTICS**, or more precisely, **LEXICAL SEMANTICS**.

The meanings of words also have to fit together in longer stretches of language in order to make meaningful propositions. For example, we order *fast food* and make *quick meals*. If we use *fast* with *meals* or *quick* with *food*, we will sound awkward, though not entirely unintelligible. This is because in the company of *food* we use, and expect to find, the adjective *fast*, and in the company of *meal* we use, and expect to find, the adjective *quick*. In other words, the adjectives *fast* and *quick* co-occur with the nouns *food* and *meal*, respectively. The 'habitual or expected co-occurrence of words' is known as **COLLOCATION** (Wales [1990] 2011: 68). Like other languages, English has its own collocational constraints. That is, it has limitations on the possibilities of word combinations based on their habitual co-occurrence. Breaking away from habitual collocational patterns, or the rules of semantic compatibility, leads to semantic deviation. The lines from e. e. cummings in Table 1.12 illustrate this point.

TABLE 1.12 Semantic deviation

Example 7
Semantic deviation

pity this busy monster, manunkind,
not. Progress is a comfortable disease;
                    (e. e. cummings, 'pity this busy monster, manunkind')

The second line is semantically odd. It violates English collocational constraints. *Progress* is not a *disease*, and *disease* does not collocate with *comfortable*. Putting together three words whose semantic content is incompatible results in what we have called semantic deviation. The use of semantic deviation invites the reader to imagine a possible world where these oddities could be resolved in order for the reader to make sense of the text.

Graphological deviation

Besides having rules governing their internal structure, languages also have their own **GRAPHOLOGY**. That is, they have writing conventions, such as the rules of spelling, punctuation, and writing patterns. They also have register-specific conventions. In English poetry, for example, lines conventionally start with capital letters, even if the beginning of the line does not correspond to the beginning of the sentence. Lines also do not run out to the right-hand end of the page, which gives poetry a unique graphological representation on the page. The discarding of capitalisation, punctuation, and spacing where they are required by genre conventions results in graphological deviation. Let us examine the lines from Michael Horovitz's 'Man-to-Man Blues' in Table 1.13, which illustrates graphological deviation.

TABLE 1.13 Graphological deviation

Example 8
Graphological deviation

– Think you're in
Heaven?
Well – you'll soon be
in H
   E
   L
   L –

(Michael Horovitz, 'Man-to-Man Blues')

The last word in the lines above constitutes a deviation from the graphological norms of the English language. Instead of being arranged horizontally in conformity with the normal graphological arrangement in English, the letters of the word *hell* are arranged vertically. Thus, the word stands out and attracts readers' attention. In this poem, the vertical arrangement serves to symbolically enact the descent from heaven into hell.

Discoursal deviation

Deviation also operates above the sentence level. The units of language structure above the sentence in spoken communication (e.g. conversations) or written communication (e.g. paragraphs) are described in linguistics as **DISCOURSE**. There are rules regulating the structure and use of discourse. In a normal discourse situation, for example, a text begins at the beginning of a sentence and also at the beginning of discourse. Besides, texts are self-contained. That is, they begin at the beginning of communication, and end where communication ends. We do not expect a text to begin in the middle of a sentence or in the middle of a conversation. If it does, it would constitute an example of discoursal deviation. The example from Adrienne Rich's 'Song' (1972) in Table 1.14 best illustrates this point (Rich 2003).

TABLE 1.14 Discoursal deviation

Example 9
Discoursal deviation

You're wondering if I'm lonely:
OK then, yes, I'm lonely.

(Adrienne Rich, 'Song')

These are the first two lines of the poem 'Song'. The poem begins with an answer to a question. The answer is in the second line. In fact, the first line of the poem contains a reported statement that repeats the missing question in order for the readers to follow the argument. The readers, therefore, are projected into the middle of a conversation, but are given a clue in order to be able to recover what is missing. The poem, or the beginning of the poem, is deviant at the level of discourse.

But the question remains. Why do authors choose to make such abnormal choices, either by repeating lexical items or structures over and over, or by deviating altogether from language or register norms?

Foregrounding

A group of scholars in Prague, capital of the Czech Republic, came up with an answer to this question in the 1930s. Jan Mukařovský, an eminent member of the **PRAGUE LINGUISTIC CIRCLE**, postulated the theory of **FOREGROUNDING** to explain why speakers and writers make such unconventional textual choices.

According to the theory of foregrounding, everyday use of language is referential. We use language to refer to entities and communicate meanings. As such, language is a 'carrier' of thoughts and feelings. When we 'extract' these messages, language is in a way 'discarded'. We got the message after all, did we not? In this view, language is 'automatised', that is, the choices are predictable and the effects can be anticipated.

The Prague School structuralists, in the tradition of the earlier Russian formalists, argued that the purpose of creative language use in the arts is to de-familiarise, that is, to present familiar themes as if they were new. For this purpose, the 'consumed' expressive potential of language offers little help. Language is not capable of expressing these unconventional views or conceptualisations of the world. According to that view, this is why these authors choose to 'de-automatise' everyday language by disrupting routine usage of language. They make use of abnormal regularity (parallelism) and/or abnormal irregularity (deviation).

These deviant choices have an important effect. By virtue of being different from the rest of the text, these choices can call attention to themselves. They come to the foreground and become more noticeable. In more technical terms, we say that these choices are 'foregrounded'. Foregrounding, therefore, may be defined as the psychological effect of linguistic deviation or parallelism on the reader or listener.

1.6 Do it yourself

The following texts contain instances of foregrounding. Identify the foregrounded parts, and specify the technique of foregrounding, that is, deviation (name the level of language at which it occurs), parallelism or repetition.

a) Break, break, break
   At the foot of thy crags, O Sea!
      (Alfred Lord Tennyson, 'Break, Break, Break')
b) Sweet day, so cool, so calm, so bright,
   The bridal of the earth and sky.
      (George Herbert, 'Virtue')
c) he sang his didn't he danced his did
      (e. e. cummings, 'anyone lived in a pretty how town')
d) this a dog barks and
   how crazily houses
   eyes people smiles
   faces streets
   steeples are eagerly
   tumbl
   ing through wonder
   ful sunlight
      (e. e. cummings, 'listen')
e) love is more thicker than forget
   more thinner than recall
      (e. e. cummings, 'love is more thicker than forget')
f) 'A tale of murder, lust, greed, revenge, and seafood'
      (A tagline for the 1988 film *Fish Called Wanda*)

Cohesion of foregrounding

But is it enough to identify the foregrounded parts of a text? Of course not. Equally important is linking the foregrounded elements to the interpretation of the text. That is, establishing how the deviant and parallel structures in a text, together with the more conventional linguistic choices, help the reader make a coherent interpretation of the text. This is known as the **COHESION OF FOREGROUNDING** (Short [1996] 2014: 36). We will see how cohesion of foregrounding is achieved in Chapter 3 when we carry out a formalist stylistic analysis of a poem.

> **Summary**
>
> In this chapter, we have considered the concept of style as variation in response to contextual factors, including the language user and the use of language in context. This concept forms the bedrock of most stylistic frameworks introduced in Part II of this book. We have also considered the concept of foregrounding, which is achieved via linguistic deviation, repetition or parallelism. While foregrounding is 'by no means absent in non-literary texts', it is 'particularly prevalent in literary texts, especially poetry' (Jeffries and McIntyre 2010: 31). In the next chapter, we look more closely at how deviant linguistic choices in poetry, against the background of more conventional textual choices, call attention to 'how' language is used to communicate meaning and achieve effect.

Further Reading

TEXTBOOKS

Haynes, J. (1995), *Style*, Routledge.
 This is a short and a readable introduction to style in literary and non-literary texts. The book examines the effect on the choice of words and structures of such factors as field, tenor, mode, personal involvement, and ideology. It has plenty of examples and each unit ends with activities for practice.

Jeffries, L. and D. McIntyre (2010), *Stylistics*, Cambridge University Press.
 The first two chapters of the book introduce the key concepts of style and foregrounding, the principles of stylistic analysis and research, and the levels of language in sufficient details. The next four chapters outline developments of pragmatic and cognitive approaches to stylistic analysis and offer rigorous analyses of literary and non-literary texts. In the last two chapters, the authors present methodological approaches for practitioners to use, highlight advances in stylistics, and consider how stylistics is likely to develop.

REFERENCES

Biber, D. and S. Conrad (2009), *Register, Genre, and Style*, Cambridge University Press.
 This is a research-based book that offers methodological techniques for the analysis of a wide range of spoken and written texts, from the perspectives of registers, genre conventions and styles. The texts analysed include conversations, service encounters, newspapers, academic prose, fiction, e-mails, and internet forums. Each chapter ends with three types of activities: reflection and review activities, analysis activities, and larger project ideas.

Simpson, P. [2004] (2014), *Stylistics: A Resource Book for Students*, 2nd edn, Routledge.
  The book is in four sections. The first two sections of the book introduce students to key linguistic concepts and techniques (such as levels of language, metre, transitivity, metaphor analysis, and the identification of point of view) which are required to replicate the stylistic analyses offered in the third section of the book and appreciate the key readings introduced in the fourth section.

van Peer, W. (2007), 'Introduction to foregrounding: A state of the art', *Language and Literature*, 16(2), 99–104, <https://doi.org/10.1177/0963947007075978> (last accessed 23 September 2021).
  This is a research paper that offers a detailed outline of foregrounding as a theory of literature. The paper traces the theory to the Prague school structuralists working on the form and function of literature, and overviews empirical research on foregrounding since the 1930s.

Part II
Into the Practice of Stylistics

2

FORMALIST ANALYSIS OF POETRY

> **Chapter Overview**
> - communication in poetry
> - formalist stylistics
> - checklist of formalist categories
> - 'Half an Hour After' by Mark O'Connor
> - formalist analysis of 'Half an Hour After'

Introduction

Chapter 1 concluded that foregrounding may be achieved by deviating from norms or by repetition of language or patterns of language use. In this chapter, we present these concepts within the framework of **FORMALIST STYLISTICS**. The first part of the chapter offers an overview of the nature of communication in poetry, an outline of the formalist framework, a checklist of formalist categories to help you see through the analysis and replicate it on the texts suggested for further practice, and the text to analyse. In the second part of the chapter, we carry out a formalist analysis of the poem by identifying the foregrounded elements in the poem and relating them to other textual choices to create intra-textual patterns of meaning contributing to a coherent interpretation of the poem.

Communication in poetry

Poetry is an unconventional mode of communication. First, unlike conventional modes of communication like books and research papers, it is vertically lined up on the printed page. Second, it is a self-contained and autonomous discourse that is dissociated from the immediate social reality. Third, it is non-referential. That is, it does not always 'refer' to reality as we know it; it often constructs it.

Fourth, it is characterised by deliberate ambiguity. Poets do not explain themselves. Instead, they leave 'gaps' for readers to fill in with reference to their own schematic knowledge of the world, and thus allow multiple interpretations. This may be a consequence of the limitations of space. A prototypical (modern) poem does not exceed the limit of a single page. There have, of course, been poems in English and other languages running into thousands of lines. Last, poetry aims at the disruption of our automatised perception of reality. In order to achieve this, poets disrupt the conventional categories of language through which we experience the world.

Because of its self-containment and its 'non-referentiality', a poem should be best read and understood with reference to authorial textual choices. Analysis of choices in the text, against the background of other possible choices, can help the reader fill in the gaps in the text and construct the reality represented through language. It is all about language, and this is one reason why we are choosing the formalist and functionalist stylistic approaches as analytical frameworks for the analysis of poetic texts in this chapter and in Chapter 3.

Formalist stylistics

The theoretical foundations of modern stylistics are traced back to **RUSSIAN FORMALISM** at the start of the twentieth century. The Russian formalists were preoccupied with the nature of a 'literary' work and the constituents of **LITERARINESS**. They argued that literature is quintessentially language and any description of literariness will have to start with the language of literature. In analysing literary language, the formalists focused on the words on the page and contributed the analytical concepts of deviation and foregrounding. These theoretical claims, and analytical concepts, laid the foundation of a stylistics that is formalist in outlook, albeit without embracing the dichotomy between literary language and conventional language use (Carter and Stockwell 2008). This section offers an outline of formalist stylistics, and you will find a more detailed account of Russian formalism in Part III of this book.

Formalist stylistics is concerned with investigating the way(s) writers exploit the 'literariness' of language in order to create the effect of **DEFAMILIARISATION**. It argues that creative writers use language in unconventional ways in order to slow down the reading of those parts of the text which aim to reorient the reader's outlook or viewpoint on the issue at hand. Accordingly, formalist stylisticians set out to analyse the linguistic structure of texts in order to uncover those linguistic choices that create the effect of defamiliarisation and thought reorientation.

Formalist stylisticians base their critical comments of (poetic) texts on retrievable observations about the formal linguistic features of the texts. The analytical toolkit of the formalist stylistician is constituted by foregrounding, which is achieved via the techniques of deviation, parallelism, and repetition. Deviation occurs when schematic expectations about the rules governing language, that is, the rules at the linguistic levels of phonology, morphology, syntax, semantics, discourse, and graphology, or when schematic expectations about the rules governing the register of poetry are broken. The deviation from normal expectations produces the effect of defamiliarisation. Parallelism is the use of repetitive structures. The repeated structures are promoted to the foreground and acquire interpretive significance. Repetition is the use of the same word, phrase, line or stanza. The repeated words, phrases, lines, or stanzas achieve prominence and merit interpretive significance (see Chapter 1 for examples of deviation, parallelism, and repetition).

A checklist of formalist categories

In this section, I suggest a list of categories to look for in carrying out a formalist stylistic analysis of a poem. The list takes the form of questions. Answering the questions will help you see how I arrived at the analysis offered in the chapter, and should guide your own independent analysis of the texts in activities 2.1 and 2.2. Questions (a) to (j) will help you spot the formalist features, and questions (k) to (l) will help you relate the uncovered features to the overall meaning and effect of the poem(s).

a) Are there instances of deviation in the text?
b) Is the deviation from the norms of the language?
c) Is the deviation from the norms of the genre?
d) Is the deviation from norms external to the text? Is it external deviation?
e) Is the deviation from norms internal to the text? It is internal deviation?
f) At what linguistic level does the deviation occur?
 – Phonology
 – Morphology
 – Syntax
 – Semantics
 – Graphology
 – Discourse
g) Relate the deviations to the normal patterns in language or the genre.
h) Do the deviations create text-internal meanings?
i) Are there instances of parallelism in the poem?
j) Is there repetition of words, phrases, lines or stanzas?
k) Do the parallel structures or the repeated parts in the text create text-internal meanings?
l) How do the deviant, parallel, and repeated structures contribute to a coherent interpretation of the poem?

The text

The poem we are analysing is 'Half an Hour After' by the Australian poet Mark O'Connor, whose poetry shows a particular interest in the environment. The poem depicts a conversation between two academics half an hour after a terrible disaster has caused considerable damage and claimed many lives. It appears in O'Connor's collection of poems *Reef Poems*, published in 1976.

'When you come to think of it,' sed Dr Hippo   1
—'Much too late of course.' sed Professor Sprong,
flicking off his trouser cuff
'—What's just happened was all but inevitable.
We never stood more than a 40% chance, I thought,   5
Of ducking the thing in our lifetimes.'
'It's sad really,' sed Professor Sprong,
watching the goldfish die in their broken bowl.
'The species, one thought, had such potential.'
'Well it's no use crying over spilt uranium.'   10
lisped Dr Hippo, regarding the ruins of the Senior Common Room
'Rum though, to think of all those bodies.
Out there, and no one around to bery them ever.'
'Not our job, thank God,' sed Sprong
'but if we last out the hour   15
We'll be able to finish this port. No more Anglo-Saxon
declensions ever! And the funny thing is
I still don't really feel enything.'

The analysis

We will now identify the foregrounded parts of the poem and the techniques through which they have been foregrounded. We will also examine the way the foregrounded parts of the poem, along with the other textual choices, contribute to the overall meaning and effect of the poem. Let us start with the linguistic features foregrounded via deviation and go on to analyse the rest of the textual choices.

Semantic deviation

The most notable deviation in the poem is at the semantic level. The poem is written in simple English and most of the words keep their habitual company. In line 10, however, an inconsistent meaning relation appears *spilt uranium*. This is not an expected collocation and the two words are semantically incompatible. The verb *spill* requires a noun that is [-solid] while uranium is a hard, dense radioactive metal whose melting point is at 1,132°C. This semantic deviation is interpretively significant in at least two ways. First, it makes clear the nature of the *disaster* that Dr Hippo and Professor Sprong have been so far only obliquely referring to. It is a nuclear disaster. Second, and perhaps more importantly, it shows the attitude of the two academics, perhaps nuclear scientists, towards such a large-scale disaster. The line *Well it's no use crying over spilt uranium* echoes the common proverb 'There's no use crying over spilt milk', which is used to suggest that it does no good to get upset over an outcome that cannot be undone. Instead of assuming responsibility for their 'miscalculations' that have led to the disaster, the two scientists seek consolation in the fact that the disaster was inevitable and the damage unleashed is unfixable. This attitude of indifference and inaction, in the context of large-scale damage to human lives and property, underscores the irresponsibility of nuclear scientists towards human lives and life at large.

Syntactic deviation

The first line in the poem is supposedly a question but it uses a declarative-sentence word order instead of an interrogative word order. It also ends with a comma in place of the expected question mark. This syntactic deviation early on in the poem serves to foreground the sense of informality that dominates a conversation about the potential extinction of the human race. Later in line 12, the end of the line is set off by a full stop even though the sentence is not complete and the next line offers the completion. In other words, line 12 is arrested and released in the next line. This creates two points of foregrounding – one at the end of line 12 and the other at the beginning of line 13. The former serves to underscore the magnitude of the disaster that has claimed so many lives, while the latter highlights the scientists' detachment from the consequences of their own actions.

Discoursal deviation

The first line of the poem casts the reader into the middle of a conversation between two scientists on a nuclear disaster. The use of the pronoun *it* in line 1 refers textually to a previously mentioned referring expression or extra-textually to the disaster that has befallen in the immediate social context of the two scientists. The former, endophoric reference, assumes previous conversational turns that are undisclosed to the reader, and the latter, deictic reference, presupposes shared contextual knowledge which is non-existent. In either case, the reader is invited to read on in order to work out the referent of the pronoun and the topic of the conversation.

In fact, the search for the withheld reference begins even earlier with the title of the poem 'Half an Hour After'. The title suggests that the conversational exchange is taking place half an hour after something has happened but again leaves the identity of this happening for the reader to figure out. In effect, therefore, the reader is projected not only into the middle of a conversation but into the middle of a disastrous event, both of which are withheld to be released later and figured out by the reader.

This discoursal deviation guides the reader's search for the poem's meaning. Line 4 uses a relative pronoun *what* to make a cross-reference to the referent but still does not reveal the identity of the referent. In line 6, it becomes *the thing* and the answer to the question is still arrested. It is later in line 10 that the reader starts to work out the nature of the disaster *spilt uranium*. Midway through the poem, the reader will have to go back to the beginning of the poem, and reread and reinterpret the previous lines in light of the new information.

In addition to starting in the middle of conversation as well as action, the poem disrupts the norms of communication in poetry. The poet is not the addresser and the reader is not addressed directly. The poem is a conversation between two academics and the reader is positioned as an eavesdropper on the conversation. The distancing of both the poet and the reader has the effect of singling out the two scientists as responsible for the disaster that has wreaked havoc on our world.

Other textual choices

The poet has used style variations to maintain thematic unity and sustain the projection of the scientists. First, there is the medium of representation. Poetry often uses written language for its medium. This poem, however, is a written record of a series of conversational exchanges in which the turn-taking is casual and language is informal. The imposition of spoken language features on a prototypically written discourse gives the poem a sense of informality and casualness which enacts the two scientists' attitude towards the unfolding disaster.

Tenor variation also sustains the attitude of the Dr Hippo and Professor Sprong towards the subject of their conversation. The words in the poem are simple and there is no technical jargon, except for *uranium*, that the reader would expect in a conversational exchange between nuclear scientists. Instead, the poem has a high incidence of informal expressions (e.g. *Of ducking the thing*), contracted forms (e.g. *What's just happened*), and truncated structures (e.g. *When you come to think of it*). The use of these informal structures carries forward the informality and indifference of the interlocutors, and the dispersion of these structures throughout the poem upholds the unfavourable image of the scientists whose irresponsibility is putting life on earth at risk.

The use of dialectical spellings is another interesting lexical choice in the poem (*sed* lines 1, 2, 7 and 14, *bery* line 13, and *enything* line 18). These are proposed spelling reforms popularised in Australia by Harry Lindgren in 1969. By using 'Australian' spellings, it may be argued that Hippo and Sprong acquire an Australian identity and represent Australian nuclear scientists. In this case, the poet is levelling an attack on the irresponsibility of Australian nuclear scientists.

Other interpretively significant lexical choices include the choice of names of the two academics. While one professor is named 'Sprong', the other is 'Hippo'. A hippo is a thick-skinned animal with a large head, a wide mouth, and short legs. The use of this name for a scientist conjures up negative connotations and is consistent with the poet's indictment of the irresponsibility of nuclear scientists. The poet's disapproval does not stop here. He gives Dr Hippo a speech defect, a lisp, which makes him pronounce sibilant fricatives, namely, /s/ and /z/ as /θ/. By giving Dr Hippo a lisp and at least twelve sibilant fricatives to pronounce, the poet is projecting Hippo as someone who bites off more than they can chew. This further enhances Hippo's unappealing image and the poet's indictment of the scientists' approach.

The absence of regularity at the phonological level is also appropriate to the poem's thematic concerns. The extra layer of rhythmic patterning that is often found in poetry is missing in the poem. The lines are not metred and they do not rhyme. The poem's rhythm is more prosaic and it is hard to identify a single recurring rhythmic pattern. The high incidence of weak forms and grammatical words contributes to the poem's prosaic rhythm. The absence of metric patterning and a regular **RHYME** scheme reflects the sense of disorderliness ensuing from the scientists' miscalculations.

The flippant attitude of the academics and the disapproval of the poet are also carried by the choice of verbs. Almost half the verbs used by the academics (nine out of twenty) are non-finite verbs, including Sprong's *flicking off his trouser cuff* and Hippo's *regarding the ruins*. Four of the remaining eleven verbs are used in reference to other entities, three are 'thinking' verbs, two are negated, and the last two are used conditionally in the context of *port*. These lexical choices underline the scientists' attitude of inaction and indifference in response to the disaster. This attitude culminates towards the end of the poem with Sprong saying it is *funny* that he does not *feel anything*.

Summary

In this chapter, we have used the formalist stylistic framework to analyse a modern, non-canonical poem. The poem depicts nuclear scientists who are unfazed by the fallout of a disaster they have unleashed upon the world. Deviations at the levels of semantics, syntax, and discourse cohere with other lexical choices to juxtapose the magnitude of the disaster with the indifferent attitude of the scientists. There are two points I would like to emphasise as we conclude the chapter. First, a given poem need not necessarily have instances of repetition, parallelism or even deviation. Second, the formalist stylistic framework is by no means applicable only to the analysis of poetry. Van Peer and Hakemulder observe that 'foregrounding devices are also encountered in everyday language' (2006: 549) and are not an exclusive property of literary texts. The formalist framework may, therefore, be applied to any text type that contains foregrounding devices. Notable applications of the framework beyond poetry include Hakemulder (2007), which explores spectators' responses to foregrounding in films, and Jensen et al. (2018), which combines qualitative and corpus tool to analyse foregrounding in fiction.

2.1 Do it yourself

Analyse the foregrounded patterns in 'Wants' by the English poet, and novelist, Philip Larkin (Larkin 2003). It is a modern poem published in 1951, which describes the wishes or 'wants' of modern man. An interesting feature of this poem is that it contains textual choices to instantiate all the techniques of foregrounding.

Hints

a) The poem has two full stops, which correspond to two sentences. Identify the two sentences.

b) The first sentence lacks a main verb, and by implication action, while the second has a dynamic verb. Identify the verb and interpret this syntactic choice in relation to the thematic concerns of the poem.
c) Explain the semantic deviation in *the sky grows dark with invitation-cards* (line 2). How does the deviation express the speaker's *wish to be alone*? (**Hint** *Compare with the normal paradigm of the sky getting overcast with dark clouds. You may look up common collocational patterns in the Online Oxford Collocation Dictionary at <https://www.freecollocation.com/>.*)
d) Explain the semantic deviation in *printed directions of sex* (line 3). How does the deviation sustain the speaker's *wish to be alone*? (**Hint** *Compare with the normal paradigm of having printed directions of a machine.*)
e) Explain the semantic deviation in *tabled fertility rites* (line 8). How does the deviation extend the speaker's *wish to be alone*? (**Hint** *Compare with the normal paradigm of having tabled obligations and examine the overtones of 'rites'.*)
f) Which lines are repeated in the two stanzas? What is the interpretive significance of the repetition? (**Hint** *Examine the way each stanza opens and closes.*)
g) The two stanzas are exact parallels of each other at the thematic and structural levels. Identify the parallel structures. How is this textual choice appropriate to the speaker's impatience with the artificiality of modern life? (**Hint** *Compare lines 2 and 7, 3 and 8, and 4 and 9. Also, examine the structure of the second, third and fourth lines in each stanza.*)
h) Compare the punctuation in the two stanzas. How is this graphological choice relevant to the poem's theme?
i) Compare the number of lines, the number of words and the rhyme scheme in each stanza. How do these textual decisions cohere with the other choices in the poem?

2.2 Do it yourself

Analyse the foregrounded patterns in 'The Brain is Wider than the Sky' by Emily Dickinson and relate them to your interpretation of the poem. The poem has no title but it often goes by its first line 'The Brain is Wider than the Sky'. Most of Emily Dickinson's poems have no titles. (There are hints below the text to guide, but not dictate, your response.)

Hints

a) How does the semantic deviation in *The brain is wider than the sky* (line 1) help convey the speaker's concept about the power of the brain? (**Hint** *'Brain' in English refers to a physical organ in the head or an abstract concept of intellectual capacity.*)
b) How does the semantic deviation in *The one will the other contain* (line 3) carry forward the speaker's construction of the human brain?

c) How does the semantic deviation in *The brain is deeper than the sea* (line 5) extend the speaker's argument about the power of the brain?
d) How does the semantic deviation in *The one will the other absorb* (line 7) sustain the construction of the brain?
e) How does the semantic deviation in *As Sponges Buckets do* (line 8) enrich the argument?
f) How does the semantic deviation in *The brain is just the weight of God* (line 9) contribute to the argument?
g) How does the semantic deviation in *they will differ . . . As syllable from sound* (line 12) conclude this construction of the human brain? (**Hint** *A syllable does not exist independently of sounds, but sounds do of syllables. Sounds are the raw material out of which syllables are made.*)
h) The poem has dashes where they are not expected, and has many of them. What effect does this graphological deviation have on reading the poem, and of course on understanding it?
i) The three stanzas are exact parallels of each other. They have the same rhythm (alternating iambic tetrametre and trimetre) and the same rhyme scheme (ABCB). Does this parallelism relate to the structure of the argument?

Further Reading

DEVIATION IN POETRY

Levin, S. R. (1965), 'Internal and external deviation in poetry', *Word*, 21(2), 225–37, <https://doi.org/10.1080/00437956.1965.11435425> (last accessed 23 September 2021).

An article on the two types of deviation (external and internal) at all levels of textual organisation in poetry.

Widdowson, H. G. (1983), 'The deviant language of poetry', in C. J. Brumfit (ed.), *Teaching Literature Overseas: Language-Based Approaches*, Pergamon Press, pp. 7–16.

This is an interesting book chapter on linguistic deviation in poetry and the need for adjustment of our reading habits when reading poetry. The chapter includes many interesting examples in support of the arguments.

FOREGROUNDING

van Peer, W. (2007), 'Introduction to foregrounding: A state of the art', *Language and Literature*, 16(2), 99–104, <https://doi.org/10.1177/0963947007075978> (last accessed 23 September 2021).

The paper offers an insight into the range of application of foregrounding by reviewing research on the effect of the density of foregrounding devices on the reader (Miall and Kuiken 1994), differences in readers' reaction to different stages in the production of a novel (Sopčák 2007), and the reactions of viewers to foregrounding in films

(Hakemulder 2007). It also refers to readers' reactions to such form, linking it to the functions of literary texts more generally.

van Peer, W. and J. Hakemulder (2006), 'Foregrounding', in K. Brown (ed.), *Encyclopedia of Language and Linguistics*, vol. 4, 2nd edn, Elsevier, pp. 546–50.

This encyclopedia entry offers one of the best introductions to the concept of foregrounding. It defines the term clearly, traces it to its historical origin, lists the devices of foregrounding, and demonstrates the existence of the devices of foregrounding across text types.

THE NATURE OF COMMUNICATION IN POETRY

Widdowson, H. G. (1992), *Practical Stylistics*, Oxford University Press.

The book is in two parts. The first part offers an introduction to the nature of communication in poetry, and the second suggests a set of principles for an approach to teaching poetry that is informed by the nature of communication in the genre.

FORMALIST STYLISTIC ANALYSIS OF POETRY

Leech, G. N. [1969] (2007), *A Linguistic Guide to English Poetry*, Longman.

The first two chapters are on the language of poetry, and the third and fourth present an analysis of foregrounding via deviation, repetition, and parallelism of extracts from poems as well as of extended poetic texts.

Short, M. [1996] (2014), *Exploring the Language of Poems, Plays and Prose*, 2nd edn, Routledge. Chapters 1 to 5 offer a stylistic analysis of foregrounding via deviation, repetition and parallelism of extracts from poems as well as of extended fictional and dramatic texts. The author also offers checklists for the reader to use when carrying out stylistic analysis.

3

FUNCTIONALIST ANALYSIS OF POETRY

Chapter Overview
- functionalist stylistics
- transitivity
- checklist of formalist categories
- 'Indian Women' by Shiv K. Kumar
- functionalist analysis of 'Indian Women'

Introduction

Linguistics took a 'functional' turn in the 1970s under the influence of M. A. K. Halliday's **SYSTEMIC FUNCTIONAL LINGUISTICS** (SFL). Halliday viewed language as a social construct, viewed style as a function of choice, and argued that a formal feature of a text is relevant to interpretation only if it contributes to the overall meaning or 'function' of the text. Stylistics also took a functional turn, with stylisticians drawing analytical frameworks from Halliday's linguistic model. This chapter offers a brief outline of **FUNCTIONALIST STYLISTICS**, suggests a checklist of functionalist stylistic categories, presents an account of transitivity as a system encoding the representation of experience, and presents the findings of our functionalist analysis of the poem 'Indian Women' by the Indian poet Shiv K. Kumar.

Functionalist stylistics

Functional, or functionalist, stylistics is informed, in theory and practice, by Halliday's systemic functional linguistics. In fact, the term has traditionally 'been used to refer to stylistics based on M. A. K. Halliday's model of linguistics' (Lin 2016: 57). Halliday views language as constructing rather than representing meaning. The linguistic choices that writers, and speakers of course, make encode meanings and perceptions of people and events. These meanings and perceptions are encoded in the grammar of the clause.

In line with Halliday's 'constructivist' outlook, functionalist stylistics views texts as a site for **IDEOLOGY** and ideological representations of the world. All texts, through choices at the different levels of language, realise ideologies and world-views. The central constituent in the toolkit of the functionalist stylistician is choice. Lexical and grammatical choices are viewed as functional and analysed for the way they encode authorial world-views. To detect these world-views, we analyse the lexicogrammatical choices in the grammar of the clause. Halliday (1971) suggests transitivity as a grammatical system through which to analyse the textual construction of the world, as well as the construction of the events, people, and circumstances in it.

TRANSITIVITY is central to the analytical toolkit of the functionalist stylistician, providing the 'lexicogrammatical resources' to account for the way texts represent the experience of the world in terms of who did what (to whom) and in what circumstances (Halliday 1985). The textual experience of the world is constructed in terms of participants (realised by nominal groups), processes (realised by verbal groups), and circumstances (realised by prepositional phrases and adverbials of time, place and/or manner), as exemplified by the sentence *The US* (participant) *invaded* (process) *Iraq* (participant) *in 2003* (circumstance).

The processes break down into six types that are claimed to cover all types of experience: material processes are processes of action, which may be intentional (*The bees attacked the children*), supervention (*He fell*), or event processes (*The bomb exploded*); verbalisation processes are processes of communication (*John told me a story*); mental processes are processes of the mind, which may be processes of perception (*John saw Mary*), cognition (*John knows Mary*), and/or affection (*John likes Mary*); relational processes are processes that express relationships, which may be relations of possession (*I have friends*), equivalence (*My boss is my neighbour*), or attributes (*John is tall*); behavioural processes are processes that express behaviour (*She laughed at me*); and existential processes are process that denote existence (*Once upon a time there was a prince*).

Related to transitivity is agency, which relates to the construction of the role of participants vis-à-vis the processes. The roles vary according to the type of process, namely, actor, goal (material), sayer, receiver (verbal), sensor, phenomenon (mental), carrier, attribute (relational), behaver (behavioural), and existent (existential). A more detailed account of the system of transitivity is available in Simpson (1988).

A checklist of functionalist categories

In this section, I propose a checklist of descriptive categories to use in carrying out a functionalist analysis of poetry. I carried out the analysis offered in this chapter using this checklist. When you use the list, make sure you tick the question you have answered. This should help you cover all functionalist categories and come up with a more systematic analysis of the poems for independent analysis in activities 3.1 and 3.2. Questions (a) to (f) on the checklist will help you spot the functionalist features, and questions (g) to (h) will help you examine the functional relevance of the patterns of transitivity and agency, as well as of the other textual choices (lexical, grammatical, and sematic), to the meaning of the poem(s), and to the way people and 'happenings' are represented through language.

a) What are the verbs in the text? List them.
b) What process type is each verb? Categorise the verbs in terms of the type of process.
c) What nominal groups are associated with each verb?
d) What semantic role does each nominal have?
e) What adverbials and prepositional phrases are associated with each process type?
f) What is the function of each adverbial and prepositional phrase?
g) How do the verbal processes, and the associated participants and circumstances, uncover the way the text constructs its world and the relationship between the characters in it?
h) How do the other textual choices sustain your interpretation?

The text

The poem to analyse here is 'Indian Women' by the Indian poet, and novelist, Shiv K. Kumar (1921–2017). It is a modern poem published in 1974, and describes the lives of rural women in India. Does the poem offer a positive or negative picture of Indian women? Let us examine authorial choices for an answer.

> In this triple-baked continent   1
> women don't etch angry eyebrows
> on mud walls.
> > Patiently they sit
> > like empty pitchers   5
> > on the mouth of the village well
> plaiting hope in each braid
> of their mississippi-long hair
> looking deep into the water's mirror
> > for the moisture in their eyes.   10
> > With zodiac doodling on the sands
> > they guard their tattooed thighs
> waiting for their men's return
> till even the shadows
> roll up their contours   15
> > and are gone
> > beyond the hills.

The analysis

Following the checklist above, we will first examine patterns of representation of rural Indian women in the grammar of the clauses in the poem. We will identify processes in which Indian women figure and the participant roles associated with them. We will then go on to consider other textual choices which sustain the construction of Indian women in the poem.

Transitivity and agency

Our point of departure is the patterns of agency and transitivity in the poem, particularly the way women are projected in relation to verbs (of action). The poem contains eight verbs: *etch, sit, plaiting, looking, guard, waiting, roll up,* and *are gone*. Indian women are the subject of the first six verbs. All six verbs are material action intentional verbs, that is, they denote action and intention. Three of these verbs, however, have been structured as non-finite verbs *plaiting, looking, waiting*. This choice is interesting in two ways. First, these verbs have no objects. Indian women are projected as involved in intentional action but action with little effect on people and life around them. Second, the choice of non-finite verbs projects women in subordinate, not main, clauses.

The other three verbs are finite. The first one *etch*, however, is negated *don't etch*; the second is a material action event with no object *sitting*; and the third is a material action intentional whose object is women themselves *guarding their tattooed thighs*.

Despite the 'apparent' agency, Indian women are embedded largely in subordinate structures, and when structured at a higher level, they appear in transitivity patterns where they initiate no action and cause no change of state. Choices related to verbs (transitivity) and subjects (agency) may therefore be said to have constructed Indian women as subordinate and powerless.

Lexical choices

Other lexical choices bear out this construction. The poem consists of three sentences. Each sentence has one independent clause and more than one subordinate clause. In fact, the poem has thirteen subordinate structures. This high incidence of subordinate constructions serves to heighten the theme of subordination in the poem.

Besides, the poem has a total of seven pronouns all of which are gender-neutral or non-sexist. Although this is a poem about women, there is not a single gender-specific pronoun (female pronoun) in the entire text. This may be explained by the poet's choice to refer to women in the plural form. Whatever the reasoning, the poet has chosen not to use any gender-specific, female pronoun in a poem unequivocally about women. There is also no female voice in the entire poem; women are silenced.

In addition to pronominal references, there is only one explicit mention of 'women' in the poem (line 2), excluding the title. Men have also only one explicit mention (line 13). This equal weight is unexpected because the poem is on Indian 'women'. This is interpretively significant. Even in a poem on women, men get almost equal representation. It may well be said that women are underrepresented in the poem. But if we count the references to women, albeit using gender-neutral pronouns, women will outnumber men.

Analysis of other linguistic choices, however, indicates that it is the men who are in control and who dominate Indian women's lives. Almost all the activities by Indian women are in the service of their men: they *sit patiently, guard their tattooed thighs and wait for their men's return*. Analysis of the language of images also contributes to the construction of Indian women. There are five images in the poem. The first offers a description of the scene where Indian women are living – a *triple-baked continent*. To bake is to make something get harder using dry heat. This is where Indian women are living. In the second image Indian women are projected as being as desperate as the land where they are living. They *don't etch angry eyebrows on mud walls*. They are incapable of anger, to the extent that they do not even sketch impressions of 'angry eyebrows' onto the mud walls of their homes. They take on everything without giving vent to their feelings. In the next image, they are compared to *empty pitchers on the mouth of the village well* waiting to be filled. Besides the sensual implications, the simile suggests that Indian women are living a life of need in the midst of abundance. There is plenty but very little for them.

The next image is of Indian women *plaiting hope in each braid of their mississippi-long hair*. When we plait cloth, we fold the cloth by doubling the material upon itself. Indian women have hopes that are folded upon themselves and awaiting realisation. The last image is of Indian women *looking deep into the water's mirror for the moisture in their eyes*. They are looking in the village well for the moisture that has dried up in their eyes. They have suffered too long. The end of the poem marks the end of the day, with women guarding their thighs in expectation of their men.

Summary

The functionalist analysis in this chapter has revealed the way language is used to textually construct Indian women. There is no female pronoun and no female voice in the entire poem. The poet speaks for them. They are constructed as having little agency, causing no change of state, and are subordinated at lower levels of textual structure. I hope that reading this chapter motivates you to read more on functionalist stylistics and SFL-informed functionalist stylistic research such as Kennedy (1982), which makes use of transitivity analysis to shed light on the role of a female character in a murder scene in fiction, and research that draws on insights from SFL to develop frameworks for the analysis of multimodal texts (e.g. Kress and van Leeuwen [1996] 2006). The reading material in the Further Reading section of this chapter should get you started.

3.1 Do it yourself

Examine the way the patterns of transitivity and agency and the way the other linguistic choices in 'I Sit and Look Out' (1860) by the American poet Walt Whitman work together to convey Whitman's criticism of people's inaction in the face of others' suffering (Whitman 1995).

Hints

a) Categorise the verbs in the poem in terms of the type of process: material (doing), verbalisations (saying), mental (thinking, feeling), relational (relation, equivalence), behavioural (behaviour), and existential.
b) Which processes are associated with the speaker?
c) What roles does the speaker assume in each process? What does the choice tell us about the speaker's reaction to other people's suffering?
d) How many sentences are there in the poem? In what way(s) does this choice contribute to the overall meaning/effect?
e) Categorise the other semantically related words. Which of them have negative/positive connotations? How does the choice contribute to the message of the poem?
f) Change the mental processes to material processes. Does the change in transitivity affect the overall tone and message?

3.2 Do it yourself

Examine the way the patterns of transitivity and agency and other linguistic choices in 'Song' (1972) by Adrienne Rich construct loneliness not as an emotional and mental state but in terms of action.

Hints

a) Categorise the verbs in the poem in terms of the type of the process: material (doing), verbalisations (saying), mental (thinking, feeling), relational (relation, equivalence), and behavioural (behaviour).
b) Which types of processes dominate the poem? Which of the processes are associated with the addressee and which are associated with the description of the speaker's loneliness? How does this choice help the speaker construct loneliness?
c) In the first stanza, the speaker compares her loneliness to a plane riding level. How does this comparison enrich the construction of loneliness?
d) In the second stanza, the speaker compares her loneliness to a woman driving non-stop. How does the comparison sustain the construction of loneliness?

e) In the third stanza, the speaker compares her loneliness to a person waking up first when others are sleeping. How does this image support the argument so far?
f) In the fourth stanza, the speaker compares her loneliness to a *rowboat ice-fat on the shore*. How does this comparison support the speaker's argument?
g) Why does the poet use *woman* not *man* (line 10)?
h) The word *lonely* is repeated nine times in the poem. What is the effect of the repetition?
i) The speaker in the poem speaks for the addressee. How does this choice contribute to the poem's overall meaning and effect?
j) Is the choice of the title 'Song' consistent with the tone and arguments in the poem?

Further Reading

TRANSITIVITY

Simpson, P. (1988), 'The transitivity model', *Critical Studies in Mass Communication*, 5(2), 166–72, <https://doi.org/10.1080/15295038809366696> (last accessed 23 September 2021).
A brief and practical introduction to the transitivity model.

TRANSITIVITY ANALYSIS: POETRY

Brooks, J. (2009), 'The growing absurdity of the South African apartheid: Transitivity in Christopher Van Wyk's "In Detention"', *Innervate*, 2, 26–34.
An essay using Halliday's transitivity model in the analysis of Christopher Van Wyk's 'In Detention' from the collection of poems *It is Time to Go Home*.

TRANSITIVITY ANALYSIS: FICTION

Halliday, M. A. K. (1971), 'Linguistic function and literary style: An inquiry into the language of William Golding's *The Inheritors*', in S. Chatman (ed.), *Literary Style: A Symposium*, Oxford University Press, pp. 330–68.
This is a seminal work in the area. Halliday demonstrates how textual choices in the novel depict one group of characters as primitive and another group as more sophisticated.

TRANSITIVITY ANALYSIS: NEWS HEADLINES

Seo, S. (2013), 'Hallidayean transitivity analysis: The Battle for Tripoli in the contrasting headlines of two national newspapers', *Discourse and Society*, 24(6), 774–91, <https://doi.org/10.1177/0957926513503267> (last accessed 23 September 2021).
This study uses transitivity analysis to highlight differences in the representation of the Battle for Tripoli during the 2011 Libyan civil war in British and Chinese online national newspapers.

4

CRITICAL LINGUISTIC ANALYSIS OF FICTION

> **Chapter Overview**
> - communication in fiction
> - critical linguistics
> - checklist of critical linguistic categories
> - *Salmon Fishing in the Yemen* by Paul Torday
> - critical linguistic analysis of an extract from *Salmon Fishing in the Yemen*

Introduction

In the previous two chapters, we analysed two modern poems using the formalist and functionalist frameworks. In this chapter, and in the next one, we analyse fiction. This chapter uses the analytical framework of **CRITICAL LINGUISTICS** to analyse an epistolary novel – a novel written in the form of letters. The first part of the chapter outlines the nature of communication in fiction and proposes a checklist of categories to use in carrying out your own critical linguistic analyses on the extracts suggested for independent study in activities 4.1 and 4.2. In the second part of the chapter, we carry out a critical linguistic analysis of an extract from the novel *Salmon Fishing in the Yemen* by Paul Torday (2011). We will look at the way **MODALITY** and modes of narration carry ideological viewpoint and authorial attitude.

Communication in fiction

A novel is a lengthy literary work written in prose containing a narrative about human experience. It offers an extended and imaginative representation of reality narrated from a particular perspective. The reader reconstructs this account of reality through the language of the text, but this reconstruction is often affected by the perspective from which the narrative is told. It could be told by one character to another, by a narrator to a narratee, or by the author to the reader. These three levels of discourse structure correspond to three possible viewpoints from which the story may be narrated. The technique of narration not only affects the way events are represented but also conditions readers' viewpoints and reactions to the narrative. This should explain why the 'study of the novel in the twentieth-century has to a very large extent been the study of point of view' (Short [1996] 2014: 256).

There are many linguistic means of presenting, and manipulating, readers' ideological outlooks on the account of experience in the narrative. This chapter focuses on modality and the modes of narration and presentation of character talk and thought as carriers of (ideological) perspective.

Critical linguistics

Critical linguistics is concerned with the role of language in ideological discourse. It investigates the way language is used to textually represent people and events, thereby constructing a social reality that maintains, or propagates, social power relations and ideological evaluations (Fowler 1991). Critical linguists maintain that language is the medium used to construct social reality, and set out to analyse language use, which they argue is always value-laden. Important linguistic carriers of viewpoint in language are modality and the modes of presentation of character speech and thought.

Modality is the expression of attitude about a proposition (such as commitment, desire, or certainty). Linguistic carriers of authorial attitudes include modal verbs, verbs, nouns, adjectives, and adverbs. Simpson (1993) classifies modality into four types. Epistemic modality is the expression of knowledge and belief realised by modal verbs *may*, adjectives *certain*, verbs *think*, or adverbs *perhaps*. Perception modality expresses commitment to the truth of a proposition (based on perception), realised by verbs *seem*, adjectives *obvious*, or adverbs *apparently*. Deontic modality is the expression of an assessment on the necessity or possibility of a proposition. It is carried by modal verbs, such as *may, should, must*. Finally, boulomaic modality, which is carried by such verbs as *wish* and *regret*, is the expression of desire.

Following Halliday, critical linguistics categorise modal operators into a system of three degrees of strength, called values. Modals with high value include *must, should, ought to, need to, have to*; modals with median value include *will, would, shall*; and modals with low value include *may, might, can, could*.

Simpson (1993) also argues that much of the effect of a text is attributable to its point of view. The narrator of the story may be a participating character (Category A) or a third person narrator or reflector (Category B). In either case, the narrative can be positively, neutrally or negatively shaded. A positively shaded text is rich in deontic and boulomaic modals of high value, resulting in an assertive and emphatic mode of narration; a negatively shaded text is characterised by low-value epistemic and perception modalities and reflects the uncertainty of the narrator; and a neutrally shaded text is narrated using non-modalised assertions.

It detaches the narrator, who does not attempt to influence the ideological perspective of the audience.

The other linguistic tool to mediate, and manipulate, the audience's perception of the narrative, and the characters in it, is the mode of presentation of characters' speech and thought. A narrative may be told in the first person and from the viewpoint of a participating character-narrator whose account of actions and events is the one we as readers must share. It may also be narrated in the third person by a detached, invisible narrator whose 'omniscience' facilitates privileged access to the thoughts and feelings of individual characters. Alternatively, it may be told in the third person, where the third person narrator is external to the action of the story and is unable or reluctant to delve at will into the thoughts and feelings of characters.

In representing characters' speech and thoughts, authors often draw on five modes of presentation of speech, paralleled by five modes of presentation of thoughts (Leech and Short [1981] 2007). The modes of speech presentation include direct speech (*Mary said, 'I am sorry for being late'*), free direct speech (*I am sorry for being late*), indirect speech (*Mary said that she was sorry for being late*), free indirect speech (*Mary was sorry for being late that day*), and narrative report of a speech act (*Mary apologised for being late*). The modes of presenting characters' thoughts, on the other hand, include direct thought (*John wondered, 'Does Mary still love me?'*), free direct thought (*Does Mary still love me?*), indirect thought (*John wondered if Mary still loved him*), free indirect thought (*Did Mary still love John?*), and narrative report of a thought act (*John wondered about Mary's love for him*).

A checklist of critical linguistic categories

This section gives you a head start by offering a set of questions to help you see how I carried out the analysis and assist you in producing your own critical linguistic analyses of the two extracts for further practice at the end of the chapter. You can use a table, like the one offered in Table 4.1, in answering the questions on the checklist.

a) What modal expressions are used? Categorise the modal expressions according to the modality type.
b) Is the text positively, negatively or neutrally shaded?
c) What is the category of narration?
d) Is the narrator a participating character in the narrative or an outsider narrating from inside or outside the consciousness of the characters?
e) Which modes of presentation of character talk are used?
f) Which modes of presentation of character thought are used?
g) How do modality, shading, and the modes of narration and presentation of character talk and thought carry attitude and ideological outlook?

The text

Salmon Fishing in the Yemen is a 2007 epistolary novel about a fisheries expert (Dr Alfred Jones) who is recruited by Ms Harriet Chetwode-Talbot, the financial consultant of Yemeni Sheikh Muhammad ibn Zaidi bani Tihama, in order to realise the sheikh's wish to introduce the sport of salmon fishing into Wadi Aleyn in the Heraz mountains of Yemen. At first, Dr Jones rejects the idea because it is scientifically absurd but later joins the team. Peter Maxwell, the British prime minister's director of communications, advises that the government support the project to improve the image of Britain in the Arab world. As the project unfolds, the sheikh survives an assassination attempt by opponents of the 'Westernisation' of the region. The project eventually loses official support but it continues. On the big day, the salmon are released into the wadi. While the team is celebrating, the weather changes. Heavy rain floods the wadi, killing the sheikh, the prime minister, and the fish. It is this tragic end, as narrated by Maxwell, that we are quoting below for analysis.

> [1]Then I heard Fred shout, 'Be careful! The water is rising! Keep an eye on it!' [2]The boss either didn't hear, or didn't want to hear. [3]He had let his fly come round and was making his next cast. [4]The rain was coming down like stair rods now, and the river looked as if it was almost boiling under the weight of water coming down out of the sky. [5]'I think you should come out now!' shouted Fred. [6]'There's a hell of a lot of water coming down!'
>
> [7]Even I could see that the water in the wadi was rising. [8]I found I had unconsciously stepped back a couple of yards, higher up the bank. [9]At the same moment, Colin began to wade into the river, I suppose to help the sheikh out. [10]I saw our security men looking at each other, wondering what to do. [11]There was a flash of lightning, or perhaps it was not lightning, but it made me turn my head and I saw the tribesman I had noticed earlier on the promontory, with his rifle raised to his shoulder. [12]He had either just fired a shot, or was about to fire one. [13]Had I heard a shot? [14]The water coming down the river was beginning to roar now. [15]One of the security people pulled a gun from under his jacket in a single fluid move, and I think he shot the tribesman. [16]At any rate the man fell backwards off the rocky crag and disappeared from my sight. [17]I don't know who he had been intending to shoot. [18]I think it must have been the sheikh, but I can't be sure.
>
> [19]There was uproar and several more shots were fired by the Yemenis, I don't know what at. [20]I don't think they had yet grasped what was going on. [21]The crowd broke up, people scrambling up the bank to get away from the river and from the shooting. [22]I found that I was several yards higher up the bank again, my heart thumping in my chest, staring down at the boss. [23]He had turned to look at the noise, but he wasn't moving. [24]I think he was smiling. [25]I don't think he had seen the tribesman either shooting or being shot, although

he knew something had happened, because he had turned to look downstream.

[26]I saw him look at the sheikh, who was bent over, supported by Colin, who was now at his side and struggling to keep his balance against the weight of water. [27]Maybe the sheikh had been shot. [28]I don't know.

[29]Behind the boss I saw a wall of white and brown water come round the corner of the canyon and surge down the wadi towards him. [30]I could see, rather than hear, Fred still screaming to him to get out. [31]Then Fred, too, turned and started to scramble towards safety, up the bank. [32]The boss was still smiling, I think. [33]I was some distance away by then, but you can tell sometimes from a person's posture that they are smiling. [34]He was facing away from the wall of water coming towards him. [35]He must have heard it. [36]I don't know. [37]Maybe he didn't. [38]They say you can get very absorbed fishing. [39]At any rate, I like to think—I am as sure as I can be—that as he lifted his rod to make another cast, he was very happy. [40]He was far away from politics, far away from wars, from journalists, from MPs, from generals, from civil servants. [41]He was in a river and there were salmon running past his feet, and with the next cast I am sure he believed he would catch a fish.

[42]Then the surge hit him. [43]A boiling torrent of brown water, mud, rocks, palm fronds raced down the wadi with a noise like a train, and in a moment Colin, the sheikh and the boss instantly vanished without trace. [44]The wave then powered on and disappeared round the next corner into the canyons far below.

[45]One second the boss was standing there; the next he was gone. [46]And I never saw him again. [47]Or the sheikh. [48]Or Colin McPherson. [50]They never found their bodies.

[51]That was what happened when we launched the Yemen salmon project, and the salmon ran in the Wadi Aleyn.

The Analysis

Guided by the checklist, we will classify the modal expressions and their values, which reflect the shading of the text. We will also identify the modes of narration and discuss their role in communicating ideological perspectives in the narrative.

Maxwell, a participating character in the narrative, is describing the situation, and narrating the events, using first person pronouns and *verba sentiendi* – verbs of mental perception, such as *feel* and *think*, that convey the speaker's viewpoint or attitude towards the events or the situation in the propositional component of the sentence. This is Category A narration.

Maxwell's description is made almost exclusively using epistemic modality – expressions of uncertainty (Table 4.1). This modality choice makes the text negatively shaded. It reflects the narrator's alienation and uncertainty about the events described. This choice is interesting because normally descriptions are made using unmodalised assertions (e.g. *he was smiling*) that do not reflect the narrator's

TABLE 4.1 Categorisation of expressions of modality in the extract

Modality type	Modal expressions	Number of expressions
Epistemic	**Modal auxiliaries** *could* (2), *must have been, can be, can't be, must have heard, would* **Modal verbs** *suppose, believed, wondering, (don't) think* (8), *don't know* (4), *knew* **Modal adverbs** *perhaps, maybe* (2) **Adjectival constructions** *I am sure he believed* **Comparative structure** *I am as sure as*	28
Perception	–	–
Deontic	**Modal auxiliaries** *you can tell sometimes*; *They say you can get very absorbed*	2
Boulomaic	–	–

attitude. Why does Maxwell choose modalised propositions to describe the scene?

Maxwell is reporting the flooding of the river. Fred is crying out to warn his boss against the rising water level. The rain is coming down heavily, and Maxwell is watching his boss, the British prime minister, drown. It was Maxwell who convinced his boss of the project in the first place. The death of the prime minister in the wadi in Yemen constitutes not only a massive shock to Maxwell but a threat to his reputation and career. It is in this state of mind that Maxwell is reporting.

Maxwell reports Fred's reaction in direct speech. He uses Fred's exact forms of words in *'Be careful! The water is rising! Keep an eye on it!'* and *'I think you should come out now!'*, which leads the reader to expect Maxwell to produce a faithful account of the situation. However, he also produces a narrative report of the speech acts of Fred *screaming to him to get out*, and his boss *He must have heard it* and *he was very happy*. He also shifts from Category A to Category B narration, giving himself the freedom to narrate from within the consciousness of other characters. He uses narrative report of thought act to report the thoughts of the security men *wondering what to do*, and his boss *he knew something had happened* and *he believed he would catch a fish*. Maxwell's interpretation of the cognition and feelings of his boss helps him convey a sense of intimate association, which has the effect of detaching Maxwell from the disaster that has befallen his boss.

Maxwell's mode of narration reflects his psychological stance. The use of estrangement devices (the expressions of epistemic modality) in a Category A mode of narration serves to distance the narrator, Maxwell, from the unpleasant reality that he is reporting. This effect is enhanced by the position of the modal operators *perhaps, either . . . or, don't know,* and *suppose*. Maxwell starts sentences with categorical assertions and before the proposition ends, he weakens it with a modalised expression. This also serves to distance the reality he is reporting and does not want to believe.

Our last comment here is on the two instances of deontic modality *you can tell sometimes from a person's posture* and *They say you can get very absorbed fishing*. The sentences contain the low-value deontic marker of possibility *can*. Although Maxwell is claiming authority over the reader by using the second person pronoun and by shifting to positive shading, the first *can* is preceded by *think* and followed by *sometimes*, and the second *can* is preceded by the generic non-referential *they* – a shift to Category B narration. In both cases, the low-value deontic is weakened even further, which enhances Maxwell's uncertainty and his attempt to detach himself from the current reality. In effect, this choice emphasises the overall epistemic shade of the narration.

> ## Summary
>
> In this chapter, we have examined the role of modality and modes of narration in the presentation of authorial point of view and manipulation of audience outlook on events and characters in narrative fiction. We have seen how Maxwell uses direct speech minimally and chooses to report the speech and thoughts of his boss using narrative report of speech act and thought act. He gives himself freedom to interpret the speech and thoughts of his boss. Maxwell's use of these modes of narration allows him to control the speech and thoughts of the other characters, particularly his boss, and thus invite the reader to see things from only his own (Maxwell's) point of view. He also uses epistemic modality markers such as *think*, *don't know*, and *cannot be sure*, which signify his confused state of mind and attempt to push back the sad reality of his boss's death and the consequent threat to his own reputation and career.
>
> We have used the critical linguistic framework to analyse fiction. This does not mean that it is applicable only to fiction. Interesting applications of the framework on other types of discourse include Iwamoto (1998), which examines modality as a marker of point of view in wartime and peacetime newspapers in Japan; Borgogni (2016), which examines modality, point of view and ideology in a letter of protestation written in prison by 'one of the most infamous radical thinkers of England in the 1650's' (2016: 636); and Alonso-Almeida and González-Cruz (2012), which describes authorial voice in a corpus of travel texts written by male and female travellers.

4.1 Do it yourself

Examine the following extract from Charles Dickens's novel *Hard Times*, published in 1854. The novel offers criticism of the English society during the Industrial Revolution in the late eighteenth and the early years of the nineteenth centuries. In the novel, Gradgrind runs his home and school by a philosophy of rationalism, utilitarianism, and facts. There is little room for imagination. His son, Tom, becomes self-interested. He persuades Louisa, his sister, to marry a factory owner who is thirty years her senior in order to make his own life easier. Louisa marries the man, Bounderby, and Tom works for him. Eventually, Louisa runs to her father's house and cries that their upbringing has made her marry a man she does not love and left her life a mess. She collapses. Tom turns to drinking, robs a bank, and escapes to the Americas, where he dies without seeing his family. Gradgrind realises that the utilitarian education has ruined the life of his children. He eventually gives up on his approach and instead devotes his life and political power (he is a Member of Parliament by now) to helping the poor people of Coketown, a fictitious industrial town where the story takes place.

In the extract below, Gradgrind is joined at a class in his own school by a government officer (the gentleman) and by the teacher, Mr M'Choakumchild. The gentleman explains to the children the nature of the education they will receive.

> 'Girl number twenty,' said the gentleman, smiling in the calm strength of knowledge.
>
> Sissy blushed, and stood up.
>
> 'So you would carpet your room — or your husband's room, if you were a grown woman, and had a husband — with representations of flowers, would you?' said the gentleman. 'Why would you?'
>
> 'If you please, sir, I am very fond of flowers,' returned the girl.
>
> 'And is that why you would put tables and chairs upon them, and have people walking over them with heavy boots?'
>
> 'It wouldn't hurt them, sir. They wouldn't crush and wither, if you please, sir. They would be the pictures of what was very pretty and pleasant, and I would fancy —'
>
> 'Ay, ay, ay! But you mustn't fancy,' cried the gentleman, quite elated by coming so happily to his point. 'That's it! You are never to fancy.'
>
> 'You are not, Cecilia Jupe,' Thomas Gradgrind solemnly repeated, 'to do anything of that kind.'
>
> 'Fact, fact, fact!' said the gentleman. And 'Fact, fact, fact!' repeated Thomas Gradgrind.
>
> 'You are to be in all things regulated and governed,' said the gentleman, 'by fact. We hope to have, before long, a board of fact, composed of commissioners of fact, who will force the people to be a people of fact, and of nothing but fact. You must discard the word Fancy altogether. You have nothing to do with it. You are not to have, in any object of use or ornament, what would be a contradiction in fact. You don't walk upon flowers in fact; you cannot be allowed to walk upon flowers in carpets. You don't find that foreign birds and butterflies come and perch upon your crockery; you cannot be permitted to paint foreign birds and butterflies upon your crockery. You never meet with quadrupeds going up and down walls; you must not have quadrupeds represented upon walls. You must use,' said the gentleman, 'for all these purposes, combinations and modifications

(in primary colours) of mathematical figures which are susceptible of proof and demonstration. This is the new discovery. This is fact. This is taste.'

The girl curtseyed, and sat down. She was very young, and she looked as if she were frightened by the matter-of-fact prospect the world afforded.

Hints

a) Categorise the modal expressions in the extract by their modality type (epistemic, perception, deontic, and boulomaic modality).
b) What is the category of narration in the passage? Is the narrator a participating character in the narrative (Category A narration) or an outsider narrating from either inside or outside the consciousness of characters (Category B narratorial or reflector mode)?
c) Is the text positively, negatively or neutrally shaded? (**Hint** *The dominant modality type decides the shading.*)
d) Which modes of presentation of character talk and thought are used?
e) How does the choice of the modes of presentation of character speech and thought carry attitude and viewpoint?
f) How does the choice of modality and shading carry attitude and outlook?

4.2 Do it yourself

Examine the following extract from William Golding's *Lord of the Flies* ([1954] 1999), a story about boys stranded on an island in the midst of a raging war back at home. The boys attempt to recreate the society they came from. They elect Ralph to lead them but he is opposed by Jack who forms the 'hunters' group. The two groups fight. Piggy is killed, and Ralph runs for his life. The kids are eventually saved by a British naval officer. The novel highlights the savagery at the heart of human beings. In the extract (from chapter 2), Piggy is telling the boys that their plane has been shot down, that nobody knows their location, and that they may be left here for a long time. Trying to comfort the boys, Ralph says he has gone around the island and that it is beautiful.

'We'll have rules!' he cried excitedly. 'Lots of rules! Then when anyone breaks 'em –'
'Whee-oh!'
'Wacco!'
'Bong!'
'Doink!'
Ralph felt the conch lifted from his lap. Then Piggy was standing cradling the great cream shell and the shouting died down. Jack, left

on his feet, looked uncertainly at Ralph who smiled and patted the log. Jack sat down. Piggy took off his glasses and blinked at the assembly while he wiped them on his shirt.

'You're hindering Ralph. You're not letting him get to the most important thing.'

He paused effectively.

'Who knows we're here? Eh?'

'They knew at the airport.'

'The man with a trumpet-thing –'

'My dad.'

Piggy put on his glasses.

'Nobody knows where we are,' said Piggy. He was paler than before and breathless. 'Perhaps they knew where we was going to; and perhaps not. But they don't know where we are 'cos we never got there.' He gaped at them for a moment, then swayed and sat down. Ralph took the conch from his hands.

'That's what I was going to say,' he went on, 'when you all, all . . . .' He gazed at their intent faces. 'The plane was shot down in flames. Nobody knows where we are. We may be here a long time.'

The silence was so complete that they could hear the unevenness of Piggy's breathing. The sun slanted in and lay golden over half the platform. The breezes that on the lagoon had chased their tails like kittens were finding their way across the platform and into the forest. Ralph pushed back the tangle of fair hair that hung on his forehead.

'So we may be here a long time.'

Nobody said anything. He grinned suddenly.

'But this is a good island. We – Jack, Simon and me – we climbed the mountain. It's wizard. There's food and drink, and –'

'Rocks –'

'Blue flowers –'

Hints

a) Categorise the modal expressions in the extract by their modality type (epistemic, perception, deontic, and boulomaic modality).
b) What is the category of narration in the passage?
c) Is the text positively, negatively or neutrally shaded?
d) Which modes of presentation of character talk is used?
e) Does the narrator have access to the characters' feelings and thoughts?
f) How does the choice of the modes of speech presentation carry attitude and viewpoint?
g) How does the choice of shading carry the children's outlook and construct Piggy's character?

h) Why does Ralph choose non-modalised language at the end? How does this choice change the children's mood?

i) If you were asked to rewrite the extract and change the mood of the children from apprehension to assurance and confidence, what changes would you introduce to the text, especially with reference to the use of modalised language?

Further Reading

THE NATURE OF COMMUNICATION IN FICTION

Leech, G. and M. Short [1981] (2007), *Style in Fiction*, 2nd edn, Routledge.
 An extensive account of language and style in fictional prose.

CRITICAL LINGUISTIC ANALYSIS OF FICTION

Simpson, P. (1993), *Language, Ideology and Point of View*, Routledge.
 An in-depth analysis of ideology and point of view in fictional texts using the critical linguistic categories of transitivity and modality.

5

FEMINIST ANALYSIS OF FICTION

> **Chapter Overview**
> - communication in fiction
> - feminist stylistics
> - checklist of feminist stylistic categories
> - *The Handmaid's Tale* by Margaret Atwood
> - feminist stylistic analysis of an extract from *The Handmaid's Tale*

Introduction

This chapter is an extension of the investigation of textual ideology in narrative fiction. In the previous chapter, we carried out a critical linguistic analysis to examine the role of modality and modes of narration in the representation of characters' outlooks and states of mind. In this chapter, we continue the exploration of authorial ideology but with reference to the textual construction of women. For this purpose, we will use the feminist stylistic framework outlined in Mills (1995). We will start by considering the ideological representation of reality in fiction, go on to sketch out the feminist stylistic framework, suggest a checklist of analytical categories, and present the findings of the feminist stylistic analysis of an extract from *The Handmaid's Tale* by Margaret Atwood.

Communication in fiction

A novel offers a representation of reality mediated by the author's ideological assumptions about the world. The represented reality, by design, perpetuates and naturalises (contested) ideologies, and seeks to manipulate the reader's perspective and outlook on the experiences represented in the narrative. The narrative representation is 'inherent in the verbal patterns' of the text (Widdowson 1992: 37).

The reader reconstructs this account of reality, and deconstructs the naturalised ideologies, through linguistic analysis of the language of the text. This chapter investigates the textual construction of gender ideology in fiction. Using the analytical framework of **FEMINIST STYLISTICS**, the chapter explores gender bias, the distribution of gender roles and the fragmentation of the female body in a twentieth-century novel.

Feminist stylistics

Feminist stylistics 'has a precursor in critical linguistics' (Mills 1995: 8). In the tradition of critical linguistics, feminist stylistics holds that language 'is not a transparent carrier of meanings, but is a medium which imposes its own constraints on the meaning which is constructed' (Mills 1995: 8). In other words, language is a medium of social control. The lexis and structures of texts encode, and even perpetuate, naturalised ideologies and social processes. Drawing on Halliday's systemic functional linguistics, feminist stylistics offers a set of strategies that aim to 'draw attention to and change the way that gender is represented' (Mills 1995: 1). It relates 'the language of texts to extra-textual political processes' in its examination of power relations and representational practices (Mills 1995: 8). In doing so, it seeks to challenge the notion of 'normality' in the representation of masculinity and femininity 'by showing alternative choices within the language and explaining the way that these alternatives can lead to different and more productive meanings' (Mills 1995: 15).

Sara Mills's (1995) *Feminist Stylistics* is a pioneering publication on the analysis of the representation of gender in different text types. Mills extends the critical linguists' effort to move stylistics away from (canonical) literary texts to a consideration of all text types, such as newspaper and advertising discourses. This is 'particularly important in feminist stylistics where "woman" is the subject of a great many discourses besides literature' (Mills 1995: 13). To empower recipients of ideological discourse, Mills offers 'a set of tools' to be used in the description and analysis of gender and gender bias in texts. The tools operate 'at a range of different levels in texts' (1995: 157). These are the levels of words, phrases/sentences, and discourse.

Analysis at the level of words covers gender-specific pronoun use, the use of generics, and gender-specific naming strategies. Although the use of words can signal gender bias in texts, words can take on new connotative meanings in textual patterns. Analysis goes on to consider word combinations at higher levels of linguistic organisation. At this level, authors make choices which represent their experience of the world. Transitivity choices may construct (fictional) characters in active control of their circumstances (by being projected in material action intention processes), as out of control (by limiting their presence to supervention processes), as introspective (by over-presenting them in internalised mental processes), or as incompetent (by the disproportionate use of externalised mental processes).

Analysis at the level of discourse involves examination of the textual construction of characters – the way characters describe themselves and the way they are constructed through descriptive vocabulary. Analysis at this level includes the fragmentation of the female body. The technique of fragmentation involves the presentation of the body not as unified physical being but in terms of its parts. The effect of the fragmentation of the female body is that the body is represented as an object, or a collection of fragmentable objects, for the male gaze.

A checklist of feminist stylistic categories

This section offers a list of questions to help you identify those parts of texts that encode ideological representations of gender. The list is short, containing only eight questions. It is by no means comprehensive. It moves systematically from the level of words and clauses to the level of discourse in order to help you carry out feminist stylistic analysis in a systematic way. I expect you to use this list in analysing the fictional extracts offered in activities 5.1 and 5.2. A longer, and more comprehensive, list is found in Mills (1995: 158–60).

a) Are the pronouns gender-specific or gender-neutral? Which characters are referred to in gender-specific pronouns and which ones in gender-neutral pronouns?
b) Are the naming strategies gender-specific or gender-neutral? How are female characters named?
c) What verbal processes are associated with female characters?
d) What world-view about women does the distribution of verbal processes perpetuate?
e) Are female body parts described?
f) What descriptive vocabulary is used to qualify the (female) body? Is it described for the male gaze?
g) Is the female body constructed as fragmentable and, as a consequence, consumable?
h) What world-views does the text perpetuate about men and women?

The text

The Handmaid's Tale is a 1985 dystopian novel that explores, among other themes, the subjugation of women in a patriarchal society. The story is set in the Republic of Gilead – a near-future totalitarian, theocratic state that has overthrown the United States government. The freedom of handmaids, and women, in the Republic is completely restricted. Handmaids can leave the house only on shopping trips and they are constantly spying on other handmaids. Because reproduction rates in Gilead are alarmingly low, handmaids are also assigned, against their will, to bear children for elite couples that have trouble conceiving.

The novel has a double narrative, Offred's tale and the handmaids' tales. The night scenes are about Offred, the Commander's handmaid, and the other scenes describe, from the perspective of Offred, the details of the lives of handmaids in the Republic. In the passage below, from chapter 4, Offred, the Commander's handmaid, is on a shopping trip talking to Ofglen, her partner handmaid, about Nick, the Commander's driver.

> ¹He's wearing the uniform of the Guardians, but his cap is tilted at a jaunty angle and his sleeves are rolled to the elbow, showing his forearms, tanned but with a stipple of dark hairs. ²He has a cigarette stuck in the corner of his mouth, which shows that he too has something he can trade on the black market.
> ³I know this man's name: *Nick*. ⁴I know this because I've heard Rita and Cora talking about him, and once I heard the Commander speaking to him: Nick, I won't be needing the car.
> ⁵He lives here, in the household, over the garage. ⁶Low status: he hasn't been issued a woman, not even one. ⁷He doesn't rate: some defect, lack of connections. ⁸But he acts as if he doesn't know this, or care. ⁹He's too casual, he's not servile enough. ¹⁰It may be stupidity, but I don't think so. ¹¹Smells fishy, they used to say; or, I smell a rat. Misfit as odor. ¹²Despite myself, I think of how he might smell. ¹³Not fish or decaying rat; tanned skin, moist in the sun, filmed with smoke. ¹⁴I sigh, inhaling.
> ¹⁵He looks at me, and sees me looking. ¹⁶He has a French face, lean, whimsical, all planes and angles, with creases around the mouth where he smiles. ¹⁷He takes a final puff of the cigarette, lets it drop to the driveway, and steps on it. ¹⁸He begins to whistle. ¹⁹Then he winks. ²⁰I drop my head and turn so that the white wings hide my face, and keep walking. ²¹He's just taken a risk, but for what? ²²What if I were to report him? . . .
> ²³I walk to the corner and wait. ²⁴I used to be bad at waiting. ²⁵They also serve who only stand and wait, said Aunt Lydia. ²⁶She made us memorize it. ²⁷She also said, Not all of you will make it through. ²⁸Some of you will fall on dry ground or thorns. ²⁹Some of you are shallow-rooted. ³⁰She had a mole on her chin that went up and down while she talked. ³¹She said, Think of yourselves as seeds, and right then her voice was wheedling, conspiratorial, like the voices of those women who used to teach ballet classes to children, and who would say, Arms up in the air now; let's pretend we're trees. ³²I stand on the corner, pretending I am a tree.

The analysis

Following the checklist, we will analyse the way female characters are textually constructed by analysing linguistic choices at the word, sentence/clause and discourse levels. The selected extract is long and the sentences have been numbered for ease of reference.

The word level

Analysis at the level of words covers the use of gender-specific pronouns and the naming strategies that serve to perpetuate a particular view of women. In the extract, Offred, the female protagonist, is talking about Nick, a male character, who works as a *Guardian* and *driver*. Nick is referred to twice by name, once as *man*, and twenty-six times in pronominal reference (nineteen references as subject, three as object, and four in possessive relations). These references construct Nick as an individual with control over the circumstances.

By comparison, Offred and Ofglen do not enjoy the same individualism. There is no mention of what they do for a living. In addition, the way the two female characters are named enhances the subordination of women. The names Offred and Ofglen are a combination of the preposition *of* and the names of the male masters they are serving, *Fred* and *Glen*, respectively. The handmaids are forbidden to use their birth names and must 'bear' the name of the male they are serving. The women are constructed in depersonalised terms as 'objects' belonging to the men they work for, not as independent personalities.

The clause level

At this level, we will compare the verbal processes that involve Offred (Table 5.1) and Nick (Table 5.2). The types of processes in which the characters are structured contribute to the construction of the individualism, or otherwise, of the female and male characters.

TABLE 5.1 Verbal processes involving Offred

Sentence	Verbal element	Transitivity pattern	Semantic role
3	know this man's name	Mental process	Sensor (Offred)
4	know this	Mental process	Sensor (Offred)
4	have heard	Mental process	Sensor (Offred)
4	heard	Mental process	Sensor (Offred)
10	don't think so	Mental process	Sensor (Offred)
12	think of how	Mental process	Sensor (Offred)
14	sigh	Material process	(Affected = none)
20	drop my head	Material process	(Affected = female body)
20	turn	Material process	(Affected = female body)
20	hide my face	Material process	(Affected = female body)
20	keep walking	Material process	(Affected = none)
22	were to report him?	Mental process	Sensor (Offred)
23	walk to the corner	Material process	(Affected = none)
23	wait	Material process	(Affected = none)
24	used to be bad	Relational process	Carrier (Offred)
32	stand on the corner	Material process	(Affected = none)
32	pretending	Mental process	Sensor (Offred)
32	am a tree	Relational process	Token (Offred)

There are eight processes in which Offred is sensor, eight processes in which she is actor, one process in which she is carrier, and one in which she is token. In this distribution of processes, it is the mental as well as the material action processes that merit attention.

The eight mental processes in which Offred appears in the position of sensor construct her as introspective. She *knows, thinks, hears,* and *pretends.* She is 'disenabled' by the clause structure in the extract. She barely reaches out of herself into the world to make decisions and take action. The other eight processes, the material action processes, in which Offred is actor do not change this construction. In five of these processes, Offred is taking action that affects nobody; for example, she *walks to the corner, stands on the* corner, *waits,* and *sighs.* In the other three processes, the action taken by Offred affects her own body parts; for example, *drop my head, turn,* and *hide my face.*

Nick, by contrast, is projected differently. Although both Offred and Nick belong to the working class serving the masters, Nick, a male character, does more material intention processes.

TABLE 5.2 Verbal processes involving Nick

Sentence	Verbal element	Transitivity pattern	Semantic role
1	is wearing the uniform	Relational process	Carrier (Nick)
1	his cap is tilted	Relational process	Carrier (cap)
1	his sleeves are rolled	Relational process	Carrier (sleeves)
2	he has a cigarette	Relational process	Possessor (Nick)
2	has something	Relational process	Possessor (Nick)
2	can trade	Material process	(Affected = cigarette)
5	lives here	Material process	(Affected = none)
6	hasn't been issued	Material process	(Affected = woman)
7	doesn't rate	Relational process	Carrier (Nick)
8	acts as if	Material process	(Affected = none)
8	doesn't know this	Mental process	Sensor (Nick)
8	doesn't care	Mental process	Sensor (Nick)
9	is too casual	Relational process	Carrier (Nick)
9	is not servile enough	Relational process	Carrier (Nick)
12	might smell	Mental process	Sensor (Nick)
15	looks at me	Material process	(Affected = female body)
15	sees me looking	Mental process	Sensor (Nick)
16	has a French face	Relational process	Possessor (Nick)
16	smiles	Mental process	Sensor (Nick)
17	takes a final puff	Material process	(Affected = cigarette)
17	lets it drop	Material process	(Affected = cigarette)
17	steps on it	Material process	(Affected = cigarette)
18	begins to whistle	Material process	(Affected = none)
19	winks	Material process	(Affected = none)
21	has just taken a risk	Material process	(Affected = Nick)

Nick participates in eleven material action, five mental, and nine relational processes. Nick, as opposed to Offred, is constructed as a character with active control of the environment. He is more affecting than reflecting. His actions are directed at objects (e.g. *He takes a final puff of the cigarette, lets it drop to the driveway, and steps on it*), people (e.g. *He looks at me*), and even at himself (e.g. *He's just taken a risk, but for what?*). In the mental processes, Nick *doesn't know, doesn't care,* and *smiles.* The relational processes also refer to attributes of Nick's clothes (e.g. *his cap is tilted*), and his possessions (e.g. *He has a French face*).

The discourse level

Let us now examine the way the character of Nick is constructed through reference to anatomical elements of his body parts. Table 5.3 presents a summary of the textual references to fragmentation of his body.

TABLE 5.3 Reference to Nick's body parts

Sentence	Nick's body parts
1	the elbow
1	his forearms (tanned)
1	a stipple of dark hairs
2	the corner of his mouth
13	tanned skin (moist in the sun, filmed with smoke)
16	a French face (lean, whimsical, all planes and angles)
16	with creases around the mouth where he smiles

Offred is describing Nick's body in unusual terms. Conventionally, male characters are described or discussed in terms of their personality type, character attributes or overall physical appearance. Little evaluation is made of the elements of their body. In this extract, Offred is fragmenting Nick's body parts. She notices his *elbow, forearms, skin, face,* and *mouth.* She even evaluates these body parts: *forearms tanned but with a stipple of dark hairs, skin moist in the sun, French face, lean, whimsical, all planes and angles,* and *creases around the mouth where he smiles.* She goes so far as thinking of how he might smell and imagines his body *filmed with smoke,* which she inhales.

Nick's body is fragmented. The description of his body parts along these terms has connotations of sexual attractiveness. Nick is constructed as a sexual object. This is unusual construction because in feminist stylistics research it has always been the female body that is 'fragmentable' and constructed as 'consumable'. The focalisation in this extract is different. It resides with a female character living in a world in which women are valued and kept, albeit as a possession, only if they are 'fertile breeders'. Has Offred assimilated into her job in the new world?

Summary

Using the 'tools' of feminist stylistics, we have seen how an ideological world-view of female characters is perpetuated through linguistic choices at the lexical, clausal, and discourse levels in a fictional extract. Offred, like the other handmaids in the novel, is a possession of her male Commander and she is named to reflect the property 'of Fred'. This construction of Offred as a passive 'victim' of the circumstances is enforced by the 'disenabling' clause structures. The mental processes in which Offred appears construct her as disempowered and inactive. Even when she figures in material action processes, Offred's actions affect no one and, at best, affect her own body parts. She assimilates into her new role as a 'breeding vessel' so much that she starts fragmenting, and evaluating, male body parts for the female gaze.

Feminist stylistic research has also explored other text types for their ideological content and representation. For example, Sunderland (2011) examines gender representation in children's fiction, Montoro (2012) analyses multimodal elements of a corpus of chick literature book covers, and Radzi and Musa (2017) offers an analysis of the representation of women in advertising.

5.1 Do it yourself

Examine the passage of text from *The Handmaid's Tale* immediately following the extract we have analysed in the chapter. In this passage, Offred is describing Ofglen, another handmaid who joins her on their daily walk. The description is in five paragraphs and twenty-two sentences starting with the words 'A shape, red with white wings around the face' and closing with the sentence 'I can't take the risk.'

Hints

a) How is Ofglen named and how is she referred to using pronouns and referential noun phrases?
b) Categorise the verbal processes that involve Ofglen, Offred, and both of them together.
c) Is Ofglen's character constructed through fragmentation of her body parts?
d) What world-view does this distribution of processes perpetuate about women in the extract?

5.2 Do it yourself

Examine the fragmentation of the female/male bodies of the characters in the following two extracts. The first extract is from chapter 16 of Charlotte Brontë's *Jane Eyre*, and the second is from Book One, chapter 4, of Charles Dickens's *Hard Times*. In the first extract, Mrs Fairfax, is describing Blanche, a female character, to Jane; in the second extract, the narrator is describing Mr Bounderby, an affluent mill owner and friend of Mr Gradgrind.

Extract 1

'¹Tall, fine bust, sloping shoulders; long, graceful neck: olive complexion, dark and clear; noble features; eyes rather like Mr. Rochester's: large and black, and as brilliant as her jewels. ²And then she had such a fine head of hair; raven-black and so becomingly arranged: a crown of thick plaits behind, and in front the longest, the glossiest curls I ever saw. ³She was dressed in pure white; an amber-coloured scarf was passed over her shoulder and across her breast, tied at the side, and descending in long, fringed ends below her knee. ⁴She wore an amber-coloured flower, too, in her hair: it contrasted well with the jetty mass of her curls.'

Extract 2

¹He was a rich man: banker, merchant, manufacturer, and what not. ²A big, loud man, with a stare, and a metallic laugh. ³A man made out of a coarse material, which seemed to have been stretched to make so much of him. ⁴A man with a great puffed head and forehead, swelled veins in his temples, and such a strained skin to his face that it seemed to hold his eyes open, and lift his eyebrows up. ⁵A man with a pervading appearance on him of being inflated like a balloon, and ready to start. ⁶A man who could never sufficiently vaunt himself a self-made man. ⁷A man who was always proclaiming, through that brassy speaking-trumpet of a voice of his, his old ignorance and his old poverty. ⁸A man who was the Bully of humility.

Hints

a) How are the bodies of Blanche and Bounderby presented? List the body parts of each character in the two extracts.
b) What descriptive vocabulary is used to qualify the body parts of each character? Whose body is described for the male or female gaze? Whose body is constructed as fragmentable and consumable?
c) What world-views of men and women does this construction perpetuate?
d) Rewrite the descriptions of Blanche and Bounderby for inclusion in a children's book. What changes would you make?

> **Further Reading**

FEMINISM AND LINGUISTICS

Montoro, R. (2014), 'Feminist stylistics', in M. Burke (ed.), *The Routledge Handbook of Stylistics*, Routledge, pp. 346–61.
  A brief survey on the development of the linguistic treatment of gender and feminism. The chapter also summarises some of the current research on feminist stylistics.

FEMINIST STYLISTICS

Mills, S. (1995), *Feminist Stylistics*, Routledge.
  An introduction to the analysis of sexism in literary texts, newspapers, pop songs, and advertisements. Drawing on Halliday's systemic functional linguistics theory, Mills offers a toolkit for the examination of how texts encode representations of men and women, and how they implicitly naturalise gendered ideologies.

FEMINIST STYLISTIC ANALYSIS

Radzi, N. S. M. and M. Musa (2017), 'Beauty ideals, myths and sexisms: A feminist stylistic analysis of female representations in cosmetic names', *GEMA Online® Journal of Language Studies*, 17(1), 21–38, <http://doi.org/10.17576/gema-2017-1701-02> (last accessed 23 September 2021).
  Using feminist stylistics, the study examines naming devices at word and clausal levels in a database of beauty produces advertised worldwide in order to examine gender representation in advertising discourse.

6

PRAGMATIC ANALYSIS OF DRAMA

Chapter Overview

- communication in drama
- pragmatic stylistics
- checklist of pragmatic stylistic categories
- *King Lear* by William Shakespeare
- pragmatic stylistic analysis of an extract from *King Lear*

Introduction

We will now turn our attention to fictional representation through dialogue. This is the literary form known as drama. A drama is also called a play, and the writer is called a dramatist or playwright. The most well-known playwright in the history of the English language is William Shakespeare. In this chapter, we offer a pragmatic stylistic analysis of an extract from Shakespeare's *King Lear* ([1605] 2004). Using insights from conversation analysis, we will examine the way power relations between characters in dramatic dialogues are built using language. Before we present the analysis, however, we will sketch the nature of communication in drama, suggest a checklist of pragmatic stylistic categories, and present the extract from the play.

Communication in drama

Like the literary **GENRES** of poetry and fiction, drama tells a story using plot, characters, setting, point of view, and theme. However, unlike some genres, it is written to be performed. Besides using stage directions, the major difference is that drama is almost exclusively written in dialogue. There is no narrative voice to provide explanation of action, description of setting, and information on characters. This information is inferred as characters communicate. All the information a reader, or analyst, needs is contained in the dramatic dialogues. For this reason, we are choosing **PRAGMATIC STYLISTICS**, with its emphasis on how character traits and power relations between characters are reflected in interactional strategies and conversational behaviour.

Pragmatic stylistics

Pragmatic stylistics uses insights from pragmatic theories (e.g. **TURN MANAGEMENT, THE COOPERATIVE PRINCIPLE,** and **POLITENESS THEORY**) in the description of how power dynamics play out in dramatic dialogues. Let us briefly introduce the main tenets of these theories and their relevance to the aims of this chapter.

One of the approaches to the description and analysis of naturally occurring interaction is conversation analysis. A basic feature of conversation analysis is the organisation of turns, that is, who initiates talks, who speaks more, and so on. This is known as turn management. In conversations, the right to speak is called the *floor*. Control of the floor is a *turn*, and exchange of the floor is *turn-taking*. Interlocutors may share the floor equally (which suggests solidarity), or compete for it (which suggests power struggle). If a participant holds the floor long, they have longer turns and dominate. Other markers of power in conversation include overlapping others or completing their turns, interruption, and the absence of pauses, hesitations, and false starts.

Another aspect of conversation analysis is the way the turns are structured and relate to each other in successful verbal interaction. H. P. Grice (1975) offers rules that we often observe when we speak or use in interpreting speech. He calls these rules the **MAXIMS OF CONVERSATION**. There are four maxims: the maxim of quantity (make your contribution as informative as is required), the maxim of quality (say what you believe to be true and for which you have evidence), the maxim of relation (be relevant), and the maxim of manner (be clear, brief, orderly; avoid ambiguity). In order for verbal communication to succeed, the maxims need to be observed. Flouting the maxim of quantity (e.g. A: *Have you written the report and sent it to the board members?* B: *I have written the report for sure!*), the maxim of quality (e.g. Teacher to late students: *Thanks for coming early!*), the maxim of relation (e.g. A: *What's that?* B: *Can we get something to drink?*), and the maxim of manner (e.g. Father: *What can I get you?* Mother *(kids present)*: *I-C-E-C-R-E-A-M*) leads to additional meanings that are inferred. The additional meanings are **CONVERSATIONAL IMPLICATURES**.

In conversation, we also need to protect our **FACE** or social image. This is the theory of politeness in language, a detailed account of which is found in Brown and Levinson (1987). Politeness in language refers to the means used to show awareness of one's or another person's *face* or public self-image. Language that is not mitigated with markers of politeness is *face-threatening*, and language that lessens the threat to positive face (the need to feel appreciated) or to negative face (the need to have freedom of action) is *face-saving*. The former shows solidarity and is marked by nicknames, inclusive terms, and appeal to a common goal; the latter, on the other hand, shows deference and is marked by modalised questions and apology for the imposition.

A checklist of pragmatic stylistic categories

To help you carry out pragmatic stylistic analyses of the dramatic extracts offered in activities 6.1 and 6.2, I provide you with a checklist that covers turn management (a–f), speech acts (g–j), the maxims of the cooperative principle (k–l), and character speaking styles (m).

a) How many turns does each participant in the conversation have?
b) How long are the turns?
c) Who has the longest or most number of turns?
d) Does a character interrupt others or get interrupted?
e) Who starts the dialogue?
f) How do the turn management and control of the floor construct the power relations between the characters?
g) What SPEECH ACTS are made and by whom?
h) Which speech acts are mitigated with politeness markers (face-saving) and which ones are face-threatening?
i) How do the characters respond to the speech acts?
j) How does the use of speech acts and politeness markers carry forward the construction of characters and the relationship between them?
k) Which maxims of the cooperative principle are flouted?
l) How does flouting the maxims contribute to characterisation?
m) How does analysis of turn management and speech acts reflect on the speech styles (high involvement or high considerateness) of the characters and sustain the representation of characters?

The text

King Lear (first performed in 1606 and published in 1623) opens with Lear, the ageing king of Britain, announcing a plan to avoid future strife by dividing his kingdom evenly amongst his three daughters, Goneril, Regan, and Cordelia. The extract we are analysing is part of this plan (Act 1, Scene 1). King Lear asks his daughters to tell him how much they love him so they might earn their share of the kingdom. Goneril and Regan respond with excessive declarations of love, but Cordelia, who loves her father the most, says she loves him as a daughter should love her father. Lear is shocked, flies into a rage, and divides his kingdom only between Goneril and Regan.

Later in the play, Goneril and Regan turn against their father. When he decides to live with them, they conspire against him and show neither hospitality nor love. Meanwhile, Cordelia raises a French army to save her father, who is going insane. She meets him, but she loses the battles and is executed. Goneril poisons Regan, and later takes her own life. The play closes with Lear carrying Cordelia's body. He dies broken-hearted.

Sennet. Enter KING LEAR, CORNWALL, ALBANY, GONERIL, REGAN, CORDELIA, *and Attendants*

KING LEAR Attend the lords of France and Burgundy, Gloucester. 1
GLOUCESTER I shall, my liege.
Exeunt GLOUCESTER and EDMUND
KING LEAR Meantime we shall express our darker purpose.
    Give me the map there. Know that we have divided 5
    In three our kingdom: and 'tis our fast intent
    To shake all cares and business from our age;
    Conferring them on younger strengths, while we
    Unburthen'd crawl toward death. Our son of Cornwall,
    And you, our no less loving son of Albany, 10
    We have this hour a constant will to publish
    Our daughters' several dowers, that future strife
    May be prevented now. The princes, France and Burgundy,
    Great rivals in our youngest daughter's love,
    Long in our court have made their amorous sojourn, 15
    And here are to be answer'd. Tell me, my daughters,–
    Since now we will divest us both of rule,
    Interest of territory, cares of state,–
    Which of you shall we say doth love us most?
    That we our largest bounty may extend 20
    Where nature doth with merit challenge. Goneril,
    Our eldest-born, speak first.
GONERIL Sir, I love you more than words can wield the matter;
    Dearer than eye-sight, space, and liberty;
    Beyond what can be valued, rich or rare; 25
    No less than life, with grace, health, beauty, honour;
    As much as child e'er lov'd, or father found;
    A love that makes breath poor, and speech unable;
    Beyond all manner of so much I love you.
CORDELIA [Aside] What shall Cordelia do? 30
    Love, and be silent.
KING LEAR Of all these bounds, even from this line to this,
    With shadowy forests and with champains rich'd,
    With plenteous rivers and wide-skirted meads,
    We make thee lady: to thine and Albany's issue 35
    Be this perpetual. What says our second daughter,
    Our dearest Regan, wife to Cornwall? Speak.
REGAN Sir, I am made
    Of the self-same metal that my sister is,
    And prize me at her worth. In my true heart 40
    I find she names my very deed of love;
    Only she comes too short: that I profess
    Myself an enemy to all other joys,
    Which the most precious square of sense possesses;

        And find I am alone felicitate   45
        In your dear highness' love.
CORDELIA [Aside] Then poor Cordelia
        And yet not so; since, I am sure, my love's
        More richer than my tongue.
KING LEAR To thee and thine hereditary ever   50
        Remain this ample third of our fair kingdom;
        No less in space, validity, and pleasure,
        Than that conferr'd on Goneril. Now, our joy,
        Although the last, not least; to whose young love
        The vines of France and milk of Burgundy   55
        Strive to be interess'd; what can you say to draw
        A third more opulent than your sisters? Speak.
CORDELIA Nothing, my lord.
KING LEAR Nothing!
CORDELIA Nothing.   60
KING LEAR Nothing will come of nothing: speak again.
CORDELIA Unhappy that I am, I cannot heave
        My heart into my mouth: I love your majesty
        According to my bond; nor more nor less.
KING LEAR How, how, Cordelia! mend your speech a little,   65
        Lest it may mar your fortunes.
CORDELIA Good my lord,
        You have begot me, bred me, loved me: I
        Return those duties back as are right fit,
        Obey you, love you, and most honour you.   70
        Why have my sisters husbands, if they say
        They love you all? Haply, when I shall wed,
        That lord whose hand must take my plight shall carry
        Half my love with him, half my care and duty:
        Sure, I shall never marry like my sisters,   75
        To love my father all.
KING LEAR But goes thy heart with this?
CORDELIA Ay, good my lord.
KING LEAR So young, and so untender?
CORDELIA So young, my lord, and true.   80
KING LEAR Let it be so; thy truth, then, be thy dower:
        For, by the sacred radiance of the sun,
        The mysteries of Hecate, and the night;
        By all the operation of the orbs
        From whom we do exist, and cease to be;   85
        Here I disclaim all my paternal care,
        Propinquity and property of blood,
        And as a stranger to my heart and me
        Hold thee, from this, for ever. The barbarous Scythian,
        Or he that makes his generation messes   90

> To gorge his appetite, shall to my bosom
> Be as well neighbour'd, pitied, and relieved,
> As thou my sometime daughter.
>
> **KENT** Good my liege,–
> **KING LEAR** Peace, Kent! 95
> Come not between the dragon and his wrath.
> I loved her most, and thought to set my rest
> On her kind nursery. Hence, and avoid my sight!
> So be my grave my peace, as here I give
> Her father's heart from her! Call France; who stirs? 100
> Call Burgundy. Cornwall and Albany,
> With my two daughters' dowers digest this third:
> Let pride, which she calls plainness, marry her.
> I do invest you jointly with my power,
> Pre-eminence, and all the large effects 105
> That troop with majesty. Ourself, by monthly course,
> With reservation of an hundred knights,
> By you to be sustain'd, shall our abode
> Make with you by due turns. Only we still retain
> The name, and all the additions to a king; 110
> The sway, revenue, execution of the rest,
> Beloved sons, be yours: which to confirm,
> This coronet part betwixt you.
>
> *Giving the crown*

The Analysis

We will now use the pragmatic stylistic framework outlined above to examine the way character traits and power relations are constructed using conversational strategies in character–character interaction in the extract from Shakespeare's *King Lear*.

Turn-taking

Analysis of turn-taking reveals that King Lear is dominant and assertive. He has complete control of the floor. He has eleven turns out of a total number of twenty-one turns – a percentage of a little over 50 per cent. The other five participants (Gloucester, Goneril, Cordelia, Regan, and Kent) do not take equal turns at holding the floor. Besides having more turns than all the other characters combined, Lear, in his turns, holds the floor longer. His turns are longer than those of all the other characters combined. The other participants get the floor only when King Lear turns it over to them. Then he takes it back. Table 6.1 provides a summary of turn management in the extract we are analysing.

Pragmatic Analysis of Drama

TABLE 6.1 Analysis of turn-taking in the extract from *King Lear*

	King Lear		Gloucester		Goneril		Cordelia		Regan		Kent	
	Turn no.	No. of lines	Turn no.	No. of lines	Turn no.	No. of lines	Turn no.	No. of lines	Turn no.	No. of lines	Turn no.	No. of lines
	1	1	1	1								
	2	19			1	7						
	3	6							1	9		
	4	8					1	1				
	5	1					1	1				
	6	1					1	3				
	7	2					1	10				
	8	1					1	1				
	9	1					1	1				
	10	13									1	1
	11	19										
Total	11	72	1	1	1	7	6	17	1	9	1	1

Speech acts

Analysis of speech acts underlines King Lear's power. The extract has a total of nineteen speech acts, all of which are made by King Lear. Lear is the only character who uses directives; other characters use statements. Table 6.2 contains an analysis of the speech acts in the extract.

TABLE 6.2 Analysis of speech acts in the extract from *King Lear*

Speech act no.	Speech act	Addressor	Addressee	Illocutionary force
1	Attend the lords of France and Burgundy.	King Lear	Gloucester	Order
2	Give me the map there.	King Lear	Unknown	Order
3	Tell me, my daughters, . . . Which of you shall we say doth love us most?	King Lear	Daughters	Order
4	Goneril, Our eldest-born, speak first.	King Lear	Goneril	Order
5	Of all these bounds, . . . We make thee lady:	King Lear	Goneril	Bequeathing
6	Our dearest Regan, wife to Cornwall? Speak.	King Lear	Regan	Order
7	To thee and thine hereditary ever Remain this ample third of our fair kingdom;	King Lear	Regan	Bequeathing
8	Speak.	King Lear	Cordelia	Order
9	Nothing will come of nothing: speak again.	King Lear	Cordelia	Threat

TABLE 6.2 (continued)

Speech act no.	Speech act	Addressor	Addressee	Illocutionary force
10	mend your speech a little, Lest it may mar your fortunes.	King Lear	Cordelia	Threat
11	Let it be so; thy truth, then, be thy dower:	King Lear	Cordelia	Disinheritance
12	Here I disclaim all my paternal care, Propinquity and property of blood, And as a stranger to my heart and me Hold thee, from this, for ever.	King Lear	Cordelia	Disowning
13	Peace, Kent!	King Lear	Kent	Order
14	Come not between the dragon and his wrath.	King Lear	Kent	Threat
15	Hence, and avoid my sight!	King Lear	Kent	Order
16	Call France; who stirs? Call Burgundy. Cornwall and Albany.	King Lear	Unknown	Order
17	With my two daughters' dowers digest this third:	King Lear	Unknown	Disinheritance
18	I do invest you jointly with my power, Pre-eminence, and all the large effects That troop with majesty.	King Lear	Burgundy Cornwall Albany	Bequeathing
19	The sway, revenue, execution of the rest, Beloved sons, be yours:	King Lear	Burgundy Cornwall Albany	Bequeathing

All the characters in the extract are recipients of King Lear's speech acts and they all, except Cordelia, carry out the actions in the speech acts in exactly the same way King Lear wishes. These nineteen speech acts are all direct speech acts, which are consistently **BALD ON RECORD**. They are face-threatening. They are not mitigated with politeness markers, do not attempt to appeal to either the positive or negative face of Lear's audience, and are fulfilled with little resistance, save from Cordelia, whose defiance incurs her father's wrath, so he disinherits and disowns her. This serves to further underline King Lear's power and his dominance.

But why does King Lear take Cordelia's answers to be an expression of ingratitude or defiance? When King Lear asks Goneril to say how much she loves him, she, as we learn later in the play, lies about her feelings and says more than she needs to. She says she loves him more than she loves life itself. She flouts the maxims of quality and quantity. King Lear knows it and likes it. It makes him feel good. Regan does the same thing, in a similar attempt to get her one third of the kingdom. Cordelia, on the other hand, starts by flouting the maxim of quantity. She answers *Nothing*, which makes the king angry. On a second request, she follows the maxim of quality. She says that she loves her father as much as she should, and that she would give half of the love she is capable of to her future husband. Lear is happier but wants to hear more. He says *How, how, Cordelia! mend your speech a little*. But, Cordelia, against her father's wishes, follows the maxim of quantity. She says:

> *You have begot me, bred me, loved me: I*
> *Return those duties back as are right fit,*
> *Obey you, love you, and most honour you.*

King Lear wants Cordelia to flout the maxim of quantity but she follows it. Following the maxim of quantity disinherits and disowns Cordelia.

> ## Summary
>
> Analysis of turn management reveals Lear as a domineering character who has total control of the floor in this speech event. He has a **HIGH INVOLVEMENT STYLE** – a fast-paced speaking style with no pauses between the turns and with overlap or completion of the turns of others (as opposed to the more accommodating style known as **HIGH CONSIDERATENESS STYLE**). He gives the floor to others as and when he wants and he takes it back as and when he wants (e.g. lines 94 and 95 when Lear interrupts Kent).
>
> King Lear's power or dominance is reinforced by analysis of the speech acts (the cooperative principle and politeness). Lear is the only character who uses direct, unmitigated speech acts, with little regard for others' face wants. He rewards Goneril and Regan for flouting the maxim of quantity and disowns his little girl Cordelia for following it.
>
> Pragmatic stylistics, like other trends in stylistics, is also applicable besides the genre selected for analysis. There have been interesting applications to conventional forms of communication. Pop (2010) examines **IMPLICATURES** derived from flouting the maxims of conversation in print advertising, Chang and Haugh (2011) investigates interactional practices leading to face threats in business communication in Taiwan, Kedveš (2013) examines the deployment of politeness strategies in summer school application calls in Europe, and Kamalu and Fasasi (2018) uses Brown and Levinson's politeness theory in the study of recorded conversations among undergraduates in Nigeria.

6.1 Do it yourself

The following extract (also from *King Lear*), comes right after the one we have analysed. In this extract, Kent, Lear's adviser, objects to dividing the kingdom between Cornwall (Regan's husband) and Albany (Goneril's husband). He calls King Lear's decision 'hideous rashness'. Enraged, Lear gives Kent five days to leave the country. Kent welcomes it and says 'Freedom lives hence, and banishment is here'.

KENT Royal Lear,   1
    Whom I have ever honour'd as my king,
    Loved as my father, as my master follow'd,
    As my great patron thought on in my prayers,–
KING LEAR The bow is bent and drawn, make from the shaft.   5
KENT Let it fall rather, though the fork invade
    The region of my heart: be Kent unmannerly,
    When Lear is mad. What wilt thou do, old man? Think'st thou that duty shall have dread to speak,
    When power to flattery bows? To plainness honour's bound,   10
    When majesty stoops to folly. Reverse thy doom;
    And, in thy best consideration, check
    This hideous rashness: answer my life my judgment,
    Thy youngest daughter does not love thee least;
    Nor are those empty-hearted whose low sound   15
    Reverbs no hollowness.
KING LEAR Kent, on thy life, no more.
KENT My life I never held but as a pawn
    To wage against thy enemies; nor fear to lose it,
    Thy safety being the motive.   20
KING LEAR Out of my sight!
KENT See better, Lear; and let me still remain
    The true blank of thine eye.
KING LEAR Now, by Apollo,–
KENT Now, by Apollo, king,   25
    Thou swear'st thy gods in vain.
KING LEAR O, vassal! miscreant!
    Laying his hand on his sword
ALBANY, CORNWALL Dear sir, forbear.
KENT Do: Kill thy physician, and the fee bestow   30
    Upon thy foul disease. Revoke thy doom;
    Or, whilst I can vent clamour from my throat,
    I'll tell thee thou dost evil.
KING LEAR Hear me, recreant!
    On thine allegiance, hear me!   35
    Since thou hast sought to make us break our vow,
    Which we durst never yet, and with strain'd pride
    To come between our sentence and our power,
    Which nor our nature nor our place can bear,
    Our potency made good, take thy reward.   40
    Five days we do allot thee, for provision
    To shield thee from diseases of the world;
    And on the sixth to turn thy hated back
    Upon our kingdom: if, on the tenth day following,
    Thy banish'd trunk be found in our dominions,   45

>   The moment is thy death. Away! by Jupiter,
>   This shall not be revoked.
>   **KENT** Fare thee well, king: sith thus thou wilt appear,
>   Freedom lives hence, and banishment is here
>   *To CORDELIA*
>   The gods to their dear shelter take thee, maid,   50
>   That justly think'st, and hast most rightly said!
>   *To REGAN and GONERIL*
>   And your large speeches may your deeds approve,
>   That good effects may spring from words of love.
>   Thus Kent, O princes, bids you all adieu;
>   He'll shape his old course in a country new.   55
>   *Exit*

Hints

a) Examine the terms of address used by Kent when talking to King Lear. How does this reflect on the power relations in the extract?

b) Examine the turn management in the extract: the number of turns to every character and the length of these turns. Also examine the control of the floor. Does King Lear still have complete control of the floor? Does he hold it longer than everyone else? Does he still turn it over and take it back as and when he wants?

c) Analyse the speech acts in the extract. Count the speech acts made by the characters. Is King Lear still the only character who is using face-threatening (unmitigated, bald-on-record) speech acts? Is he still unopposed?

d) Is King Lear's style still a high involvement style?

6.2 Do it yourself

The following extract is from *Pygmalion* – a play written by George Bernard Shaw in 1912 (Shaw [1916] 2004). The play tells the story of Henry Higgins, a professor of phonetics, who bets his friend, Pickering, that he can pass off the Cockney flower girl, Liza, as a duchess by teaching her to speak with a refined, upper-class accent. In the extract, Higgins and Pickering are talking to Liza, in the presence of Higgins's housekeeper Mrs Pearce, about the fee she must pay for the lessons. Examine the way language is used in the extract to suggest power differences between Liza and the other three characters involved.

> **HIGGINS**: Come back to business. How much do you propose to pay me for the lessons?
>
> **LIZA**: Oh, I know what's right. A lady friend of mine gets French lessons for eighteen pence an hour from a real French gentleman. Well, you wouldn't have the face to ask me the same for

teaching me my own language as you would for French; so I won't give more than a shilling. Take it or leave it.

HIGGINS [walking up and down the room, rattling his keys and his cash in his pockets] You know, Pickering, if you consider a shilling, not as a simple shilling, but as a percentage of this girl's income, it works out as fully equivalent to sixty or seventy guineas from a millionaire.

PICKERING: How so?

HIGGINS: Figure it out. A millionaire has about 150 pounds a day. She earns about half-a-crown.

LIZA [haughtily]: Who told you I only—

HIGGINS [continuing]: She offers me two-fifths of her day's income for a lesson. Two-fifths of a millionaire's income for a day would be somewhere about 60 pounds. It's handsome. By George, it's enormous! it's the biggest offer I ever had.

LIZA [rising, terrified]: Sixty pounds! What are you talking about? I never offered you sixty pounds. Where would I get—

HIGGINS: Hold your tongue.

LIZA [weeping] But I ain't got sixty pounds. Oh—

MRS PEARCE: Don't cry, you silly girl. Sit down. Nobody is going to touch your money.

HIGGINS: Somebody is going to touch you, with a broomstick, if you don't stop snivelling. Sit down.

LIZA [obeying slowly] Ah–ah–ah–ow–oo–o! One would think you was my father.

HIGGINS: If I decide to teach you, I'll be worse than two fathers to you. Here [he offers her his silk handkerchief]!

LIZA: What's this for?

HIGGINS: To wipe your eyes. To wipe any part of your face that feels moist. Remember: that's your handkerchief; and that's your sleeve. Don't mistake the one for the other if you wish to become a lady in a shop.

Liza, utterly bewildered, stares helplessly at him.

Hints

a) Examine the turn management in the extract – the number of turns to every character and the length of these turns. Who is in control of the floor? Do they hold it longer than everyone else? Do they turn it over and take it back as and when they want?

b) Analyse the speech acts in the extract. Who makes them? Are they face-threatening (direct, bald on record) or face-saving (mitigated with politeness markers)? How do the characters respond to these speech acts? And how do these choices construct power relations between the characters?

c) How does the speech style of the characters (in terms of high involvement and high considerateness styles) sustain the power relations between the characters?
d) If Liza had a social status equal to that of Professor Higgins and still wanted to take language lessons, how would turn-taking, turn length, and control of the floor change? Also, would Professor Higgins make the same speech acts and hold on to his speech styles? Rewrite the conversation in light of your changes.

Further Reading

PRAGMATIC STYLISTICS

Black, E. (2006), *Pragmatic Stylistics*, Edinburgh University Press.
   An introduction to pragmatic stylistics and the way pragmatic theories such as politeness and relevance can be used to explain how we interpret literary figures in literary texts.

THE NATURE OF COMMUNICATION IN DRAMA

Short, M. [1996] (2014), *Exploring the Language of Poems, Plays and Prose*, 2nd edn, Routledge.
   Chapter 6 offers an account of the nature of dramatic conversation and the way it differs from naturally occurring conversation.

PRAGMATIC STYLISTIC ANALYSIS

Culpeper, J., M. Short and P. Verdonk (eds) (1998), *Exploring the Language of Drama: From Text to Context*, Routledge.
   Twelve papers offering analysis of turn management, politeness, implicature, and conversation in different types of dramatic texts.

Kedveš, A. (2013), 'Face threatening acts and politeness strategies in summer school application calls', *Jezikoslovlje*, 14(2), 431–44.
   The paper examines politeness strategies in a corpus of verbal application calls.

7

COGNITIVE ANALYSIS OF LINGUISTIC HUMOUR

> **Chapter Overview**
> - communication in linguistic humour
> - cognitive stylistics
> - relevance theory
> - checklist of relevance theoretic categories
> - relevance theoretic analysis of jokes

Introduction

In the previous chapter, we introduced pragmatic stylistics, which is informed by the Gricean approach to pragmatics. In this chapter, we introduce **RELEVANCE THEORY**, which is a theory of communication that shares the pragmatic stylistic concern with utterance interpretation and grounding on Gricean pragmatics but offers a cognitive account of interpretation. The chapter applies the relevance theoretic cognitive framework to the analysis of jokes. After outlining the nature of communication in linguistic humour, the chapter presents the relevance theoretic framework, suggests a checklist of categories to use in analysing humorous texts using relevance theory, and offers cognitive stylistic analyses of five short jokes.

Communication in linguistic humour

Humour created in and through language is called linguistic humour. The effect in linguistic humour is not a property of the text but is best understood in terms of the mental processes the hearer goes through during interpretation (Yus 2003).

The humourist has the ability to 'predict which mental procedures the addressee is likely to go through in the relevance-seeking extraction of the information that utterances convey' (Yus 2003: 1308). This knowledge is manipulated to humorous effect. Let us take jokes by way of example. The language used by the humourist in the first part of a joke (the set-up) creates cognitive expectations of optimal relevance that are defeated in the second part of the joke (the punchline). That is, the set-up misleads the audience into anticipating the optimally relevant interpretation, and the punchline surprises them by revealing an interpretation that yields fewer contextual (or cognitive) effects and demands additional processing effort. To resolve the ambiguity, the audience goes back to the set-up in search of the intended meaning. Realisation of the intended interpretation resolves the ambiguity and leads to humour.

The ambiguity, or the manipulation of the communicative potential of language, operates at all levels of language structure. The joke teller could exploit the phonological, morphological, lexical, syntactic, semantic, or pragmatic possibilities for making meaning to create the incongruity between the expected optimally relevant interpretation and the intended interpretation that is inconsistent with the **PRINCIPLE OF RELEVANCE**.

Cognitive stylistics

Stylisticians in the late 1970s developed an interest in exploring the reading process and the way readers interpret texts. One of the pioneering works in the area of **COGNITIVE STYLISTICS** is Reuven Tsur's *Toward a Theory of Cognitive Poetics*, which attempted to describe the 'perceptual effects of literary texts in readers' drawing on both cognitive psychology and cognitive linguistics (Harrison and Stockwell 2014: 218). The application of cognitive science to literary-linguistic analysis is known as cognitive stylistics (Stockwell 2015), and because of its particular concern with literature, it is also known as **COGNITIVE POETICS**.

Mainstream cognitive stylistic frameworks include **SCHEMA THEORY** (Cook [1992] 2001), **TEXT WORLD THEORY** (Werth 1999), **CONCEPTUAL BLENDING** (Dancygier 2006), and **CONCEPTUAL METAPHOR THEORY** (Steen 1994). The choice of relevance theory in this chapter over mainstream cognitive stylistic theories is justifiable. The theory, with its pragmatic roots traceable to H. P. Grice, is in line with the focus on pragmatic stylistics in other parts of the book, and our choice of humour is driven by the nature of communication in linguistic humour, as we have seen in the previous section.

Relevance theory, developed by Dan Sperber and Deirdre Wilson, is a cognitive theory of human communication in which decoding is minor to inference (Sperber and Wilson 1986). Sperber and Wilson's 'dissatisfaction with Grice's co-operative principle' led them to develop a cognitive theory of communication 'which holds that only the maxim of relation (relevance) is necessary' in the search for meaning (Black 2006: 80). For this reason, the theory is called the relevance theory.

Relevance theory maintains that the perceptual mechanism of the human mind engages in a cost–benefit procedure that aims at picking out the most relevant interpretation from among an array of possible interpretations. This is the principle of relevance. According to the principle of relevance, an utterance is optimally relevant if it achieves an adequate range of contextual effects (i.e. if it interacts with existing cognitive assumptions about the world to strengthen them, contradict them, or combine with them to yield contextual implications) for the minimum justifiable processing effort (cognitive analytical effort to generate a satisfactory interpretation of the input information). The greater the contextual effects, the greater the relevance. The smaller the processing effort, the greater the relevance.

A checklist of relevance theoretic categories

In this section, I will offer a checklist to help you identify 'the linguistically encoded and contextually inferred conceptual features' in jokes (Sperber and Wilson 1995: 182). Using the checklist, you will be able to detect the way the joke tellers exploit the human cognition tendency to maximise relevance and manipulate our optimal relevance expectations about the world and about language in order to create humour.

a) Identify the set-up and punchline of the joke.
b) What are the two possible interpretations of the joke?
c) Which of the two interpretations of the set-up is the hearer or reader likely to pick out?
d) How is our previous knowledge of the word used in the set-up to make this interpretation yield positive cognitive effects? In other words, how does this interpretation interact with existing cognitive assumptions about the world to strengthen them, contradict them, or combine with them to yield contextual implications?
e) What linguistic elements are deployed in the set-up to minimise the processing effort needed to derive this interpretation?
f) At what linguistic level is the ambiguity in the punchline (phonetic, lexical, syntactic, semantic, pragmatic, or discourse)?
g) How does the communicator exploit the relevance-orientation of the human cognition to create humour in the punchline?

Text 1

    A: What is black and white and /red/ all over?
    B: A newspaper.

Structure

In the spoken version of this joke, the set-up is *What is black and white and /red/ all over?*, and the punchline is *A newspaper*. The set-up contains a homophone. It is a set of words that have the same pronunciation but different spellings. In the set-up, there is a sound combination /red/ that can be represented in spelling by either of the two words *read* or *red*, with two possible readings (1a) and (1b) as follows:

(1a) What is black and white and red all over?
(1b) What is black and white and read all over?

Which of these readings is the listener promoted to choose?

Analysis

The first reading is optimally relevant. The fact that the sound combination /red/ occurs in the contextual company of the two colour words *black* and *white* prompts the listener to derive (1a). The listener has easy access to a context in which (1a) has an adequate range of contextual effects that are derived at minimal processing effort. The input connects with (and upholds) background information that relates to national striped flags bearing the three colours such as those of Egypt, Iraq, Sudan, Syria, and Yemen. This interpretation is consistent with the principle of relevance.

The second reading (1b), on the other hand, is less easily accessible. The two adjectives *black* and *white* are followed by the past tense form of the verb *read* in a parallel structure, thereby putting the listener to some extra processing effort in order to recover (1b). The listener will eliminate (1b) as the intended interpretation out of the expectation that the speaker would not have used a third colour word homophonous with the past tense of 'read' if the intended interpretation was (1b). It is inconsistent with the principle of relevance because of the extra demands on processing effort.

The phonetic string /red/ is the source of ambiguity in the joke. The choice of a phonetic string corresponding to two differently spelled words is a deliberate choice by the joke teller. The speaker could have spared the listener the effort of accessing and processing interpretations (1a) and (1b), and then engaging in an inference process to choose the more relevant interpretation, by rephrasing the utterance to eliminate the unwanted interpretation. The unjustifiable processing effort in recovering (1b) leads the listener to choose, on optimal relevance grounds, interpretation (1a) as the intended interpretation. The punchline, however, reveals that (1b) is the intended interpretation. The listener realises that they have been deceived, by design, into inferring (1a) to be the intended interpretation. The element of surprise resulting from recognising the manipulation of optimal relevance expectations, and of knowledge of English sounds, is the source of humour.

Text 2

> **MOTHER:** Did the doctor treat you?
> **DAUGHTER:** No, mom. I paid for the check-up.

Structure

The set-up contains the lexical item *treat*, which has at least two different meanings. The first is *to use drugs to cure a person of a disease or heal an injury*; the second is *to buy or pay for something for another person*, giving rise to two possible interpretations of the mother's turn as follows:

> (2a) Did the doctor use drugs to cure you?
> (2b) Did the doctor pay for your treatment?

Which of these two meanings does the mother intend and which one is her daughter prompted to pick up?

Analysis

The first reading (2a) is consistent with the principle of relevance. By using *treat* after *doctor*, the listener is driven to conclude that the mother is picking out the first meaning of *treat*, and prompted to derive interpretation (2a). There is an easily accessible context in which (2a) has a manifestly adequate range of contextual effects obtained at minimal processing effort. The input interacts with existing cognitive assumptions about the doctor–patient relationship to strengthen them, and the use of *doctor* and *treat* minimises the processing effort needed to derive (2a).

On the other hand, the second interpretation (2b) is less easily accessible for two reasons. First, it is more demanding to access a context in which (2b) yields positive cognitive effects, that is, a context in which existing schematic knowledge about the doctor–patient relationship interacts with the incoming input and is relevant. Second, the search for relevance in (2b) requires unjustifiably more processing effort. On these two counts, the listener excludes (2b) as the intended interpretation. It is not an optimally relevant interpretation.

The lexical ambiguity (the association of the word *treat* with two distinct meanings) is a calculated choice. The speaker could have reduced the listener's effort in accessing and processing interpretations (2a) and (2b), and then implying the more relevant interpretation, by replacing the word *treat* with another word such as *examine* in order to eliminate the unwanted interpretation. Following a path of least effort, the listener takes interpretation (2a) to be the intended interpretation, which is the optimally relevant interpretation. The punchline, however, takes us by surprise. It reveals (2b) to be the intended interpretation. The listener has been intentionally misled into a miscalculated inference. The 'pleasant' surprise stemming from a recognition that our expectations of optimal relevance have been manipulated leads to humour.

Text 3

> **WAITER:** We do not serve Muslims here.
> **MUSLIM CUSTOMER:** That's fine by me. I just want some roast chicken.

Structure

The set-up contains the verb *serve*, which functions as a transitive verb with different meanings depending on the semantic properties of its direct object. If *serve* takes a direct object with the semantic feature [-animate], it means *to provide food or drink* as in *We serve breakfast here*. If it takes, especially in British English, a direct object with the semantic feature [+animate], it means *to deal with customer* as in *They would not serve me because I am too young*, giving way to two possible interpretations (3a) and (3b) as follows:

> (3a) We do not deal with customers who are Muslims.
> (3b) We do not provide Muslims as food on our menu.

Which of these two meanings is intended by the waiter and which one is picked up by the customer?

Analysis

The first interpretation (3a) is optimally relevant. Existing knowledge of the semantic features of direct objects of the verb *serve*, whose direct object in Text 3 bears the semantic feature [+animate], prompts the listener to pick out the meaning *deal with customer* and derive interpretation (3a). It is the most relevant interpretation. There is an easily retrievable context in which this interpretation has a range of positive cognitive effects obtained at minimal processing effort. The input interacts with existing cognitive assumptions about the treatment of Muslims in some communities to strengthen them, and the use of an animate object of the verb *serve* minimises the processing effort needed to derive (3a).

The second reading (3b), on the other hand, is inaccessible. The input fails to interact with existing cognitive assumptions about restaurant menus. There is no context in which (3b) yields positive (cognitive) contextual effects, and it takes unjustifiably extra processing effort to derive interpretation (3b). Because of this inconsistency with the principle of relevance, the listener disregards (3b) and opts instead for (3a) as the intended interpretation.

The semantic ambiguity (the choice of a verb whose meaning changes as do the semantic features of its direct object) is intentional. The speaker could have eliminated the unwanted interpretation by choosing another verb, thereby sparing the listener the effort of accessing and processing interpretations (3a) and (3b) and then engaging in an inference process to choose between them. Following a path of maximum relevance and least effort, the listener takes (3a) to be the intended interpretation. The punchline, however, reveals that the interpretation that is inconsistent with the principle of relevance is indeed the intended interpretation. Rather than take offence, the customer in the joke interprets *Muslims* not as the direct object, which would include him as one of the people not served at the restaurant, but as the indirect object – the food that is served. He says *I just want some roast chicken*. The element of surprise following from recognising that our expectations of optimal relevance have been defeated is the source of humour.

Text 4

MAN IN SHOP: Can I try on that suit in the window?
SALESPERSON: No, you will have to use the changing room like everyone else.

Structure

The set-up contains the prepositional phrase *in the window* that can function either as a post-modifier in the nominal group headed by *suit* (giving rise to interpretation (4a) below) or as an adjunct qualifying the clause structure (giving rise to interpretation (4b)) as follows:

(4a) Can I try on that suit which is in the window? (post-modifier)
(4b) Can I get in the window to try on that suit? (adjunct)

Analysis

The second reading (4b) is inconsistent with the principle of relevance. The input fails to connect in any meaningful way with schematic knowledge about the world and yield positive cognitive effects. For contextual effects to be derived, additional unnecessary processing efforts are called into action. On optimal relevance grounds, the listener will disqualify (4b) as the intended interpretation.

The first reading (4a), on the other hand, is more easily accessible at much reduced processing effort. The listener has easy access to a context in which the input interacts with existing cognitive knowledge about shopping and about trying on garments in clothes shops to yield an adequate range of contextual effects, namely, strengthening existing assumptions. The processing effort required is minimal, making (4b) an optimally relevant interpretation.

The syntactic ambiguity at the interface between the nominal and prepositional groups gives rise to interpretations (4a) and (4b), which are processed by the listener and weighed against the principle of relevance. The speaker could have spared the listener the effort in processing both interpretations by rephrasing the structure at the interface between the nominal and prepositional groups to eliminate the unwanted interpretation. Following the principle of relevance, the listener takes interpretation (4b) to be optimally relevant; it produces positive cognitive effects and spares the listener processing effort. However, the listener is 'punchlined' into interpretation (4b), which is revealed to be the intended interpretation. The element of surprise following the realisation that our expectations of optimal relevance have been defeated and that our inference has misfired is the source of humour.

Text 5

DOCTOR: There's something wrong with her! (said of a stricken woman) We need to take her to a hospital.

OFFICER: What is it?
DOCTOR: It is a place where people who are ill or injured are treated and taken care of by doctors and nurses.

Structure

The set-up contains the referring expression *it*, which has anaphoric reference. The doctor in the punchline is expected to pick out the appropriate antecedent of the anaphor *it* in the set-up. There are two possible antecedents. The first is the most immediate noun *hospital*, which is dictated by the rules of grammar. The second constituent *the woman's health condition* is less immediate, less explicit, and demands that we invoke assumed, shared knowledge to work out the anaphoric connection. It requires pragmatic inference. These two antecedent–anaphor patterns give rise to the following two possible interpretive expectations in the punchline:

> (5a) It is (reference to the health condition of the stricken woman).
> *Pragmatic inference*
> (5b) It is (offering the sense of the most immediate noun *hospital*).
> *Grammatical rule*

Which of these interpretive expectations is more relevant and which one does the doctor pick up?

Analysis

There is an easily accessible context in which the first reading (5a) has a manifestly adequate range of contextual effects. The input interacts with existing cognitive assumptions about post-accident medical measures and yields positive effects. This interpretation, however, involves a deliberate increase in processing effort. The listener needs to exert more effort by invoking assumed schematic knowledge about post-accident situations in order to infer (5a).

The other interpretation (5b), on the other hand, requires much less processing effort. The listener identifies the referent of the referring expression *it* to be the most immediate noun *hospital* and proceeds to define it. The input, however, fails to interact with existing cognitive assumptions about post-accident medical measures. There are no accessible contexts in which this interpretation yields positive contextual effects. It states the obvious.

The pragmatic ambiguity (triggered by the interpretation of the antecedent–anaphor pattern) is a deliberate choice. The speaker could have reduced the listener's effort in accessing and processing interpretations (5a) and (5b), and then implying the more relevant interpretation, by rephrasing the set-up to eliminate the unwanted interpretation. Interpretation (5a) has an adequate range of contextual effects obtained at additional processing effort, whereas interpretation (5b) reduces the processing effort but yields few positive cognitive effects. The listener picks interpretation (5a) as the intended interpretation because the additional processing effort is offset by the positive contextual effects. The punchline, however, exposes that we have been deliberately misled into inferring the more relevant but unintended interpretation. The recognition that our inference has misfired leads to humour.

> ## Summary
>
> In this chapter, we have offered an account of relevance theory as a cognitive stylistic theory of utterance interpretation rooted in the Gricean maxim of relation. We have applied the theory to the interpretation of humour in language by highlighting the way the joke teller exploits the addressee's cognitive tendency to pick out the interpretation that is consistent with the addresser's communicative intention and the principle of relevance. The theory has also been applied to a wide range of text types, including analysing the communicative effects of literary texts (Clark 1996), interpretative possibilities in media discourse (Yus Ramos 1998), implicatures in ordinary conversations (Taguchi 2002), the interpretation of irony (Yus 2016), and literary interpretation (Wilson 2018).

7.1 Do it yourself

Examine the way our expectations of optimal relevance are manipulated to create humour in the following jokes.

1) **TEACHER:** The Mississippi River flows in which state?
   STUDENT: Liquid.
   - Set-up
   - Punchline
   - Linguistic element in the set-up that creates ambiguity
   - Interpretation (1a)
   - Interpretation (1b)
   - Which interpretation yields positive cognitive effects? How is it achieved?
   - Which interpretation is obtained for the minimum justifiable processing effort? How is it achieved?
   - Which interpretation is revealed to be intended in the punchline?
   - Is the intended interpretation consistent with the principle of relevance?
2) **TEACHER:** How can you prevent diseases caused by biting insects?
   JOSE: Do not bite any.
   - Set-up
   - Punchline
   - Linguistic element in the set-up that creates ambiguity

- Interpretation (2a)
- Interpretation (2b)
- Which interpretation yields positive cognitive effects? How is it achieved?
- Which interpretation is obtained for the minimum justifiable processing effort? How is it achieved?
- Which interpretation is revealed to be intended in the punchline?
- Is the intended interpretation consistent with the principle of relevance?

3) **A:** How do you make a turtle fast?
   B: Take away his food.
   - Set-up
   - Punchline
   - Linguistic element in the set-up that creates ambiguity
   - Interpretation (3a)
   - Interpretation (3b)
   - Which interpretation yields positive cognitive effects? How is it achieved?
   - Which interpretation is obtained for the minimum justifiable processing effort? How is it achieved?
   - Which interpretation is revealed to be intended in the punchline?
   - Is the intended interpretation consistent with the principle of relevance?

4) **POSTMASTER:** Here is your five-cent stamp.
   SHOPPER: Do I have to stick it on myself?
   POSTMASTER: No, sir. On the envelope, please.
   - Set-up
   - Punchline
   - Linguistic element in the set-up that creates ambiguity
   - Interpretation (4a)
   - Interpretation (4b)
   - Which interpretation yields positive cognitive effects? How is it achieved?
   - Which interpretation is obtained for the minimum justifiable processing effort? How is it achieved?
   - Which interpretation is revealed to be intended in the punchline?
   - Is the intended interpretation consistent with the principle of relevance?

5) **TEACHER:** Where was the Declaration of Independence signed?
   STUDENT: At the bottom of the page.
   - Set-up
   - Punchline
   - Linguistic element in the set-up that creates ambiguity
   - Interpretation (5a)
   - Interpretation (5b)

- Which interpretation yields positive cognitive effects? How is it achieved?
- Which interpretation is obtained for the minimum justifiable processing effort? How is it achieved?
- Which interpretation is revealed to be intended in the punchline?
- Is the intended interpretation consistent with the principle of relevance?

Further Reading

COGNITIVE STYLISTICS

Stockwell, P. (2002), *Cognitive Poetics: An Introduction*, Routledge.
  The book outlines cognitive poetic approaches to the reading of literature and applies them to literary genres across different historical periods. For example, it applies deictic shift theory to a nineteenth-century novel, scripts and schemas to an old English poem, possible worlds and mental spaces to science fiction, and parable and projection to Middle English allegories.

THEORY OF HUMOUR AND AMBIGUITY IN LANGUAGE

Ross, A. (1998), *The Language of Humour*, Routledge.
  This textbook is an accessible and reader-friendly introduction to the theory of humour in language. It has a number of annotated examples of humour resulting from ambiguity at the different levels of linguistic structure.

RELEVANCE: THEORY AND RESEARCH

Clark, B. (2013), *Relevance Theory*, Cambridge University Press, <https://doi.org/10.1017/CBO9781139034104> (last accessed 23 September 2021).
  This is a comprehensive introduction to relevance as a theory of cognition and communication. The book is in two parts. The first part (Overview) presents a reader-friendly account of the theory, traces the origins of the theory to the work of Paul Grice, and zooms in on the two principles of relevance which form the main thrust of the theory. The second part (Details and Developments) focuses on theory-internal notions, such as explicatures and implicatures. The book contains many exercises to test understanding of theory and mastery of analytical skills. The book is accompanied by a website which offers more exercises for further practice.

Wilson, D. and D. Sperber (1994), 'Outline of relevance theory', *Links & Letters*, 1, 85–106, <https://doi.org/10.7146/hjlcb.v3i5.21436> (last accessed 23 September 2021).
  The paper offers an outline of the theory as an approach to utterance interpretation in which relevance plays a central role. After defining relevance, the authors explain how utterances create expectations of optimal relevance and illustrate the theory by applying it to different examples.

8

MULTIMODAL ANALYSIS OF ADVERTISEMENTS

Chapter Overview
- multimodal stylistics
- communication in advertising
- checklist of multimodal categories
- multimodal stylistic analysis of two adverts

Introduction

In our analysis of all the different text types in the previous six chapters, we have focused exclusively on verbal texts. In this chapter, we use mainstream stylistic frameworks along with the tools of visual grammar in the analysis of multimodal advertisements. We will be looking at the way verbal and visual elements in advertisements interact to create meaning and effect. The chapter is in two parts. The first part offers an overview of the nature of communication in advertising, an outline of the multimodal framework, and a checklist of categories for the analysis of multimodal texts. In the second part of the chapter, we carry out multimodal analyses of two adverts by relating features in the verbal and visual components in the adverts.

Communication in advertising

An advertisement is a discourse situation. It involves an addresser who is exchanging thoughts with an addressee about a particular subject. It involves an advertiser promoting (for sale) to a consumer or consumers goods or services through print media, television, internet, or any other advertising medium. Not all advertisements, however, sell products or promote services. Non-product advertisements promote charitable, political, or social events.

The meaning and effect of an advertisement are often carried linguistically by words and by other modes of representation, notably the visual mode. This multimodal nature of communication in the advertising register calls for an analytical methodology that treats meaning and effect as a configuration of textual and visual choices, hence **MULTIMODAL STYLISTICS**.

The approach combines mainstream stylistic approaches to the verbal text, in our context pragmatic stylistics, with Gunther Kress and Theo van Leeuwen's visual grammar approach to other semiotic modes. Analysis of the verbal text covers the way consumers are targeted directly or via speech acts and presuppositions, the use of directives and politeness markers, and the way the participants in the advert are located in time and space via deictic expressions. Analysis of the visuals, on the other hand, covers the construction of meaning via the visual material, the positioning of the viewer in relation to the participants, and the placement of the visual material on the printed page.

Multimodal stylistics

In 1996, Kress and van Leeuwen expanded the stylistics toolkit with a terminology for the analysis of, beyond verbal forms, visual modes of communication such as typography, layout, colour, distance, and other visual effects. This is multimodal stylistics. Basing their descriptive grammar on Halliday's social semiotics, multimodal stylisticians propose three levels of meaning, namely, representational, interactive, and compositional meanings in visual communication that correspond to Halliday's three metafunctions of language: the ideational function (the representation or construction of experience through language), the interpersonal function (the relationship between speakers and hearers in communication), and the textual function (the organisation of information in a text).

Representational meaning is the way the visual elements construct meaning through a configuration of processes, participants, and circumstances. Two process types are common in the literature of advertising: the first is action (in which a **VECTOR** emanates from an actor and affects a goal), which may be *transactional* involving an actor 'doing to' a goal or *non-transactional* with no goal or no doing. The second type is reactional (in which the vector is formed by an eyeline or the direction of a gaze), which is also *transactional* involving a reactor and the phenomenon being looked at, or *non-transactional* with a reactor but no phenomenon. Circumstances refer to amount of detail, colour saturation, and lightness in the setting.

The interactive meaning (the positioning of the viewer in relation to the participants) includes the gaze (the way participants in an image gaze directly – a demand, or are positioned as observers – an offer), angle of interaction (horizontal or vertical), distance (the way the participants are represented in a close, medium, or long shot to suggest intimacy or detachment), and modality (the way an image is stylised by a decrease or exaggeration of modality markers such as detail, background, depth, light, shadow, tone, and colour to indicate to the viewer how the image should be taken).

The third aspect is compositional meaning (the spatial organisation of elements on the page), which is constrained by the principles of information value (the placement of visual material on the left (given), right (new), top (ideal), bottom (real)), framing (the way the elements of the visual material are (dis-)connected by means of frames and contrast), and salience (the way elements of a visual are foregrounded due to their relative size, colour, focus, or tone).

A checklist of multimodal stylistic categories

The checklist in this chapter is divided into two sets. The first set helps you identify the aspects of the verbal text that are relevant to the meaning and effect of the advert. This set draws its analytical categories mainly from pragmatic stylistics. This second set draws its categories from Kress and van Leeuwen's terminology. It should help you identify the visual aspects of the adverts and relate them interpretively to the textual patterns.

Verbal text

a) Does the advert use a question? Whom does the question target? What is the effect intended?
b) Are there any speech acts in the advert? Are there any directive speech acts? Who makes them? Do they use any markers of politeness? What is the effect intended?
c) Does the advert have pronouns? How do they serve to delimit the identity of the target audience?
d) Are there other linguistic elements of the verbal texts that contribute to the overall effect of the advert?

Visual text

Representational meaning

e) What are the processes, participants, and circumstances that construct the representational meaning in the visual?

Interactive meaning

f) How is the audience positioned in relation to the participants in the advert? What is the effect of this positioning?
g) Are the participants in the advert gazing at the audience? What is the effect of this choice?
h) How close is the shot? What is the effect intended?
i) What are the markers of modality used in the advert? What is the intended effect?

Compositional meaning

j) Where is the visual material placed in the advert? What effect is intended by this choice?
k) How does the framing contribute to the effect of the advert?
l) Which part of the visual is salient? How does this contribute to the overall effect of the advert?
m) How do the verbal and visual elements of the advert together produce a coherent interpretation and achieve the intended effect?

Advert 1

FIGURE 8.1 Dettol advertisement

The product

Dettol, a brand name for a line of antiseptic products manufactured by Reckitt Benckiser, has been in use since the early 1930s when Dettol was first used for cleaning and disinfecting skin during surgical procedures. Since its introduction, the brand has covered most germ-killing tasks, from surgery rooms to kitchen utensils. The advert we are analysing here promotes Dettol as a kitchen gel.

Advert structure

The advert has four main constituents to it. There is the Indian Medical Association logo, which is irrelevant to our purpose, at the top right-hand corner, the advertising text at the bottom left-hand corner, the image of the Dettol kitchen gel product at the bottom right-hand corner, and a picture of a doctor and a mother with her child at the top left-hand corner and stretching to occupy the centre of the visual. We will start by analysing the verbal text, move on to examine the representational, interactive, and compositional meanings of the family picture, and conclude with a note on how the different modes in a multi-modal advert combine to carry its communicative intent.

Analysis: verbal text

The verbal text *GET 100% BETTER PROTECTION* uses no direct form of address and targets a wide group of consumers. It leaves the range of possible addressees unrestricted, and it is the accompanying visual that defines the family as the intended audience.

The audience is targeted directly using a directive speech act *GET X*. Directive speech acts (such as commands and requests) are used to get the addressee to perform some action. In English, directive speech acts often use linguistic politeness markers to show concern for others and minimise the threat to their face. They may use, for example, tag questions, as in *Open the window, will you?*, or discourse markers, as in *Pass the salt, please!*, in order to mitigate the force of the directive, that is, to make it less direct and less forceful. The directive speech act is used unmitigated by politeness markers, however, if it is considered to be beneficial to the recipient in one way or another, as in *Have a seat*. In this advert, we have a directive that is unmitigated with any markers of politeness. The effect of using a directive unmitigated with politeness markers is to construct the buying of Dettol gel as beneficial to the consumer, not the advertiser.

Analysis: visual text

The picture shows the doctor standing closer to the viewer and the mother standing not far behind, hugging a female child. They are all looking at the audience with big smiles on their faces.

Analysis of the representational meaning reveals the picture to be a reactional process in which the vector is formed by an eyeline or the direction of a gaze (Kress and van Leeuwen [1996] 2006). It is a non-transactional reactional process. That is, it is uni-directional, involving a reactor but no phenomenon. The reactors are the three participants in the advert (the doctor, mother, and child) who are looking the viewer straight in the eye. The eyeline between the reactors and the audience constitutes the vector, which indicates that the reactional process is one of complete satisfaction following the use of Dettol gel.

The interactive aspects of the visual composition add up to the meaning. The choice of a loving mother hugging her child to promote the gel creates a personal connection with every viewing mother and family (member). This personalised connection is enhanced by the gaze. The doctor and the small family are gazing and smiling at the viewer, thereby creating 'a visual form of address' in which the subject of the photograph 'demands' something from the viewers (Kress and van Leeuwen [1996] 2006: 117). It is a demand picture. The doctor and family in the picture demand that the viewing families use Dettol gel in order to attain the same level of well-being, comfort, and happiness.

The angle of the photograph accentuates the demand. It is eye level, with all three subjects in the photograph turning their heads slightly to face the viewer. This active choice to face the viewer makes the demand even more pressing.

In addition, the interactive element of social distance further enhances the personalised connection between the subjects and the viewer. It is a close shot, which intensifies the level of intimacy.

The last interactive dimension of the photograph concerns modality. It is a formally stylised photograph. The choice of the white colour for the background and garments along with articulation of the different colours of clothing, hair, and teeth serve to highlight the healthiness and the sense of gratification issuing from the use of the Dettol product.

The third dimension of visual analysis is the compositional meaning. Let us examine the information value in the image. The photograph is positioned in the upper half of the advert, occupying the left corner as well as the centre. This positioning constructs the family as the ideal towards which consumer families should strive. To attain this ideal, consumers will have to start from the realm of the real (the Dettol gel), which, along with the relevant verbal text, occupies the bottom half of the advert. It is through the real-world choices in response to the invitation that the idealised family extends that the status of healthiness and contentment can be attained.

The other compositional value of framing contributes to the meaning of this multimodal advert. The photograph is bordered by two layers of frames that suggest double protection from germs. The absence of framing at the top and the left, on the other hand, serves to communicate connectedness to the world of the viewer and leaves the door open for the viewer to join the world of protection and well-being.

In conclusion, the verbal and visual elements in the advert interact multimodally to create the advertising effect. The verbal text uses speech acts without redressive action in order to construct buying the Dettol gel as beneficial to the viewer, and the reactional process of satisfaction in the visual complements this effect. Other visual choices contribute to sustaining this effect. The gaze at the viewer, the head-on angle and the closeness of the shot, the positioning of the photograph as an ideal, the dominant white tone, and the articulation of colours combined bring into salience the good health of the family, as well as the feelings of satisfaction and delight resulting from the use of the advertised product.

The combination of verbal and visual modes is also employed to heighten the protection that the Dettol gel offers. The verbal text, using upper-case letters throughout and the enlarged font size of the verb *get*, gives a categorical assurance about the protection offered. The visual mode enhances this effect. The use of a two-layered frame to border the bottom half of the photograph enhances this assurance of protection that the verbal text makes.

Advert 2

FIGURE 8.2 United Way Movement advertisement (danger)

The service

The United Way Movement is a volunteer-based organisation engaged in hundreds of communities in more than forty countries and territories worldwide. In Canada, it has a network of over ninety United Way offices, which offer different support programmes that aim to help children graduate from school and college, build healthier environments, and make opportunities broadly available to local community members. This advert promotes a community-based support programme that targets schoolchildren.

Advert structure

The advert has a verbal text at the top, and the rest of the advert is a picture of three adults and a child in a local neighbourhood. Two of the men in the picture are sitting, with a bottle of beer next to them, and the third one is standing, with another bottle of beer and a boom box by his feet. This man is also smoking and offering a cigarette to the child, who is wearing his school backpack and holding a basketball with his left hand. The wall behind the three men has unintelligible graffiti in red and black, while the part of the wall behind the child is, as it were, unsullied, a blank canvas. An adult left hand stretches in-between the child and the three young men to separate them and interrupt the communication. Like with the first advert, we will analyse the verbal text and the different meanings in the visual, and then examine the way these textual and visual meanings combine to produce a coherent interpretation of the advert and achieve its intended effect.

Analysis: verbal text

The verbal text has two parts. The longer section written in small font reads, 'When you give to United Way, you're helping create positive environments for young people by providing things like after-school programs, employment assistance and counseling. With United Way-funded agencies helping so many in our community, making a difference is easier than you think. Visit www.unitedway.ca'. This text is followed by a shorter, bigger-sized and upper-case, slogan than reads, 'WITHOUT YOU, THERE WOULD BE NO WAY'.

Let us start with the longer text. The text uses the second person deictic pronoun *you* three times to address the target audience. The choice of second person pronouns creates the effect of a shared context. The audience is projected into the middle of the discourse and hence the middle of the action.

This effect of shared context and shared purpose is enhanced by the use of the inclusive pronoun in *our community*. After building the case for the proximity of the audience to the targeted schoolchildren, the advert uses the directive speech act *Visit X*, unmitigated with any markers of politeness. At this point, taking action to protect children is construed as beneficial to the viewer, who has already been constructed as a member of the community.

The shorter text uses bigger font and capital letters to underscore the urgency, and significance, of the audience's intervention for the future of the children. If you do not stretch your hand in support, the advert tells the viewers, these children will have no way of getting a better future.

Analysis: visual text

Analysis of the representational meaning reveals that there are three narrative processes at work. First, there is a reactional process in which the vector is formed by the eyeline between the child and the three men. It is a transactional process in which the child and the men are both reactor and phenomena at the same time. The second process is a process of action in which the vector is realised by the hand of the man standing against the wall and offering the child a cigarette. The actor is the man making the offer and the child is the goal of the action process.

The third process is also an action process and is related in significant ways to the other two narrative processes. The vector of this process of action is realised by the extended hand forming an oblique line with the eye contact between the child and the men (the vector of the first process of reaction) in order to protect the child from the encroachment of the adult world (the goal and actor of the second process of action).

The second aspect of visual design is the interactive meaning. The absence of a gaze at the viewer constructs the photograph as an 'offer' to participate in saving the child from street gangs, and singling out one child as the victim personalises the connection with the viewers and invites them to save the child from the imminent danger. The angle of the photograph enhances the meaning. It is a frontal angle, which reinforces the urgency for the viewer to get involved.

The authenticity of the dangers of the encroachment of gang life on the world of children is emphasised by the modality in the photograph. This is a high modality photograph. In other words, it is a non-modalised expression of the threats to children in local communities. The colours, background, lighting, and tones are all real, and so is the hand that extends to insulate the child.

The third aspect is the spatial organisation of elements on the page. This is a centred composition, that is, all elements of the visual, save the text, are placed at the centre. The hand forcibly divides the composition into left and right, with the child placed to the right and the three men to the left. This positioning constructs gang life as given, which is to be separated from child life, which is constructed as new.

The other compositional concepts of framing and salience enrich the findings. The absence of framing stresses connectedness of the version of community life in the photograph with life in the larger community outside, and the sharper focus on the extended hand brings it, and brings the need to intervene to save children by implication, into salience.

To sum up, verbal choices and visual elements combine to produce the intended advertising effect. The deviation from schematic pragmatic expectations about pronominal reference in the verbal text combines with the absence of framing in the visual to create the effect of shared context. The use of the inclusive pronoun and the unmitigated directive in the text, along with the high modality in the visual, construct the viewer as an insider community member. Finally, the capital letters and the enlarged font size in the printed slogan *WITHOUT YOU, THERE WOULD BE NO WAY* combine with choice of vector in the third process of action, that is, the extended hand, the frontal angle of the photograph, the positioning of the hand in the middle of the photograph, and the sharper focus on the hand to bring into salience the importance of the need to take action.

> **Summary**
>
> In this chapter, we have carried out multimodal stylistic analyses of two print advertisements. We have seen textual choices combine with visual modes to create meaning and enhance effect. Multimodal stylistic analysis has also been used in the analysis of literary texts. Nørgaard (2009) offers a methodological framework for describing the semiotic potential of typography in literary texts, and Nørgaard (2010) offers a practical demonstration of the semiotic contribution of typography, layout, and images to the meaning and effect of a multimodal novel. Other interesting applications include Gibbons (2013), which explores multimodal metaphors in experimental literature, McIntyre (2008), which analyses multimodal elements in a scene from a film version of a Shakespearean play, and Moya Guijarro and Pinar Sanz (2008), which examines the role of verbal and visual elements in creating meaning in a children's picture book. More recently, Nørgaard (2019) has offered a more comprehensive analytical framework for the analysis of multimodal meaning-making resources in the novel.

8.1 Do it yourself

Examine the following two multimodal advertisements for the way the verbal and visual elements create meaning and effect.

1)

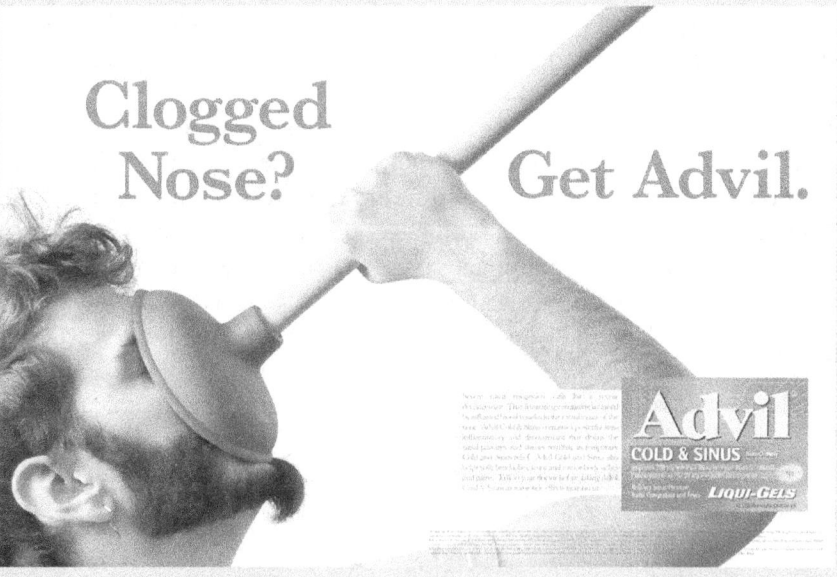

FIGURE 8.3 Advil advertisement

Hints

Advil is a pain reliever, used for treating several kinds of pain, including headache and muscle aches. The drug has been sold as an over-the-counter medication for over thirty years in the USA and abroad.

Verbal text

a) How does the use of a question position the viewer?
b) What is the effect of using an elliptical question?
c) Is the directive mitigated with politeness markers? What is the effect?

The visual

d) Identify the vector, actor, and goal in this action process.
e) Is it a close, medium, or long shot? What is the effect of this social distance choice?
f) Is this a high or low modality photograph? What is the effect of this choice?
g) Examine the ideological significance of information value (or positioning) in the advert. What is brought into salience? How?
h) How do these verbal and visual elements cohere to produce the advertising effect?

2)

FIGURE 8.4 United Way Movement advertisement (homeless)

> **Hints**
>
> The United Way Movement is a volunteer-based organisation with different support programmes that target local community members.
>
> **Verbal text**
>
> a) Use the findings from our analysis of advert 2 in the chapter. You may edit the analysis if you disagree with the findings.
> b) Add a new verbal text to communicate the message of the advert. Include the following:
> - Address the target audience directly.
> - Use a second person pronoun.
> - Use a directive unmitigated with politeness markers.
>
> **The visual**
>
> c) Identify the vector, actor, and goal in this action process.
> d) Is it a close, medium, or long shot?
> e) What is the angle of the photograph?
> f) Is this a high or low modality photograph?
> g) Examine the ideological significance of information value (or positioning) in the advert. What is brought into salience? How?
> h) How do these verbal and visual elements cohere to produce the advertising effect?

> **Further Reading**

THE LANGUAGE OF ADVERTISING

Goddard, A. (1998), *The Language of Advertising*, Routledge.

This textbook offers an introduction to the language of advertising. It defines advertising, and lists the visual and verbal attention-seeking devices used in advertisements. The book offers plenty of practical activities on the way advertisements communicate meaning and make effect, and closes with a comprehensive glossary of advertising terms.

THE DISCOURSE OF ADVERTISING

Cook, G. [1992] (2001), *The Discourse of Advertising*, Routledge.

A more advanced book that examines British adverts from TV, magazines, and posters. It relates texts to their context of communication and considers the effect of verbal, visual, as well as semiotic (signs) modes of communication on consumers' behaviour and ideology.

THE GRAMMAR OF VISUAL DESIGN

Kress, G. and T. van Leeuwen [1996] (2006), *Reading Images: The Grammar of Visual Design*, Routledge.
The book offers a descriptive framework for the description of visual communication, including children's drawings, school textbook illustrations, advertisements, magazine layout, and three-dimensional forms. The methodology includes tools for the analysis of patterns of representation (the ways we encode experience visually), patterns of interaction (the relations between the makers and viewers of visual texts), and patterns of composition (the spatial organisation of the visual and its elements on the page).

MULTIMODAL STYLISTICS

Nørgaard, N. (2014), 'Multimodality and stylistics', in M. Burke (ed.), *The Routledge Companion to Stylistics*, Routledge, pp. 471–84.
Drawing on Hallidayan stylistics and Kress and van Leeuwen's grammar of visual design, this book chapter offers an introduction to multimodal stylistics and considers future directions.

Nørgaard, N. (2019), *Multimodal Stylistics of the Novel: More than Words*, Routledge.
The book offers a systematic framework for the analysis of multimodal as well as 'visually conventional novels' (p. 3). The book explores the semiotic potential for meaning of a novel's verbal text, typography, layout, photographs, drawings, book-cover design, and physical form.

9

CRITICAL STYLISTIC ANALYSIS OF POLITICAL DISCOURSE

> **Chapter Overview**
> - critical stylistics
> - communication in political discourse
> - checklist of critical stylistic categories
> - Obama's statement on the events in Tunisia
> - critical stylistic analysis of Obama's statement

Introduction

In Chapter 4, we used critical linguistics to investigate ideology and power in fiction. This chapter revisits the concern with ideology but explores political discourse. We use **CRITICAL STYLISTICS**, which offers a more comprehensive toolkit for the investigation of ideology in language, to analyse a statement by the 44th American President Barack Obama on the events in Tunisia in 2011. Before presenting the findings of the critical stylistic analysis, we will offer an overview of the nature of political communication, sketch out the critical stylistic approach, and suggest a checklist of critical stylistic categories to help you see how I arrived at the findings of the analysis and assist you in making your own critical stylistic analysis of the other statement suggested for further practice in activity 9.1.

Communication in political discourse

Political discourse refers to spoken or written communication (such as debates, statements, press releases, and speeches) by individuals who are professionally engaged in the affairs of government, parliament, and political parties. In other words, it is the text and talk of politicians, political institutions, and ordinary citizens in relation to the use of power to achieve social, economic, and political ends.

Political discourse is a means to an end. Its aim is to spread ideologies, influence behaviours, and win supporters. In order for political discourse to achieve this effect, it employs linguistic means to help achieve its goal. These include, but are not limited to, choice of words, repetition, deletion, the use of metaphors, speech acts and politeness strategies, choice of words and **DEIXIS** to manipulate the audience's perspectives, change of part of speech to achieve ideological effect (e.g. nominalisation), syntactic subordination (e.g. passivisation), creation of text-specific relationships of opposition and equivalence, manipulation of the speech and thoughts of others, repetition or deletion of parts of the proposition, and the use of metaphors, speech acts, and politeness strategies.

Analysis of how political discourse manipulates the ideological outlook of its recipients necessarily entails analysis of how these linguistic tools are deployed in political text and talk. The present chapter focuses on ten of the tools listed in the previous paragraph, which together form the analytical toolkit of our analytical framework – critical stylistics.

Critical stylistics

Critical stylistics is an attempt to offer a more coherent analytical toolkit for the investigation of ideology in language use. A detailed outline of the approach is found in *Critical Stylistics* (2010) by Lesley Jeffries. Jeffries acknowledges that the approach is an extension of the concern in critical linguistics and **CRITICAL DISCOURSE ANALYSIS** with the investigation of the ideological import of texts. Her contribution is a coherent set of analytical tools covering lexical choice and widening up to include structural, semantic, and pragmatic aspects of texts to make up for the lack of 'comprehensive coverage of linguistic features' in other approaches to ideology (Jeffries 2010: 13). Jeffries argues that the comprehensiveness of the toolkit allows the analyst to analyse ideological content in a systematic way and expose the way texts 'influence the ideological outlook of their recipients' (2010: 6).

Critical stylistics offers a set of ten textual functions to uncover the way ideologies are 'communicated, reproduced, constructed and negotiated using language' (Jeffries 2010: 20). These functions may be instantiated by more than one linguistic form, as we will see in the next three paragraphs.

The first function is naming and describing, which is realised lexically by the choice of nouns, morphologically by the process of **NOMINALISATION** (turning a verb into a noun), and syntactically by noun modification. The second function is representing actions, events, and states. Using transitivity options, text producers choose verbs carefully to represent a situation as an action, event, or state, with ideological consequences for the way text recipients conceptualise the represented world (see Chapter 3 for more on transitivity). The third function is equating and contrasting. It refers to the construction of the world in the text in terms of opposition, using such linguistic carriers as NP apposition, parallelism, and metaphor, or in terms of equivalence, using textual opposition, contrastives, and so on.

The fourth function is exemplifying and enumerating. A text producer may use linguistic carriers like *for example, for instance*, or *to exemplify* to instantiate members of a list or suggest comprehensiveness of the members of a list. The fifth function is prioritising, which refers to manipulating the default focus to signal ideological priorities. This is carried linguistically by subordination, clefting, and passive transformation. The sixth function is implying and assuming. Text producers may use definite NPs, factive verbs, change-of-state verbs, comparative structures, implicatures, iteratives, and clefts to naturalise debated ideologies and present them as if they were common knowledge. The seventh function is negating, which has a 'persuasive power' (Jeffries 2010: 107). It allows text producers to produce a hypothetical reality in order to inspire fear, belief, or hope in the text recipients and influence their actions and reactions.

The eighth function is hypothesising. This function is linguistically carried by modal auxiliary verbs, modal verbs, modal adjectives, modal adverbs, and conditionals. These linguistic choices allow authors to express assertions about propositions or different degrees of commitment to the truth or desirability of the propositions. The ninth function is presenting the speech and thoughts of others. A text producer may exercise degrees of control over the speech and thoughts of textual characters, thereby mediating the audience's experience of the textual world (see Chapter 4 for more on the presentation of others' speech and thoughts). The last function is representing time, space, and society. Text producers choose deictic expressions of time, place, and person to construct a textual deictic centre and influence the text percipients' viewing position.

A checklist of critical stylistic categories

This section provides a checklist for you to follow in carrying out critical stylistic analyses of political texts. The checklist has ten items corresponding to the ten textual functions making up the toolkit of critical stylistics. Answering all the questions will help you cover all linguistic features which may be ideologically manipulative, thereby making systematic critical stylistic analyses.

a) What are the nouns, nominal groups, and nominalised verbs used in the text? Who are they associated with? How does the choice of nominals carry the text producer's ideological outlook?
b) What verbs are used in the text? Classify them into the patterns of transitivity and the associated semantic roles. How do these choices sustain the text producer's ideological outlook?
c) Does the text construct relations of equivalence or opposition? How does the choice relate to the reality propagated by the text?
d) What lists are made in the text? Are the lists comprehensive or suggestive? How does listing sustain the text producer's ideology?
e) What ideological priorities are structured in the text? Examine the patterns of subordination, clefting, and transformation.

f) How do the textually prioritised patterns manipulate the text recipient's outlook on the reality in the text? How is language deployed to naturalise debatable propositions? Look for instances of **EXISTENTIAL PRESUPPOSITION** (triggered by definite NPs), **LOGICAL PRESUPPOSITION** (triggered by factive verbs, iterative words, and change-of-state verbs), and implicatures.

g) How do these choices tacitly build a consensual reality? List the negative particles, negated words, and structures. What hypothetical reality is conjured up by negation for the text recipient to believe desire or fear?

h) Which parts of the text are categorically asserted and which are modalised to give an opinion about the truth or desirability of the propositions contained in it?

i) How does the text producer present the speech and thoughts of other people? Look for examples of direct speech, free direct speech, indirect speech, free indirect speech, or narrative report of speech. Also look for examples of direct thought, free direct thought, indirect thought, free indirect thought, or narrative report of thought. How do these choices manipulate the text recipient's outlook on the projected reality?

j) What deictic terms of place, time, person, and address are used in the text? How do they construct the time, space, and human relationships that make up the world of the text? How does the effect from this choice cohere with the overall effect of the text?

The text

The text to analyse is a statement by Barack Obama on the Tunisian uprising in 2011. The written statement was released by the Office of the Press Secretary at the White House on 14 January 2011 as part of the US official response to the Tunisian chapter of the Arab Spring (The White House 2011a).

The Arab Spring started on 17 December 2010 when a Tunisian fruit vendor who had been humiliated by police set himself on fire. Buazizi's frustration resonated with the Tunisian people and led to a revolution that ousted President Bin Ali, and triggered a wave of popular protests in five other countries, namely, Egypt, Yemen, Libya, Bahrain, and Syria. These revolutions are collectively known as the Arab Spring.

Tunisia, under Bin Ali, was a US strategic ally in containing terrorism in North Africa, and Bin Ali was instrumental in maintaining the American interests in Tunisia and the region. This speech by Obama was made on 14 January 2011, which is the day Bin Ali fled the country and the popular revolt was practically over.

> ¹I condemn and deplore the use of violence against citizens peacefully voicing their opinion in Tunisia, and I applaud the courage and dignity of the Tunisian people. ²The United States stands with the entire international community in bearing witness to this brave and determined struggle for the universal rights that we must all uphold, and we will long remember the images of the Tunisian people seeking to make their voices heard. ³I urge all parties to maintain calm and avoid violence, and

call on the Tunisian government to respect human rights, and to hold free and fair elections in the near future that reflect the true will and aspirations of the Tunisian people.

[4]As I have said before, each nation gives life to the principle of democracy in its own way, grounded in the traditions of its own people, and those countries that respect the universal rights of their people are stronger and more successful than those that do not.[5] I have no doubt that Tunisia's future will be brighter if it is guided by voices of the Tunisian people.

The analysis

Not all texts make use of the same set of linguistic resources to articulate or propagate ideological positions. Different text producers make different selections that reflect their perspectives and ideological priorities. In the analysis below, therefore, we will focus only on the textual functions that uncover Obama's ideological evaluation of the Tunisian revolution. For this text, these functions are naming; representing events; prioritising; equating and contrasting; implying and assuming; hypothesising; and representing time, space, and society.

Naming

Obama's ideological evaluation of the Tunisian uprising is reflected in his manipulation of names and naming conventions. He avoids any reference to the ousted Tunisian president and labels Tunisian revolutionaries *citizens* and *Tunisian people*. What binds the revolutionaries in this qualification is more a national identity than socio-political and economic grievances. Obama abstains from calling it 'a popular revolt' and refrains from honouring the revolutionary cause. Consistent with this attitude is the construction of the uprising as a *struggle* for *universal rights*. Tunisians' aspirations are generalised, rather than localised, and this helps Obama avoid detailing the specifics of the Tunisian situation under Bin Ali. Although this construction implies a negative qualification of the Tunisian regime being in opposition to universal rights, Obama's condemnation is at best an implication. Elsewhere in the statement, this 'struggle for universal rights' is constructed as *opinion* and a *voice*.

Obama also uses metaphorical nominalisation to ideological effect. In *I condemn and deplore the use of violence*, Obama packages up a potential proposition (x used violence against y) inside the headword of the noun phrase *use*, thus nominalising a possible proposition. The fully-fledged propositional version would require naming the agent of using violence and goal of the use of violence, which Obama is unwilling to spell out. A similar nominalisation of an evaluative proposition occurs in *this brave and determined struggle*. Again, the propositional version of this nominalised structure would require specifying who struggled and against whom or against what. Obama's preference to block agency and blur intentionality throughout the statement is an ideological decision that is consistent with his ideological outlook on the Tunisian uprising.

Representing events/actions/states

The patterns of agency and transitivity are also ideologically significant. The statement contains twenty-two verbal elements, as shown in Table 9.1.

TABLE 9.1 Transitivity and agency in Obama's statement on Tunisia

No.	Verbal element	Sentence no.	Transitivity pattern	Semantic roles
1	condemn	1	Verbiage	Sayer (Obama)
2	deplore	1	Verbiage	Sayer (Obama)
3	applaud	1	Verbiage	Sayer (Obama)
4	stand with	2	Mental process	Sensor (US)
5	uphold	2	Mental process	Sensor (US and world)
6	remember	2	Mental process	Sensor (US and world)
7	seek	2	Material action process	Agent (Tunisians)
8	urge	3	Verbiage	Sayer (Obama)
9	maintain	3	Material action process	Agent (Tunisians and other parties)
10	avoid	3	Material action process	Agent (Tunisians and other parties)
11	call on	3	Verbiage	Sayer (Obama)
12	respect	3	Mental process	Sensor (Tunisian government)
13	hold	3	Material action process	Agent (Tunisian government)
14	reflect	3	Mental process	Sensor (elections)
15	say	4	Verbiage	Sayer (Obama)
16	give	4	Material action process	Agent (nation)
17	respect	4	Mental process	Sensor (countries)
18	be	4	Relational process	Carrier (countries)
19	not respect	4	Mental process	Sensor (countries)
20	have	5	Relational process	Carrier (Obama)
21	be	5	Relational process	Carrier (Tunisian future)
22	guide	5	Material action process	Agent (Tunisians)

Obama's ideological evaluation of the Tunisian president and revolution is borne by his deployment of the patterns of agency. There is a marked absence of agency in the statement. Only six processes, out of twenty-two processes, involve agents, and the most notable absent agents are the ousted Tunisian president and the United States. The former is left out altogether and the latter, along with the international community, assumes the semantic roles of sayer or sensor throughout the statement.

The only recurring agent in the statement is the Tunisian people, and this observation merits attention. The Tunisians are projected in the semantic role of agent four times in the statement, and these references are embedded at low levels of textual subordination. The first reference is placed at the last level of subordination in the second sentence, the second and third are placed higher up at the second level in sentence number 3, and the fourth reference is at the third and last level of subordination in the last sentence. In their first agent role, the Tunisian people are only *seeking* to make their voices heard; in the second and third, they are urged *to maintain calm and avoid violence* and in effect are framed as sharing the status of their oppressors; and in the fourth reference, there is a metonymic reference to their *voices*, which is predicated upon a conditional proposition. The only other agents in the statement are the Tunisian government, which appears three times in reference to a future course of action, and the nations of the world that champion democracy.

Related to causation are the patterns of transitivity – the representation of power relations. The statement has six material action intentional verbs, six verbalisation processes, seven mental processes, and three processes of relation. Although Obama and the US government are the grammatical subjects of all the main clauses, which gives an illusion of agency, they do not constitute any of the material action intentional structures of the statement. Obama appears in six verbalisation processes *condemn, deplore, applaud, urge, call on,* and *said* in which he offers 'verbiage' to communicate an unfavourable attitude towards the use of violence. He appears once in a relational process of possession *have no doubt* which speculates on the future of Tunisia. The US government along with the international community are the 'sensor' in three mental processes of 'bearing witness', 'upholding', and 'remembering' the images and voices coming out of Tunisia. It is also interesting to note all the material action intentional verbs are embedded at subordinated levels and the main clause is always constituted by a non-action verbal element.

Prioritising

Obama's ideological evaluation is also signalled by the textual priorities. Each of the five sentences making up the statement has at least three levels of embedding, creating a structure for ideological prioritisation. The first sentence prioritises Obama's verbalisation *I condemn* and subordinates the brutality of the Tunisian regime, which is nominalised *the use of violence*, and the defiance of the Tunisian revolutionaries. The second sentence prioritises the United States and the international community and downplays the cause and human cost of the popular uprising. Sentences 3 and 5 place Obama's verbalisation at the highest level of subordination, and the Tunisians' will and voices at the lowest, while sentence 4 prioritises Obama's verbiage and makes no reference to the Tunisian people. The other interesting choice in this regard is the adjectival transformation *in this brave and determined struggle*. Obama prefers the transformation because the propositional version would turn it into a material action intentional structure that requires specifying an agent and patient for the action verb, that is, who struggled against whom or what.

Equating and contrasting

Obama also constructs textual opposites with ideological consequences. The *use of violence against civilians peacefully voicing their opinion* is projected in opposition to the *courage and dignity of the Tunisian people* by virtue of being predicated on verbs with opposite semantic content *condemn* vs *applaud*. This textual opposition triggers two semantic implications: first, the use of violence against civilians becomes an act lacking in courage and dignity; and second, with courage and dignity being attributes of the Tunisian people, the textual opposite becomes an attribute of the Tunisian regime against which they are protesting.

Implying and assuming

Obama's ideological evaluation of the Tunisian situation continues to be tacitly advanced. Regime repression is logically presupposed in *seeking to make their voices heard*. Another logical presupposition is triggered by the change-of-state verb in *avoid violence*, which presupposes the use of violence by 'all' parties, and a third presupposition is triggered by the comparison in *Tunisia's future will be brighter*, in reference to Tunisia's past under Bin Ali. The Tunisian regime's authoritarian practices are logically presupposed in *to respect human rights* and *hold free and fair elections*. Other evaluations are triggered by flouting the maxim of quantity, leading to implied pragmatic meanings. The revolutionary cause is referred to as *opinions* and the tens of deaths and casualties are *images*, both signalling a slanted ideological standpoint.

Hypothesising; representing time, space, and society

The last sentence of the statement is interesting. Obama uses epistemic modality *have no doubt* to suggest a highly certain version of reality, but it contains a negative particle which serves to conjure up the negated scenario. Within the scope of this modal is a conditional, which serves to mitigate the strength of the epistemic modality *will be brighter if it is guided by the voices of the Tunisian people*. The last remark on this speech concerns the use of deictic expressions. The text constructs a default deictic field in which Obama's time/place is at the centre. Noteworthy is the use of *this* in *this brave and determined struggle*, which projects Obama in proximity and projects Obama with an insider's perspective on the Tunisian situation.

> ## Summary
>
> Critical stylistic analysis of the statement reveals Obama's ideological slant towards the Tunisian revolution. Reference to Tunisian President Bin Ali is blocked by transformation and morphological nominalisation. Obama's criticism of the Tunisian regime's repression is at best logically presupposed in the use of change-of-state verbs and comparisons, and in flouting of the maxim of quantity. It is never explicit. In comparison, Obama refers to the

Tunisian revolutionaries as *citizens* and *people*, and to the uprising as an *opinion*. The Tunisian president is never allocated the role of agent in any of the twenty-two verbal structures. It is always the Tunisian people who assume this role, but their actions, nevertheless, are subordinated at lower levels of structure to Obama's verbiage.

Like the other trends in stylistics introduced in this book, critical stylistics is applicable beyond the genre it has been used to analyse in this chapter. The framework has been used to analyse the representation of men in women's magazines (Coffey 2013), and to examine the ideologies behind the construction of the speaker and the fictional world in a collection of political poems (Ibrahim 2018), to name a couple of examples.

Remarks

The analysis of Obama's statement on Tunisia is part of a research project published in the *Journal of Language Aggression and Conflict*, 2(1), 2014 (Alaghbary 2014).

9.1 Do it yourself

The following is President Obama's statement, released on 25 February 2011, on the Libyan popular revolt against President Qaddafi (The White House 2011b). Make a critical stylistic analysis of the statement.

Statement by the President on Libya Sanctions

> The Libyan government's continued violation of human rights, brutalization of its people, and outrageous threats have rightly drawn the strong and broad condemnation of the international community. By any measure, Muammar el-Qaddafi's government has violated international norms and common decency and must be held accountable. These sanctions therefore target the Qaddafi government, while protecting the assets that belong to the people of Libya.
>
> Going forward, the United States will continue to closely coordinate our actions with the international community, including our friends and allies, and the United Nations. We will stand steadfastly with the Libyan people in their demand for universal rights, and a government that is responsive to their aspirations. Their human dignity cannot be denied.

Hints

a) Examine the naming conventions in the statement. How is President Qaddafi referred to?

b) Identify the nominalisations in the first paragraph. What do they tell us about Obama's, and the US's, attitude towards the Libyan regime?
c) Examine the agency and transitivity choices. Who is structured as agent in the material processes? What role do the Libyan government, Libyan people, and the US government have in the statement? What do these choices tell us about Obama's attitude towards the Libyan revolution?
d) Examine the way ideological priorities are structured into the text. Who is prioritised in every sentence in the text? Where are the protesters and the repressive practices of the Libyan regime structured? How do these choices relate to your answers to the previous questions?
e) Examine the other linguistic choices in the statement. How do they contribute to a coherent interpretation of Obama's (or the US's) ideological outlook on the Libyan president, government, people, and the popular revolution?
f) Rewrite Obama's statement on the events in Tunisia to give it the assertive and committed attitude that is present in the Libya statement. In your rewriting, use the following hints:
- The Tunisian president's name at the time was Bin Ali.
- Replace the mental and verbalisation processes with material processes.
- Package evaluations inside nominals to pass them as assumptions.
- Use one or two levels of subordination to communicate clarity of objectives and priorities.
- Use non-modalised language to sustain the assertive mood.
- Report the thoughts of the international community and presuppose its agreement.

Further Reading

CRITICAL STYLISTICS

Jeffries, L. (2010), *Critical Stylistics: The Power of English*, Palgrave Macmillan.
A comprehensive and reader-friendly account of critical stylistics. The book offers ten tools for the investigation of the power of spoken and written texts on their recipients. It contains a wealth of annotated examples drawn from different genres.

CRITICAL STYLISTIC ANALYSIS OF POLITICAL DISCOURSE

Alaghbary, G. S. (2014), 'The United States' reaction to the Arab Spring: A critical stylistic analysis', *Journal of Language Aggression and Conflict*, 2(1), 151–75, <https://doi.org/10.1075/jlac.2.1.06ala> (last accessed 23 September 2021).

This paper uses the ten tools of critical stylistics in the investigation of ideological embedding in US presidential rhetoric on aggression and conflict. In particular, it examines Obama's first official statements on each of the 2011 popular uprisings in Tunisia, Egypt, Yemen, Libya, Bahrain, and Syria. You could compare your answer to the practice exercise with the analysis of the Libyan statement in the paper.

Alaghbary, G. S. (2019), 'Ideological positioning in conflict: The United States and Egypt's domestic political trajectory', in M. Evans, L. Jeffries and J. O'Driscoll (eds), *The Routledge Handbook of Language in Conflict*, Routledge, pp. 83–102.

This book chapter offers a critical stylistic analysis of two statements by President Obama and the Egyptian Armed Forces on the removal of Egyptian President Morsy from office in 2013. Analysis reveals the way political actors deploy language resources to naturalise ideologies and manipulate our perception of the 'truth'.

10

CORPUS ANALYSIS OF ONLINE JOURNALISM

> **Chapter Overview**
> - corpus stylistics
> - communication in online journalism
> - checklist of corpus stylistic categories
> - the English Web 2018 (enTenTen18) corpus
> - the Arabic Web 2012 (arTenTen12, Stanford Tagger) corpus
> - corpus stylistic analysis of the subcorpus

Introduction

This chapter is slightly different from the previous eight chapters. In this chapter, we combine techniques from **CORPUS LINGUISTICS** with stylistic analysis. In other words, we combine qualitative with quantitative analysis. For this reason, the layout of the chapter is slightly different. We are not analysing a text. We are analysing a large collection of texts, or a body of language data, that is available online and not presented in physical form in the chapter. The checklist is also different. It takes the form of steps to follow in retrieving the corpus, looking up the patterns, and reporting the findings. In the activities for further practice, there are also no texts to present. You will be carrying out corpus stylistic analyses of data in a number of corpora.

Communication in online journalism

The internet is now the most widely used medium of communication. It is convenient and accessible round the clock. It has made available vast resources of texts. Online newspapers, magazines, and e-books, for example, are one click away, and almost free. The introduction of hand-held technology and mobile applications has further enhanced the accessibility of information. Many young people today find much of what they are looking for on the internet, which is accessible on their smartphones. My students report that Twitter is where they read news, watch games, make friends, communicate, and learn. In other words, it is their TV, radio station, virtual coffee shop, newspaper, and so forth.

Information gathered from different sources is presented in websites. A website is a collection of web pages, much like a book. There are many types of websites, classified according to content and purpose. These include blogs, information websites, government websites, business websites, personal websites, and news websites. Huge amounts of data gathered from these websites are stored electronically in what are known as corpora.

Online journalism is progressively moving away from limiting itself to the written mode. Most websites today are multimodal. They communicate in at least five different modes. They use texts (the most common mode) but supplement this mode with other semiotic modes, such as images, sound tracks, videos, animations, or links to other texts or websites, in order to offer a more dynamic narrative, keep readers engaged, and enable a higher level of interactivity. In this chapter, we focus on textual communication in online journalism.

News websites present political, social, economic, and personal news, or news of general interest. The writer's account of the story, despite their best attempt, is not 'factual'. It necessarily reflects an ideological outlook. The choice of story, interviewees, time, location, and language are all affected by the author's ideological take on the story.

Corpus stylistics

The application of the techniques of corpus linguistics to the analysis of large amounts of literary, and conventional, text types has improved the 'systematicity and rigour of stylistic analysis' (McIntyre and Walker 2019: 2). The result of this integration is known as **CORPUS STYLISTICS**.

Corpus stylistics refers to the computer-aided analysis of a (large-scale) collection of electronically stored samples of naturally occurring texts (or **CORPUS**) for the purpose of identifying patterns of language that constitute meaning, style, and ideological outlook. A corpus may be created of written or spoken texts, or both, in any language, depending on the purpose of the corpus compiler.

An electronically stored corpus is processed with the help of computer applications that enable researchers to run through the corpus, create lists of words, and compare frequency of occurrence. The patterns of meaning obtained from a corpus stylistic analysis are measured against a reference corpus in order to establish what the norm is and how the patterns uncovered relate to the norm.

Popular, and free, reference corpora include the British National Corpus (BNC), which is a 100-million-word collection of written and spoken British English texts, and the Corpus of Contemporary American English (COCA), which contains over 560 million words. Software tools for corpus management may be designed for use on a server (e.g. Sketch Engine) or to be installed on a computer (e.g. WordSmith and AntConc). In this chapter, we are using Sketch Engine, which contains, at the time of writing, 500 ready-to-use corpora in over 90 languages.

Of all the available corpora on Sketch Engine, we will be working on two. The first is English Web 2018 (enTenTen18), the largest corpus on Sketch Engine in terms of size, and the second is Arabic Web 2012 (arTenTen12). The set of tools available on Sketch Engine for these two corpora include 'word sketch', which generates collocations categorised by grammatical relations, 'keywords', which extracts the terminology in the corpus, 'word lists', which offers lists of the parts of speech in the corpus organised by frequency, and 'concordance', which displays the search word/phrase in context. Sketch Engine also allows you to create a user corpus by downloading relevant texts from your laptop or from the internet to which you can apply the same set of tools to obtain the desired results. In this chapter, we are interested in the 'word sketch' and 'concordance' tools, which will help us generate the collocates of the words in the two corpora and examine their collocational behaviour in context. We will categorise the resulting collocates in terms of positive and negative shading in order to make conclusions about the favourable representation or negative online portrayal of the search word in the two corpora.

A checklist of corpus stylistic categories

This section offers steps to follow in selecting a software, choosing a corpus, and running corpus tools. This list is complemented by a procedure of analysis that I offer prior to the presentation of findings later in this chapter.

a) What is the research hypothesis you want to test out using the corpus?
b) Which corpus is most appropriate for your research purpose?
c) Do the available corpora contain the texts needed to test out the hypothesis?
d) What kind of information do you need to extract from the corpus?
e) Which text analysis software will you use?
f) Which corpus tools do you need to run in order to extract the information you need (e.g. wordlists, collocational behaviour, concordance lines)?
g) Do you need to compare your results with relevant patterns in a reference corpus?
h) Which reference corpus is appropriate for your purpose?
i) Do you need to create your own (sub-)corpus?
j) What are the findings from the quantitative analysis? Combine qualitative information with the quantitative data to test out your research hypothesis and draw conclusions based on a solid linguistic basis.

The analysis

In this section, we will examine the impact of language choice on the representation of religion/faith in online journalism. In particular, we will be comparing patterns of representation around the word *Islamic* in the English Web 2018 corpus (enTenTen18) with patterns of representation around the Arabic word اسلامي (meaning *Islamic*) in the Arabic Web 2012 (arTenTen12, Stanford Tagger) corpus. Our specific focus will be on the noun collocates of the words in the two corpora. The purpose of examining collocational behaviour in two corpora in two different languages is to compare the way *Islamic* is represented via collocation for the English-speaking audience in the English corpus, and the way it is constructed for the Arabic speaking world in the Arabic corpus.

The corpora

English Web 2018 (enTenTen18) is the largest corpus in Sketch Engine. It contains, at the time of writing, 21.9 billion words in about 37 million web pages that include newspaper articles and blog entries crawled from World Wide Web domains (i.e. .com, .org, .net, etc.). The corpus contains several subdomains such as the UK domain, the Australian domain, the Canadian domain, the EU domain, the Indian domain, the US domain, the New Zealand domain, and the Irish domain. Because of this wide range of domains, the construction of *Islamic* in the corpus is considered representative of international news coverage.

The construction of *Islamic* in international news websites in English is compared with the representation of اسلامي (*Islamic*) in the largest Arabic corpus on Sketch Engine in terms of size. The Arabic Web 2012 (arTenTen12, Stanford Tagger) corpus contains 7.5 billion words in 11.5 million web pages that also include newspaper articles and blog entries crawled from World Wide Web domains. The domains in the corpus cover all states in which Arabic is the official language, including the Saudi Arabia domain, the Egypt domain, the Syria domain, the Jordan domain, the UAE domain, and the Morocco domain. Because of the distinctive character of the domains, the construction of اسلامي (*Islamic*) in the corpus is representative of regional news coverage.

Procedure of analysis

Analysis proceeds as follows:

1. Sign up for a 30-day free trial user account on the Sketch Engine web page at <https://www.sketchengine.co.uk>. You will need to subscribe or have access to an institutional subscription upon expiry of this period.
2. Switch to the new interface (if prompted).
3. When you log in, select the English Web 2018 (enTenTen18) from the drop-down menu at the top of the dashboard.
4. Select 'Concordance (examples of use in context)'.
5. Type the target word *Islamic* in the simple search box to generate the concordance lines of the search word in the entire corpus.
6. Click 'search'. At the time of writing this chapter, the search returns 706,243 concordance lines for the Key Word in Context (KWIC).
7. At the top right-hand side, select 'collocations (...)' to generate a list of collocation candidates of the target word.

8. We want to look for collocation candidates for the search word and its other morphologically related forms, so we will change the default option of query type from 'word' to 'lemma'.
9. The default options are 'word' and 'range −3 to 3', which means that the software will look for up to three collocation candidates before and after the search word. Keep this unchanged. Click 'go'.
10. Four options are important in the displayed table. These are T-score, MI, cooccurrences, and logDice. The Sketch Engine online glossary (<https://www.sketchengine.eu/guide/glossary/>) offers the following definitions for these terms:
    a) *T-score* 'expresses the certainty with which we can argue that there is an association between the words, i.e. their co-occurrence is not random. The value is affected by the frequency of the whole collocation which is why very frequent word combinations tend to reach a high T-score despite not being significant collocations.'
    b) *MI* (Mutual Information) score 'expresses the extent to which words co-occur compared to the number of times they appear separately. MI score is affected strongly by the frequency, low-frequency words tend to reach a high MI score which may be misleading.
    c) *Cooccurrence* 'expresses how often two terms from a corpus occur alongside each other in a certain order. It usually indicates words which together create a new meaning. We call them as [sic] phraseme or multi-word expression, e.g. *black sheep* or *get on*.'
    d) *logDice* expresses the 'typicality of ... co-occurrence of the node and collocate'. It is calculated on the basis of 'the frequency of the node and the collocate and the frequency of the whole collocation'.
11. For our purpose, we will look closely at the logDice statistical measure. The other measures, such as T-score and cooccurrence, would include function words (such as *the*) and punctuation marks (such as the comma) based on frequency of occurrence only. Click on all four statistical measure to compare the findings.
12. Copy the search results of the collocations of *Islamic* in English Web 2018 (enTenTen18). We will compare them later with the patterns from the Arabic corpus.
13. Repeat step 3 above. This time select Arabic Web 2012 (enTenTen12, Stanford Tagger) from the dropdown list at the top of the dashboard.
14. Repeat steps 4 and 5 above but use the search word إسلامي (*Islamic*) to generate the concordance lines of the search word in the entire corpus.
15. Click 'search'. At the time of writing this chapter, the search returns 153,529 concordance lines for the KWIC.
16. Repeat steps 7, 8, and 9 above. Click 'go'.
17. Compare the results from steps 9 and 16. In particular, examine the logDice statistics of the search words. We will consider the top ten collocates in both corpora.

Findings

Figure 10.1 summarises the collocational behaviour of *Islamic* in English Web 2018 (enTenTen18).

	Lemma	Cooccurrences	Candidates	T-score	MI	LogDice
1	State	79,034	3,951,692	280.75	9.51	9.12
2	Republic	22,775	756,814	150.78	10.10	8.99
3	militant	11,878	212,274	108.93	11.00	8.73
4	Jihad	9,321	41,609	96.53	13.00	8.67
5	extremist	9,704	159,515	98.46	11.12	8.52
6	Iran	14,568	866,975	120.50	9.26	8.25
7	fundamentalist	7,148	89,552	84.52	11.51	8.20
8	terrorist	12,884	754,244	113.33	9.29	8.18
9	terrorism	9,051	467,466	95.00	9.47	7.98
10	fundamentalism	5,490	36,050	74.08	12.44	7.92
11	Iraq	11,559	915,403	107.28	8.85	7.87
12	radical	9,114	673,743	95.27	8.95	7.76
13	extremism	4,738	72,093	68.80	11.23	7.64
14	scholar	8,825	1,019,085	93.64	8.31	7.39
15	Front	4,768	263,531	68.95	9.37	7.33
16	Movement	4,161	187,534	64.43	9.66	7.25
17	caliphate	3,450	36,313	58.72	11.76	7.25
18	Sharia	3,359	31,154	57.94	11.94	7.22
19	jurisprudence	3,355	63,179	57.89	10.92	7.16
20	Isis	3,982	225,630	63.01	9.33	7.13

FIGURE 10.1 Collocational behaviour of *Islamic* (range −3 to 3) in English Web 2018 (enTenTen18)

1. The target word occurs 706,243 times in the 37 million web pages in the corpus.
2. The strongest collocate of *Islamic* in the corpus is *State*, with the highest logDice of 9.12. The collocation *Islamic state* refers to a militant group that is designated as a terrorist organisation by the United Nations, the United

States, the UK, and most Arab and Muslim countries. The group is also known as ISIS (Islamic State in Iraq and Syria).

3. The second strongest collocate of *Islamic* in the corpus is *Republic*, with a logDice of 8.99. Only four countries in the world are Islamic republics, namely, Pakistan, Mauritania, Iran, and Afghanistan. If you click on the three dots after logDice and choose *only this* to generate the concordance lines, you will see all four republics mentioned, with Iran being the main referent. Iran also ranks third in terms of cooccurrence count with 14,568 hits or appearances.
4. The third strongest collocate *Islamic* in the corpus is *militant*, with a logDice of 8.73.
5. *Jihad* ranks fourth on the list of collocates, with a logDice of 8.67. The fourth collocate in terms of cooccurrence count, however, is *terrorist* with 12,884 hits or appearances.
6. The other six collocates in the list of top ten, in descending order, are *extremist*, *Iran*, *fundamentalist*, *terrorist*, *terrorism*, and *fundamentalism*.

Now let us examine the collocational behaviour of the search word اسلامي (*Islamic*) in the Arabic Web 2012 (arTenTen12, Stanford Tagger) corpus (Figure 10.2). Below is a list of the top ten collocates.

	Word	Cooccurrences	Candidates	T-score	MI	LogDice
1	عربي	12,858	492,173	113.31	10.47	9.35
2	منظور	3,406	108,610	58.33	10.73	8.73
3	مفكر	2,134	34,461	46.18	11.71	8.54
4	داعية	2,544	74,653	50.41	10.85	8.51
5	بلد	8,355	810,294	91.24	9.13	8.15
6	ذك	3,211	267,655	56.58	9.34	7.96
7	مسيحي	1,731	74,176	41.57	10.30	7.96
8	اسلامي	2,066	153,529	45.39	9.51	7.78
9	تيار	2,262	211,400	47.48	9.18	7.67
10	مجتمع	4,000	528,505	63.09	8.68	7.59
11	معتدل	1,038	27,653	32.20	10.99	7.55
12	مصرف	1,371	87,419	36.98	9.73	7.54

FIGURE 10.2 Collocational behaviour of اسلامي (*Islamic*) (range −3 to 3) in Arabic Web 2012 (arTenTen12)

	Word	Cooccurrences	Candidates	T-score	MI	LogDice ↓
13	علماني	1,010	29,342	31.76	10.87	7.50 ...
14	متطرف	770	20,943	27.73	10.96	7.18 ...
15	ديني	1,298	142,278	35.95	8.95	7.17 ...
16	جمهوري	765	21,599	27.64	10.91	7.16 ...
17	عالمي	1,060	111,240	32.49	9.01	7.04 ...
18	اصيل	869	64,200	29.44	9.52	7.03 ...
19	متشدد	664	12,946	25.76	11.44	7.03 ...
20	قومي	986	107,293	31.34	8.96	6.95 ...

FIGURE 10.2 (continued)

1. The search returns 153,529 concordance lines in the 11.5 million web pages in the corpus.
2. The strongest collocate of اسلامي (*Islamic*) in the corpus is عربي (*Arab*), with the highest logDice of 9.35. It is also, according to the cooccurrence count, the most frequent collocate, with 12,858 hits or appearances.
3. The second strongest collocate of اسلامي (*Islamic*) in the corpus is منظور (*perspective*), with a logDice of 8.73. It is not the second highest in terms of cooccurrence count, however.
4. The third and fourth strongest collocates of the search word are مفكر (*thinker*) and داعية (*preacher*), with logDices of 8.54 and 8.51, respectively.
5. The noun بلد (*country*) ranks fifth in the list of strong collocates and second in terms of cooccurrence count. It has a logDice of 8.15 and occurs 8,355 times with the search word.
6. The next candidate on the list is ﺑﻨﻚ (*bank*). The correct spelling in Arabic is بنك (*bank*). If you click on the three dots after logDice and choose *only this* to generate the concordance lines, you should confirm that the collocate is بنك (*bank*), but the first letter is incorrectly spaced out.
7. The remaining four collocates in the list of top ten, in descending order, are مسيحي (*Christian*), اسلامي (*Islamic*), تيار (*trend*), and مجتمع (*society*).

Summary

In the English Web 2018 corpus, negative construction of the search word accounted for 80 per cent of the results. The collocates of *Islamic* in the corpus are mainly nouns associated with militancy and armed aggression. These collocates are *Islamic State, militant, Jihad, extremist, fundamentalist, terrorist, terrorism,* and *fundamentalism,* in a descending order of typicality of co-occurrence. It may be argued, therefore, that international online media, represented by the domains in the corpus, propagate an image around *Islamic* that associates it with extremism and terrorism. This association is reinforced through frequency of occurrence in the data and it is the construction to which the English-speaking audience are exposed.

The representation of اسلامي (*Islamic*) in the Arabic corpus for the Arabic-speaking audience, on the other hand, is more positive. The search word is associated with an ethnicity (*Arab*), organised community (*society*), intellectual activity (*thinker*), religious activity (*preacher*), economic institutions (*bank*), and religious faiths (*Christian, Islamic*). The representation of اسلامي (*Islamic*) in the corpus is one that encourages thinking, fosters conversation with other faiths, and intertwines with socio-economic institutions. It does not disseminate hatred and death; it radiates life.

In this chapter, we have used corpus linguistic tools to analyse representation in online journalism. Stylisticians have also used the corpus linguistic toolkit on a wide range of text types. For example, Walker (2011) investigated characterisation in Julian Barnes's novel *Talking It Over*, Murphy (2015) carried out a corpus stylistic analysis of a corpus of soliloquies from thirty-seven Shakespearean plays, and Jeffries and Walker (2018) combined corpus tools with critical stylistics in analysing keywords from two corpora of broadsheet news articles from three British national broadsheet newspapers under British Prime Minister Tony Blair. Corpus tools are applicable to potentially any collection of texts gathered from the internet or compiled by the researcher.

Remarks

1. English Web 2018 (enTenTen18), just like any other corpus, is continually updated with new texts. So if you repeat the same procedure on the same corpus at the time of reading the book, which will be removed from the time of writing it, you should expect to see different results. You did it right but the corpus size is different. The same thing may hold true for Arabic Web 2012 (arTenTen12).

2. Analysis here is confined to collocation and only to one search word. The purpose is to introduce you to corpus analysis and my hope is that this chapter arouses your interest and gets you started.

Resources and tools

AntConc

Available at <http://www.antlab.sci.waseda.ac.jp/> (last accessed 23 September 2021).

British National Corpus (BNC)

Available at <http://bncweb.lancs.ac.uk/bncwebSignup/user/login.php> (last accessed 23 September 2021).

Corpus of Contemporary American English (COCA)

Available at <http://corpus.byu.edu/coca/> (last accessed 23 September 2021).

Sketch Engine

Available at <https://www.sketchengine.co.uk/quick-start-guide/> (last accessed 23 September 2021).

WordSmith

Available at <http://www.lexically.net/wordsmith> (last accessed 23 September 2021).

10.1 Do it yourself

Examine the next ten collocations of *Islamic* in English Web 2018 (enTenTen18) and Arabic Web 2012 (arTenTen12, Stanford Tagger) in Figures 10.1 and 10.2, respectively. Do they support, enrich, or invalidate the findings of our analysis above? Repeat the analysis in English Web 2018 (enTenTen18) after changing the KWIC range from the default 'range −3 to 3' to 'range −1 to 1'. Compare your findings with all the results reported so far. Do the new collocates have more positive semantic prosodies?

Hints

a) Collocates numbers 11 to 20 on Arabic Web 2012 (arTenTen12, Stanford Tagger) translate like this: 11 *moderate*, 12 *bank*, 13 *secular*, 14 *extremist*, 15 *religious*, 16 *republic* (Iran-related), 17 *international*, 18 *authentic*, 19 *hard-line*, 20 *national*.

At the top right-hand side, select 'collocations (. . .)' and change the default 'range −3 to 3' to 'range −1 to 1' to generate the list of collocation candidates.

10.2 Do it yourself

Analyse the collocational behaviour of the word *terrorist* in the English Web 2018 (enTenTen18) corpus. This time use *Word Sketch*.

Hints

a) Repeat the procedure from the chapter to get to the corpus. After selecting the corpus, click on *Word Sketch* and type in the word *terrorist* to generate collocation candidates of the search word. Click on the 'change view' option at the top left-hand side. Check 'show scores', 'show frequencies', and 'show examples'. Keep the other

options unchecked. This will give you the logDice (or the typical collocates), the frequency of collocation, and an example of each collocate.
b) Examine the top ten lexical items modifying *terrorist* (you'll find them in the third column 'terrorist' and/or . . .).
c) What countries, religions, or affiliations appear in each list?

10.3 Do it yourself

Use *Word Sketch Difference* to compare the collocational behaviour of the word *good* in the written academic and the spoken transcripts subcorpora of the British National Corpus. *Sketch diff* (Sketch Difference) is used to compare the collocational behaviour of a word in two different (sub-)corpora.

Hints

a) Select the British National Corpus (BNC). Click *Word Sketch Difference* on the left-side panel on the main menu screen. Click on 'Advanced' and change the default option from 'lemmas' to 'subcorpora'. Type *good* under 'lemma', select 'written academic' as subcorpus number 1, select 'spoken transcripts' as subcorpus number 2, and select 'adjective' as the part of speech. Keep all other options unchanged and click 'go' to compare the collocational behaviour of the adjective *good* in academic writing and spoken English. There are two colours in the collocational behaviour summary table. The words shaded in green (top four) are strong collocates of *good* in academic writing, and those shaded in red (bottom five) are strong collocates of *good* in spoken English.
b) Examine the *nouns and verbs modified by good*. Change the default 'view option' from 'show counts' to 'show scores' to generate the typical or strong collocates only. How useful are the results of your search? Where else might you apply the same search, especially in relation to online journalism?

Further Reading

CORPUS STYLISTICS

McIntyre, D. and B. Walker (2019), *Corpus Stylistics: Theory and Practice*, Edinburgh University Press.
The book outlines corpus stylistics as a 'systematic approach to the techniques of using corpora in stylistic analysis' and explains 'the theoretical and methodological issues that underlie this practice' (p. 2).

CORPUS ANALYSIS OF DIFFERENT TEXT TYPES

Stubbs, M. (1996), *Text and Corpus Analysis: Computer-Assisted Studies of Language and Culture*, Blackwell.
A reader-friendly introduction to the interplay between critical linguistics and corpus analysis. The book theorises on the investigation of ideology in corpora and offers practice on using corpus analysis to investigate ideological outlook in diverse text types such as political speeches, summing-ups in criminal trials, and school textbooks.

SKETCH ENGINE

Kilgarriff, A., V. Baisa, J. Bušta, M. Jakubíček, V. Kovář, J. Michelfeit, P. Rychlý and V. Suchomel (2014), 'The Sketch Engine: Ten years on', *Lexicography*, 1, 7–36 <https://doi.org/10.1007/s40607-014-0009-9> (last accessed 23 September 2021).
The paper offers an introduction to development of Sketch Engine as a corpus analyser and describes different functions that the analyser performs such as lemmatisation, POS-tagging, input format and grammatical relations.

CORPUS ANALYSIS USING SKETCH ENGINE

Pearce, M. (2008), 'Investigating the collocational behaviour of MAN and WOMAN in the BNC using Sketch Engine', *Corpora*, 3(1), 1–29. <https://doi.org/10.3366/E174950320800004X> (last accessed 23 September 2021).
A lexical analysis of the collocational behaviour of *man* and *woman* using Sketch Engine. The paper is useful to those interested in the representation of women and men in corpora.

Part III
Extension

11

THE STORY OF STYLISTICS

> **Chapter Overview**
> - stylistics
> - why stylistics emerged
> - turns and trends in the story of stylistics
> - future directions

Introduction

In Part I of the book, we introduced key terms in the study of style in language, such as register, and key stylistic techniques, such as foregrounding, that create textual patterns encoding (ideological) meaning and creating (literary) effects. In Part II, we introduced stylistic frameworks and applied them to the analysis of meaning and effect in different text types. This part of the book offers a brief overview of the development of stylistics through the twentieth century. The chapter aims at extending your knowledge in the area by relating the concepts and frameworks introduced earlier to the relevant trends in stylistics, and positioning the stylistics frameworks along a timeline that tells the story of stylistics. The chapter also suggests a list of key publications to further your knowledge of the theory and practice of stylistics.

Beginning of the story

The story begins with the school of literary criticism and literary theory known as Russian formalism in the early years of the twentieth century. Russian formalists, such as Roman Jakobson, and Prague school structuralists, such as Jan Mukařovský, Boris Eichenbaum, and Viktor Shklovsky, believed that art defamiliarises reality, that is, it presents familiar concepts and objects from a strange, unfamiliar perspective. It challenges automatised perception of the world. Everyday language, as we agreed in Chapter 1, is referential and its expressive potential is somewhat consumed. It does not help much as a medium for defamiliarising reality. To achieve the effect of defamiliarisation, creative writers use unconventional language (see the poetry of e. e. cummings in Chapter 1) that has the effect of slowing down the reading and reorienting the reader's world-view. Shklovsky, in 'Art as Technique', contends that:

> The technique of art is to make objects 'unfamiliar', to make forms difficult, to increase the difficulty and length of perception because the process of perception is an aesthetic end in itself and must be prolonged. *Art is a way of experiencing the artfulness of an object; the object is not important.* (Shklovsky [1917] 1965: 4; original emphasis)

Because of the centrality of language to defamiliarisation, Russian formalists and Prague school structuralists focused primarily on the 'formal' features of literary texts. They examined phonological, lexical, and grammatical structures in works of art and isolated such features as parallelism, deviation, and foregrounding, which they described as characteristics of literary language. The formalists' focus on literature and their use of linguistics as a means of systematically analysing the language of poetry inspired literary criticism in Europe and America, as we shall see as the story unfolds.

11.1 Do it yourself

Consider the following two lines from e. e. cummings's 'pity this busy monster, manunkind', discussed in Chapter 1 and reproduced here for ease of reference. What linguistic resources does cummings use, and manipulate, to defamiliarise our conception of 'man**kind**' in the lines below?

> pity this busy monster, manunkind,
> not. Progress is a comfortable disease;
>   (e. e. cummings, 'pity this busy monster, manunkind)

The Russian formalist notion of literariness (literary language being different from non-literary language, and having genre-specific formal features) was argued by later stylisticians to be incompetent. Such textual features as deviation and parallelism are common in poetry as well as in the register of advertising, to take an example (see Example 4 in Table 1.9). Literariness is in fact today viewed more as a continuum, with the different registers occupying different positions along the scale, than as a property of a particular register. The effect of Russian formalism, however, continued and, indeed, continues to date. Early stylisticians, in the tradition of Russian formalists, focused largely on literary texts, and on poetry in particular, which was regarded as the most 'literary' of literary texts.

Why did stylistics emerge?

Well, the driving impulse for stylistics was to offer an alternative, linguistics-based approach to literary text interpretation. There was a growing body of theories in the emerging field of linguistics, and a parallel growing belief that the descriptive field of linguistics is capable of contributing more 'precise' interpretations of literary texts than traditional literary criticism. After all, the meaning and effect of a literary text are a function of linguistic choices. No wonder, therefore, that primacy of place was assigned to language in literary text analysis.

Let us take an example. Geoffrey N. Leech (2008) makes a stylistic analysis of Keats's 'Ode to a Nightingale', which had already been analysed by the literary critic F. R. Leavis. Leech chooses two aesthetic judgements from Leavis's interpretation. The first refers to the poem's 'rich local concreteness' that is a manifestation of 'a sureness of a touch that is the working of a fine organization'; the second relates this 'fine organization' to the 'balancing of contrasting emotional movements' (Leavis, cited in Leech 2008: 43). Nice as they sound, it is hard for the reader to work out how the critic arrived at such aesthetic judgements. Equally hard for the reader is to come up with a similar statement on another text.

Leech uses linguistic analysis to give evidence-based support to Leavis's interpretation. He analyses the poem at the phonemic, metrical, and syntactic levels. Close analysis of the patterns of sounds, **METRE** and structure bears out Leavis's 'fine organization' critical comment. Changes in mood are accompanied, and reinforced, by changes in rhyme scheme and the distribution of phonemes, and changes in thematical structure are accompanied, and reinforced, by the balancing of the two contrasting parts of the stanza. In short, the textual evidence garnered from the stylistic analysis bears out Leavis's 'vague aesthetic terms' (Leech 2008: 50). Leech's purpose in examining an already established interpretation of a literary text is to explicate the aesthetic effects that Leavis had discovered but did not explicate, perhaps for lack of descriptive terminology or interest in doing so.

Leech concludes that even with its imperfections and limitations, stylistics is capable of offering 'a more secure basis for critical arguments' since the techniques of stylistics allow us to 'reduce the critic's reliance on "mere assertion of judgment"' (2008: 50, 51).

Stylistics, therefore, was seen as an attempt to make literary criticism more 'scientific'. In fact, literary criticism of the time was viewed as characterised by 'subjective emotionalism' (Jeffries and McIntyre 2010: 22). Stylisticians argued that the critical analyses consisted largely of aesthetic and value judgements with little textual evidence, and where evidence is provided it is selective evidence in support of pre-formulated intuitions. A literary text may be described as 'marked by an extensive use of esoteric elements' or as 'full of symbolic depth'. These are nice-sounding critical judgements, but how can the reader work out how the critic arrived at these aesthetic judgements, and how can the reader replicate the analysis on other texts?

The 1920s: the impact of formalism

In fact, the ambition to make literary criticism have the precision of science was first articulated by the English literary critic I. A. Richards (1929). Impatient with the impressionism of literary criticism and its heavy reliance on extra-textual information, Richards turned to the formalist literary theory. He argued that attention to historical or social information about the text diverts the readers from the text and from understanding themselves in relation to the text. In a series of classroom experiments at Cambridge University, Richards gave his students thirteen short poems, without any authorial or historical/cultural contextual information. He encouraged his students to make individual responses to the text based on 'the words on the page' only – a reading strategy that came to be known as **CLOSE READING**.

The British chapter: practical criticism

In his 1929 book *practical criticism* (the literary critical approach which the book advances is also called **PRACTICAL CRITICISM**), Richards reports findings from the students' close analysis of the poems. The students concentrated on the thoughts in the poems, had no resources to relate these thoughts to except their own thoughts and emotions, and came up with 'organised' responses to the texts. Reading the poems in 'clinical' isolation, Richards argued, had the psychological advantage of focusing the students' attention on their own thoughts and emotions. So, beside the attention to the text, practical criticism had an interest in the reader's text-processing skills, to be picked up later by cognitive linguists.

The 1940s: Jakobson in America

The story took a new turn ten years later. In 1941 Roman Jakobson escaped war-torn Czechoslovakia, where he and Jan Mukařovský were working on their formalist critical theory, to America. This move opened up new doors for work in the linguistics–literature interface. Jakobson's ideas spread in America and gave rise to **NEW CRITICISM**.

The American chapter: new criticism

New criticism is, in fact, closely related to Richards's practical criticism. New criticism, like practical criticism, was a literary critical movement whose interest was more in the 'words on the page' than in authorial intentions and contextual considerations. However, new criticism had the advantage of building on the work of its predecessor, practical criticism.

Exemplified in the work of Cleanth Brooks and Robert Warren, new criticism considers the text as self-contained and self-referential – it contains everything the reader needs in order to understand it with no need to refer to anything outside the text. Like practical criticism, new criticism emphasises 'close reading'

– close attention to the words and structures in a literary text (such as theme, setting, plot) in order to describe its aesthetic qualities.

But new critics find faults with practical criticism. They de-emphasise the practical critics' concern with the reader's emotional and psychological reactions, and focus on the linguistic description via close reading of the aesthetic qualities of literary texts. New criticism, with its undivided attention to the words on the page, to the exclusion of any consideration of author or reader, is often regarded as the direct precursor of the discipline of stylistics.

The theories of practical and new criticism together constitute what is sometimes referred to as the Anglo-American literary critical theory of the 1920s to the 1940s. Important features of this critical school are that:

- it was a reaction against biographical and philological traditions of literary study
- it was inspired by the formalist interest in the language of literature
- it viewed a literary work as a self-contained unit of meaning
- it focused critical attention on the words on the page using the technique of close reading
- it attributed the effects of a literary work to linguistic choices in the texts
- it used the descriptive apparatus of linguistics as a means of systematically analysing language in literature and identifying its aesthetic effects.

11.2 Do it yourself

Which of the following descriptions apply to practical criticism and which ones apply to new criticism? Write *practical criticism* or *new criticism* against each statement. Some descriptions apply to both theories.

a) It was inspired by formalism.
b) It attempted to offer a less 'impressionistic' model of literary studies.
c) It started in Britain.
d) It started in America.
e) It started in the 1920s.
f) It started in the 1940s.
g) It focused on the text.

Modern stylistics

Modern stylistics, as we have seen, originated in the literary theory of formalism, and is a logical extension of the legacy of practical criticism and new criticism. In the tradition of its formalism-inspired precursors, stylistics is interested in the language of literature and uses linguistics to describe literary effects.

In its early years of analysing literary texts, stylistics used the analytical toolkit of the formalist literary critic, namely, the analysis of linguistic foregrounding via deviation, repetition, and parallelism (see Chapter 1). A stylistician would ascribe the aesthetic effects of a literary text to such abnormal patterning as deviation at the level of syntax (such as an unusual word order), semantics (such as unusual meaning relations), morphology (such as unusual morpheme combinations or the invention of new words), graphology (such as unusual punctuation or graphic presentation), and phonology (such as unusual pronunciations). They might also attribute these effects to extra-linguistic regularity or parallelism imposed on the text at the level of phonology (such as **ALLITERATION**, **ASSONANCE**, rhyme, and **RHYTHM**), syntax (such as repetition of clausal structures), morphology (such as repetition of lexical structures), semantics (such as repetition of meaning relations), or graphology (such as repetition of italics, punctuation, or spacing to achieve some effect).

Of course, the concepts of foregrounding, parallelism, and deviation continue to have a firm place in the stylistician's toolkit to date. Some of the most prominent stylisticians in the twentieth century, namely, Geoffrey Leech and Mick Short, relied quite heavily on the concepts of foregrounding and deviation in their publications. These include Leech's *A Linguistic Guide to English Poetry* ([1969] 2007), Leech and Short's *Style in Fiction* ([1981] 2007), and Short's *Exploring the Language of Poems, Plays and Prose* ([1996] 2014). However, over the years, stylistics has also developed an association with linguistics and has also always updated its analytical methodology in response to the development of new theories of language. In the rest of this chapter, we will be looking at the way linguistics has provided stylisticians with descriptive vocabulary and analytical techniques for the systematic description and analysis of meaning and effect in literary, and non-literary, texts.

The 1960s: the impact of Chomsky

In the late 1950s, Noam Chomsky proposed a theory of grammar, which had a profound effect on modern linguistics. Chomsky's theory, also known as **GENERATIVE GRAMMAR**, was first presented in his influential book *Syntactic Structures* (1957). Chomsky argues that all humans are born with an innate ability to learn language – any language. The human brain contains general principles governing all natural languages. The input a child receives from the linguistic surrounding determines which particular language the child will acquire. In his book, Chomsky also argues that sentences have a surface structure and a deep structure. The surface form of sentences is generated from an underlying syntactic structure by application of the generative transformational rules of addition, deletion, movement, and so on. Chomsky's proposals about language acquisition and about transformational grammar ushered in a new phase in psycholinguistics as well as in modern linguistics.

Generative stylistics

Chomsky himself was not concerned with language use in literary texts, but his ideas appealed to the stylisticians of the time. Chomsky's theory of language was somewhat related to the stylisticians' own theory of style, namely, that style is a matter of selection of linguistic features (surface structure) stylised to represent an underlying thought (deep structure). Taking on Chomsky's theory of generative grammar, stylisticians in the 1960s, whose work has come to be known as **GENERATIVE STYLISTICS**, viewed stylistic variation in literary texts as the result of the application of transformational rules to underlying structures. This explains why most generative stylistic analyses of the 1960s were confined to investigations of syntax and semantics.

Examples of this trend in stylistics include Ohmann (1964) and Levin (1971). Richard Ohmann (1964) examines truncated and kernel sentences in D. H. Lawrence, nominalisation in Hemingway, and embedding in Henry James, and concludes that the writers' individual styles are the result of differences in the choice of syntactic transformational rules. Harvey J. Levin (1971) accounts for the 'deviant' structures in e. e. cummings's poetry in terms of generative transformational operations to underlying forms.

Stylisticians adopting Chomsky's analytical framework showed more interest in demonstrating the efficacy of the transformational generative grammar theory than in describing the aesthetic effects of literary works. In other words, the stylistics of this time used literary texts to test linguistic theories. It was more linguistics oriented than literature oriented. For this reason, this kind of stylistics is also known as **LINGUISTIC STYLISTICS**.

Ohmann, however, goes one step further and argues that 'forms carry meanings' (1966: 261). He assigns a semantic value, or functional significance, to the formal features of the text. In this way, the syntactic preferences in a text become reflective of certain meanings. This move that Ohmann makes from description to interpretation, or the shift from formal analysis to functional significance, prepares the ground for the next chapter in our story.

The 1970s

After Ohmann, the interest of stylisticians shifted from a consideration of the transformational operations responsible for an author's deviant stylistic choices to a consideration of the functional significance of these choices. But Ohmann and other generative stylisticians of the time (Milic 1967; C. Thorne 1965; J. P. Thorne 1970) had opened up a gap between analysis and interpretation. A formal feature of the text was ascribed meaning without a clear-cut association between the two. In other words, there were no criteria for correlating formal patterns with functional significance.

Fish's attack

The formalists' interpretive leaps from textual patterns to patterns of meaning brought them under severe criticism by the American critic Stanley Fish. What these stylisticians seem to aim at, Fish argues, is the establishment of automatic interpretive procedures based on an inventory of 'fixed relationships between observable data and meanings'. These interpretations do not vary with context and can be read out 'independently of the analyst or observer who need only perform the operations specified by the "key"' (Fish [1973] 1996: 94).

Affective stylistics

The explanation for that interpretation, Fish counter-argues, is not the capacity of a syntax to express it, but the ability of the reader to confer it. To narrow down the interpretive gaps, Fish calls for an **AFFECTIVE STYLISTICS** (aka **READER RESPONSE STYLISTICS**) in which 'the focus of attention is shifted from the spatial context of page and its observable regularities to the temporal context of a mind and its experiences' ([1973] 1996: 109). Instead of ascribing meaning to formal patterns, affective stylistics focuses on what readers do when they read, the expectations they bring to the reading act, and the conclusions they draw from textual patterns.

Response 1: pedagogical stylistics

One direction which stylistics took in response to Fish's attack was a move towards the reader. Stylisticians started focusing on stylistic analysis as 'a *way* of reading' and how it can be 'of direct use to students, both in mother-tongue language learning and in an English as a foreign language context' (Weber 1996b: 3). The use of stylistic analysis as an aid in reading literature gave rise to **PEDAGOGICAL STYLISTICS**. The aim of pedagogical stylistics is not to 'produce the next generation of stylisticians' or 'create even more accurate users of language' but 'to promote linguistically aware readers who can perceive the qualities of language which are manipulated for particular effects' (Clark and Zyngier 2003: 342). In order to sensitise students to the expressive potential of language and to help them produce individual responses to texts, stylisticians use established language-based teaching activities such as cloze procedure, gap filling, prediction, and paraphrase (Carter 1986, 1989; Collie and Slater 1987; Widdowson 1975, 1992; Lazar 1993). The aim of the activities is to increase students' awareness of textual structure and the interpretative significance of language in different contexts. Besides, the activities eventually deepen the students' knowledge of the language itself (Lazar 1993).

Response 2: close the gap

The other direction stylistics took was to narrow down the formalists' 'interpretive gap'. This stylistic trend, inspired by Halliday's theory of language, argues that a formal feature of a text is relevant to interpretation only if it has meaning or function.

The impact of Halliday

In the 1970s, Halliday articulated a theory of language that was totally different from Chomsky's. Halliday's theory is based on the view that language is a social, not mental, phenomenon. It is an account of grammar based not on transformation operations resulting in surface structures, but on choice that is available to all language users. While stylisticians working in the cognitive school in the

US focused more on deviation as a consequence of transformational operations on an underlying form, stylisticians in the functional school in Britain viewed style as a function of choice (see our discussion of style as choice and deviation in Chapter 1).

Halliday's theory of language is known as systemic functional linguistics. According to the theory, meaning is socially and linguistically constructed. By adopting a particular style, a writer privileges certain linguistic choices over others, and by implication, certain ideologies and world-views. Unlike the generative linguists whose interest was in the internal structure and patterning of language at the sentence level, the functional linguists focused on the use of longer stretches of language in relation to context. The grammatical labels employed by functionalists, such as register, tone, mode, genre, modality, and transitivity, reflect this concern with function and context.

Functionalist stylistics

Many stylisticians soon adopted systemic functional linguistics, resulting in a functionalist stylistics – a stylistics driven by functional considerations, in answer to Fish's attack, but which is also characterised by a concern with longer texts such as narrative fiction and with contextually created and ideologically motivated meanings.

The most well-known application of the functional theory of linguistic in stylistics comes from Halliday himself (1971). Analysing the style of William Golding's novel *The Inheritors*, Halliday focuses on the way the transitivity choices construct character types. Analysis reveals that the linguistic choices made by two groups of characters in the novel help construct one group as primitive and the other as more sophisticated.

11.3 Do it yourself

Which of the following descriptions apply to formalist stylistics and which ones apply to functionalist stylistics? Write *formalist stylistics* or *functionalist stylistics* against each statement. Some descriptions apply to both theories.

a) It was popular in the 1960s in the USA.
b) It was popular in the 1980s in Britain.
c) It was influenced by Chomsky's view of language as a mental phenomenon.
d) It was influenced by Halliday's view of language as a social phenomenon.
e) It viewed style as deviation from an underlying form.
f) It viewed style as choice from available options.
g) It showed an interest in analysis of language in context.
h) It mostly analysed poetry and prose.

i) It analysed poetry, prose, and drama.
j) It was criticised for assigning meanings to forms.
k) It asserted that only linguistic forms with functional significance are relevant to interpretation.

The 1980s

Other examples of the investigation of contextually created meanings using functionalist stylistic analyses include Burton's (1982) analysis of Sylvia Plath's novel *The Bell Jar*, Kennedy's (1982) analysis of Joseph Conrad's novel *The Secret Agent*, and Nørgaard's (2003) analysis of James Joyce's short story *Two Gallants*. All these studies focus on how characters are constructed linguistically via the representation of action and participants in clausal structures.

Critical linguistics

Another group of functionalists shifted attention from the linguistic construction of fictional characters to investigating authorial ideology. Using the Hallidayan functional categories of modality, transitivity, and point of view, these stylisticians examined literary, and non-literary, texts for the way language signposts authorial attitudes, and constructs power relations and ideology. Because of their focus on 'critiquing' authorial intentions and because of the heavy reliance on linguistics for analytical techniques, this trend in stylistics is called critical linguistics.

Critical linguistics originated in Roger Fowler, Bob Hodge, Gunther Kress, and Tony Trew's *Language and Control* ([1979] 2019). What these academics at the University of East Anglia shared was an interest in the potential of texts to influence people's opinions on socio-political issues such as politics and religion, and the potential of texts to shape people's beliefs and assumptions about social values and the world at large.

The text types analysed by critical linguists include poetry, fictional extracts, newspaper articles, political texts, and even humorous texts. Fowler's *Language in the News: Discourse and Ideology in the Press* (1991) is a seminal work in the critical linguistic literature. Using the Hallidayan analytical tools of lexical choice, naming conventions, nominalisation, transitivity, and modality, Fowler critically examines the newspaper discourse for the way language stereotypes groups of people, the way it represents gender and power, and the way it constructs consensus or differences. The newspaper stories Fowler samples for his analysis cover issues that are political (the American bombing of Libya in 1986), medical (the 1988 infection of Britain's egg production with the salmonella bacterium), and social (the controversy of youth and contraception).

Two years later, in 1993, Paul Simpson developed Halliday's analytical toolkit for the examination of the role of language in mediating reality. His book *Language, Ideology and Point of View* offers a more elaborate procedure for the analysis of the 'semantic-syntactic choices in the structure of the clause' (1993: 166). Simpson calls it the 'transitivity model'. The model offers a framework for the investigation of the way texts encode ideological outlooks and influence the perception of readers. It is one of the most quoted and most referenced frameworks for the investigation of ideology and world-view in news, narratives, and beyond.

Gender and ideology: feminist stylistics

Inspired by research into language and ideology, Sara Mills extends this stylistics trend to the investigation of language and gender. In her book *Feminist Stylistics* (1995), Mills examines a wide range of text types including narrative fiction, advertisements, and even humorous texts for the way language choice at the word, sentence, and discourse levels encodes ideologically loaded messages and ideological evaluations of women. This approach is named feminist stylistics after the title of Mill's book.

Critical discourse analysis

The work of critical linguists was revitalised a decade later in what has come to be known as critical discourse analysis. The most prominent proponent of this method is Lancaster University Professor Norman Fairclough. In the tradition of critical linguistics, critical discourse analysis (CDA) maintains that language constructs, rather than represents, reality. Also, in the tradition of critical linguistics, CDA heavily draws on Halliday's systemic functional linguistics for its descriptive vocabulary and analytical toolkit.

From text to speaker: the Austin effect

In fact, well before Halliday proposed systemic functional linguistics, there was already a growing interest in language-in-context studies in Britain. One of the earliest theories was proposed by the Lancaster philosopher J. L. Austin (1962) – the **SPEECH ACT THEORY**. Austin argued that we use language not only to convey information but to perform action. These actions, or speech acts, include requesting, warning, apologising, confessing, promising, and so on.

In *How to Do Things with Words* (1962), Austin offers a systematic classification of speech acts, and a theory of how speakers communicate more than they say and how hearers infer the speakers' intended meanings. Austin's theory did not catch the attention of stylisticians in the 1960s, but it caught the attention of an American philosopher at the University of California. John Searle developed Austin's ideas in his book *Speech Acts* (1969). Stylisticians, however, had not adopted the theory.

Meanwhile, research on Austin's theory continued in Britain. H. P. Grice (1975) developed Austin's and Searle's ideas further into a more coherent theory of meaning, conversation, and communication. Leech, who had himself published a number of books and articles on stylistics, laid the foundations of the discipline more clearly in his book *Principles of Pragmatics* (1983). Four years later, Brown and Levinson contributed a theory of politeness in language, and now stylisticians are on board.

Pragmatic stylistics

Austin and Searle's speech act theory, Grice's theory of the cooperative principle and the maxims of conversation, and Brown and Levinson's politeness theory constitute the analytical apparatus for what is known as pragmatic stylistics. The topics covered by pragmatic stylisticians include the way conversation is structured to build dramatic characters (Short 1989), investigating speech acts in Bernard Shaw's plays (Leech 1992), analysis of intentional communication using relevance theoretic principles (Clark 1996), analysis of turn-taking in drama (Herman 1998), and analysis of participants' roles in press releases (Jacobs 1999). While it focused on all text types, the major contribution of pragmatic stylistics has been the study of conversation and characterisation in dramatic texts.

Discourse stylistics

Because of the shared interest in context and how it can affect sentence and speaker meaning, there is an expected crossover between the work of pragmatic stylisticians with that of critical linguists. Some scholars would lump the two approaches under the term **DISCOURSE STYLISTICS**.

The 1990s: the impact of cognitive linguistics

The story took yet another turn. The 1990s saw the rise and growth of cognitive science theories, which were adopted by language scholars. This might sound like a revival of the Chomskyan preoccupation with human cognition; however, the cognitive linguists of the 1990s were interested in the way the mind processes texts and 'creates' meanings.

A popular cognitive linguistic theory is schema theory. According to schema theory, meaning is not contained in the text. Instead, it is built up by the reader by combining background knowledge with clues from the text. This is known as a top-down approach to text interpretation, as opposed to the classic bottom-up approach that starts with the words on the page. In this view, existing background knowledge of the world is organised in the mind into units called schemata. New knowledge from reading a new text, or new schemata, makes sense if it fits into already existing schemata. This is why readers comprehend some texts but not others. Culpeper offers an interesting account of the way characters 'arise as a result of a complex interaction between the incoming textual information on the one hand and the contents of our heads on the other' (2002: 251).

Another popular cognitive theory is Sperber and Wilson's relevance theory. According to this theory, meaning is not in the text to be extracted by the reader, but is a potential to be constructed by the reader based on textual evidence that guides interpretation. Evidence leads to inferences that are guided by the principle of relevance. This principle helps the reader decide which of the 'weak' implicatures that are triggered by the text are more 'relevant' to interpretation.

The cognitive linguists' concern with reading and interpretation found an echo with stylisticians in the 1990s. Cognitive stylistics is concerned with the reader's role in the creation of textual meaning. But cognitive stylistics is not one strand; it refers to a number of approaches to the role of the reader in the process of meaning-making, each with its own view on the reader–text relationship. Cognitive stylisticians working within relevance theory, for example, explore what readers do when they read a text, that is, what mental moves they make in order to decide which of the implicatures created by the text are more likely to be 'intentionally communicated'. Other mainstream cognitive stylisticians, such as those working within text world theory, are more interested in the way readers conceptualise the world described by a (literary) text.

Cognitive stylisticians focus largely on literary texts. There has been much research in the area, and seminal cognitive stylistic analyses are published in *Cognitive Stylistics: Language and Cognition in Text Analysis* (2002) – a collection of essays edited by Elena Semino and Jonathan Culpeper. In this book, Freeman applies blending theory to poetic texts, Semino applies a cognitive stylistic approach to the analysis of narrative fiction, Culpeper focuses on characterisation, and Attardo offers a cognitive stylistic analysis of humorous texts. Analysis reveals how knowledge of the world and of genres is represented and processed in the human mind, and how that existing knowledge is used by readers to process texts and arrive at different interpretations.

The 2000s: the impact of technology

Advances in computer technology at the turn of the twenty-first century had a significant impact on the study of human languages. Linguistics used this expanding knowledge of computer technology to investigate issues of author attribution and gain insights about the use of language in forensic contexts of crime investigation and legal documents. More recently, it has used knowledge of computer technology to develop software tools that have the ability to recognise and generate human languages, and to translate from one language into another. The sub-field of linguistics concerned with the computerised processing and modelling of natural languages is known as **COMPUTATIONAL LINGUISTICS**.

Linguists would also use computer technology to do a large-scale analysis of a collection of written or spoken texts, known as a corpus. Analysis of collections of texts was a tedious, time-consuming manual task before the use of computers. The work of Randolph Quirk in the late 1950s (the Survey of English Usage Corpus) is an example of corpus data created and annotated manually. It consisted of 200 texts and one million words of (spoken and written) British English. The use of computers in the construction and annotation of corpora started about ten years later at Brown University in the USA. It was called the Brown Corpus, and consisted of one million words of (written) American English. 'The success of the Brown Corpus led to the creation of other similarly structured corpora' including the LOB Corpus (Lancaster, Oslo, and Bergen) in 1978, the COBUILD project (Collins Birmingham University International Language Database) started by Professor John Sinclair in 1980, and the BNC (British

National Corpus), which consisted of 100 million words of spoken and written British English and was accomplished over a period of three years from 1991 to 1994 (McIntyre and Walker 2019: 7). This sub-field of linguistics, called corpus linguistics, has been of particular interest to stylisticians because of the shared interest in text analysis. Stylisticians adopted this methodology in their analyses, which has led to the development of corpus stylistics.

Corpus stylistics

Corpus stylistics is concerned with the computer-aided analysis of (very large) collections of literary, and non-literary, written or transcribed texts for the purpose of investigating (bottom-up or top-down) patterns of language that constitute style. This is an important turn in the story of stylistics for a number of reasons.

First, statistical analysis of corpora has added yet another analytical tool to the already rich and growing toolkit of the stylistician. This has contributed significantly not only to the descriptive apparatus of the stylistician but also to the explanatory power of stylistics.

Second, the construction and analysis of large-scale corpora of language has made it possible for stylisticians to support qualitative analyses of texts with quantitative, statistical analyses. For example, analysis of the relative frequency of words, word forms, collocations, and structures has also enabled stylisticians interested in the investigation of authorial ideologies and points of view to support their subjective remarks with quantitative data. Stylistics can now make confident claims to analytical objectivity.

Third, this new development has enabled stylisticians to revisit one of the classic concerns of their discipline, namely, analysis of style to establish text authorship. This is now possible. Windows-based applications such as *WordSmith* have enabled corpus stylisticians to create lists of words (and word forms) and compare the frequency of occurrence of these forms against a reference corpus. This helps stylisticians make decisions regarding authorship attribution.

One of the pioneers of using statistical measures to identify stylistic factors that are characteristic of text types and genres is Douglas Biber. His analysis of the co-occurrence patterns of large numbers of linguistic features across a wide range of spoken and written texts has led to *The Longman Grammar of Spoken and Written English* (Biber et al. 1999) – the first grammar book based on corpus analysis of stylistic features.

There has also been extensive corpus analysis of literary texts. Stubbs (2005) analyses the frequency and distribution of individual words and recurrent phraseology in Joseph Conrad's *Heart of Darkness*. Analysis not only provides support for established literary interpretations of the novel, but also identifies markers of style significant for interpretation but which have not been noticed before. Other studies offering analyses of literary texts using corpus linguistic techniques include Louw (1997), Semino and Short (2004), Starcke (2006), Wynne (2006), O'Halloran (2007), Mahlberg (2007, 2009, 2010, 2013a, 2013b), McIntyre (2010), Hoover et al. (2014), and McIntyre and Walker (2019).

11.4 Do it yourself

Which of the following descriptions apply to critical, pragmatic, cognitive, or corpus stylistics? Write the name of the stylistic trend against the statement that best describes it. Some descriptions apply to more than one stylistic trend.

a) It draws on theories of the human mind.
b) It draws on systemic functional linguistics.
c) It is computer-aided.
d) It focuses more on readers than on texts.
e) It investigates authorial ideologies and power relations in texts.
f) It focuses on dramatic conversation.
g) Analysis is qualitative and quantitative.
h) It analyses large collections of texts.

From words to images

The use of computer technology in linguistic and stylistic research has generated an interest in visual communication. Computer communication depends a great deal on graphics. This involves the use of colours, pictures, sounds, and movies.

Stylisticians, who have predominantly and traditionally been concerned with the analysis of meaning and effect in written and spoken texts, are now taking on semiotic modes other than language. Their investigations have broadened to include a description of the way the page layout, its typography, colours, and images interact with each other and with the words on the page to create meaning and effect. Because of the interest in analysing multiple semiotic modes, this new trend in stylistics is known as multimodal stylistics.

Multimodal stylistics

The methodology of multimodal stylisticians draws analytical tools from Kress and van Leeuwen's visual grammar ([1996] 2006), which is itself based on Halliday's functional linguistic theory. The multimodal stylistic approach is applicable to the analysis of written texts as well as to multimodal genres like children's books, iconic poetry, graphic fiction, drama performances, comics, pamphlets, magazines, advertisements, films, and internet websites.

Multimodal stylisticians have contributed to the analytical toolkit of the stylistician a methodology, borrowed from multimodal theory, for the analysis of the material aspects of texts. The tools they have contributed include ways of analysing the placement of the words on the page, the use of images and colours on the page and on the book cover, and ways of analysing how these material aspects add an extra layer of meaning and effect to the text. But how do multimodal stylisticians, or analysts in general, do that?

Here is how. In *Reading Images: The Grammar of Visual Design*, Kress and van Leeuwen ([1996] 2006) suggest that the analyst examine the gaze, distance, and salience. When the participants in an image, for example, are presented as 'gazing' at the reader, the invitation is for the reader to get involved and to engage with the image. However, if the participants are looking elsewhere, the reader is positioned as an observer rather than a participant. In addition, the closer up the image, the more intimate the reader's relation with the participants in the image; and the more distant the shot, the more detached the reader. Lastly, an image or a text may be made salient, or 'foregrounded', because of its relative size, colour, or other typographical features, thus inviting extra attention and processing on the part of the reader.

Multimodal stylistics has drifted somewhat from the traditional concern of stylisticians with the mode of language. Besides, the concern with the new semiotic modes of expression would necessarily entail knowledge of the theory and practice of the allied fields of **TYPOGRAPHY, MUSICOLOGY, SEMIOTICS**, and the visual arts. This has not only made stylistic analyses less text-centred but has also greatly increased the theoretical and practical demands on practitioners in the field.

11.5 Do it yourself

How would the overall effect of this chapter change if we changed the semiotic presentation of its content by, for example, adding pictures of prominent stylisticians?

Hints

a) Consider using pictures of stylisticians gazing at you. What is the effect of the gaze?
b) Consider using close-up pictures of stylisticians. What is the effect of this choice?
c) Consider using pictures without frames. How does choice sustain the effect created by the gaze and closeness of the shot?

Back to the text

In 2010, Lesley Jeffries revisited the stylisticians' concern with the textual construction of ideology. In her book *Critical Stylistics: The Power of English*, Jeffries offers a text-based framework for the analysis of ideology, which she describes as developing 'in reaction to the rise of critical discourse analysis as an increasingly influential approach to ideology in language' (2014: 408). Jeffries's argument is that critical discourse analysis was more interested in contextual considerations and less concerned with the provision of a text-based analytical framework or methodology for the investigation of ideological bias in texts. Critical stylistics was her response to the 'feelings of frustration in the face of critical discourse analysis's deliberate lack of methodology or framework' (Jeffries 2014: 410).

Critical stylistics

The title of Jeffries's book refers to the approach that characterises the methodology. Critical stylistics investigates of the power of texts to ideologically manipulate readers. That is, it investigates the way(s) ideologies are implicitly built into texts and passed as assumptions. The book offers a set of ten conceptual functions to help the reader expose implicit manipulative uses of language. This toolkit is the main contribution of critical stylistics. In addition to being textually oriented, the toolkit is 'more comprehensive than any provided in the literature on CDA and other similarly politically motivated linguistic studies' (Jeffries 2010: 1). It examines the way the lexical, syntactic, and meaning resources of language could be mobilised to package up or slant information with consequences for ideology.

The approach is, of course, not altogether new. It adopts Halliday's functional approach, which is based on the ideational metafunction of language. The critical stylistic toolkit is used to question power and ideology in language use and describe the way language represents the world. This concern is an extension of work in critical linguistics in the 1970s, in CDA in the 1980s, and all research in the area since then.

The story continues

Is this the end of the stylistics story? No. New trends will always continue to emerge. Stylisticians are reaching out to such registers as comics (Forceville et al. 2014), films (Toolan 2014), hypertext fictional works (Trimarco 2014), and even emotion and neuroscience (Hogan 2014). They are also carrying out research in order to enrich the analytical methodologies in such existing fields as corpus, multimodal, and critical stylistics.

Stylistics has, therefore, come a long way since the story began in the early years of the twentieth century. It has been a little under a hundred years but there has been extensive research in the area generating several trends in stylistics, each with its own analytical toolkit that is drawn from such allied fields as linguistics, literary theory, semiotics, cognitive science, cultural studies, theories of reading, and beyond. Stay tuned for more exciting work in stylistics by reading collections and handbooks by major publishers, which offer a comprehensive overview of developments in the field, and research articles in journals that seek to promote the study of style in language, such as *Language and Literature*, which is the journal of the international Poetics and Linguistics Association (PALA).

> **Further Reading**

GENERAL REFERENCES

Nørgaard, N., R. Monotor and B. Busse (2010), *Key Terms in Stylistics*, Continuum.
   This is a very useful reference book, especially if you are new to the field. The book is structured in four main parts, introducing key branches, key terms, key thinkers, and key texts in stylistics.

Wales, K. [1990] (2011), *A Dictionary of Stylistics*, 3rd edn, Pearson.
   This dictionary, in its third edition, is an essential reference book which beginner and practised stylisticians refer to for information on concepts and terms, trends and methodologies, and historical and recent developments in the field. The dictionary offers over 600 entries.

STYLISTICS

Gibbons, A. and S. Whiteley (2018), *Contemporary Stylistics: Language, Cognition, Interpretation*, Edinburgh University Press.
   In addition to introducing stylistics, key concepts in the field, and the basic units of structure in language, the book applies contemporary trends in stylistics to the analysis of contemporary literary texts, with a focus on pragmatic, cognitive, and corpus stylistic frameworks.

Jeffries, L. and D. McIntyre (2010), *Stylistics*, Cambridge University Press.
   A comprehensive, reader-friendly introduction to style and stylistics. The book highlights methodologies available for stylisticians across stylistic trends, and offers several 'objective, replicable and falsifiable' analyses, as well as exercises, on literary and non-literary texts.

DEVELOPMENT OF STYLISTICS

Burke, M. (ed.) (2014), *The Routledge Handbook of Stylistics*, Routledge.
   A reference book that contains a collection of thirty-two essays by authorities in the field, providing a comprehensive outline of historical (part I of the book) and contemporary issues in stylistics (part III of the book), and introducing emerging and future trends in the area (part IV of the book).

Weber, J. J. (ed.) (1996a), *The Stylistics Reader from Roman Jakobson to the Present*, Arnold.
   The collection of essays in the book document the development of stylistics since the formalist days, covering such trends as functionalist, affective, pedagogical, pragmatic, critical linguistic, feminist, and cognitive stylistic trends.

FORMALIST STYLISTICS

Burke, M. (2014), 'Formalist stylistics', in M. Burke (ed.), *The Routledge Handbook of Stylistics*, Routledge, pp. 31–44.
   This book chapter presents formalism in its historical context, introduces the work of three Russian formalists, zooms in on the concept of foregrounding, and closes with a presentation of formalist stylistic work adopting Chomsky's generative grammar.

Shklovsky, V. [1925] (1991), *Theory of Prose*, trans. B. Sher, Dalkey Archive Press.
An introduction to formalist concepts in the arts, especially defamiliarisation.

FUNCTIONALIST STYLISTICS

Halliday, M. A. K. (1985), *Introduction to Functional Grammar*, Edward Arnold.
An indispensable introduction to Halliday's systemic functional linguistics, which forms the bedrock of many stylistic frameworks introduced in this book.

Lin, B. (2016), 'Functional stylistics', in V. Sotirova (ed.), *The Bloomsbury Companion to Stylistics*, Bloomsbury Academic, pp. 57–77.
This book chapter traces the origins of functional (or functionalist) stylistics to Halliday's SFL, presents an overview of functionalist stylistics, introduces key concepts in the framework (such as transitivity and mood), and offers an overview of research inspired by SFL, including some trends in multimodal stylistics and a practical demonstration of functionalist stylistic analysis in action.

PRACTICAL CRITICISM

Peck, J. and M. Coyle (1995), *Practical Criticism: How to Write a Critical Appreciation*, Palgrave Macmillan.
A practical step-by-step guide to close reading of poetry, prose, and drama.

NEW CRITICISM

Brooks, C. and R. Warren (1938), *Understanding Poetry*, Holt, Rinehart and Winston.
A coherent presentation of new criticism and a practical demonstration of the relevance of its methodology to educational contexts where poetry is taught. The book was supplemented by *Understanding Fiction* (1943, 1979), and the two books revolutionised the teaching of literature in the 1950s and 60s.

AFFECTIVE STYLISTICS

Fish, S. (1970), 'Literature in the reader: Affective stylistics', *New Literary History*, 2(1), 123–62, <https://doi.org/10.2307/468593> (last accessed 23 September 2021).
In this journal paper, Fish argues that the reader's response to a literary text should be a central concern of literary criticism.

Fish, S. (1980), *Is There a Text in this Class? The Authority of Interpretative Communities*, Harvard University Press.
The book contains sixteen essays which present Stanley Fish's model of reading and arguments against locating meaning within the verbal structure of the text. Fish contends that meaning is a function of the reader's goals and experiences rather than the form of the text or the intentions of the author. He introduces the concept of interpretive communities to constrain the relativity and subjectivity of interpretations.

PEDAGOGICAL STYLISTICS

Brumfit, C. and R. Carter (eds) (1986), *Literature and Language Teaching*, Oxford University Press.

The book includes a collection of twenty essays by prominent practitioners of stylistics on the teaching of literature and the use of literature in the language classroom.

Lazar, G. (1993), *Literature and Language Teaching: A Guide for Teachers and Trainers*, Cambridge University Press.

The book develops an approach to teaching literature for language learners at an intermediate level or lower. It includes several tasks and activities, to use in class or independently, and a set of tools for teachers to use in designing their own teaching materials.

CRITICAL LINGUISTICS

Fowler, R. (1991), *Language in the News: Discourse and Ideology in the Press*, Routledge.

The book outlines the critical linguistic tools of transitivity, modality, syntactic transformations, and speech acts, and applies them to the study of 'how language is used in newspapers to form ideas and beliefs' (p. 1).

Simpson, P. (1993), *Language, Ideology and Point of View*, Routledge.

The book introduces critical linguistics and draws on Halliday's systemic functional linguistics to examine a range of texts such as narrative fiction, advertisements, and newspaper articles for the way in which language is used to encode beliefs, interests, and ideological biases.

FEMINIST STYLISTICS

Mills, S. (1995), *Feminist Stylistics*, Routledge.

An introduction to the analysis of sexism in literary texts, newspapers, pop songs, and advertisements. Drawing on Halliday's systemic functional linguistics theory, Mills offers a toolkit for the examination of how texts encode representations of men and women, and how they implicitly naturalise gendered ideologies.

Montoro, R. (2014), 'Feminist stylistics', in M. Burke (ed.), *The Routledge Handbook of Stylistics*, Routledge, pp. 346–61.

This book chapter presents 'a general overview of language and gender so that feminist stylistic concerns are diachronically and thematically contextualised in relation to other linguistic treatments of gender and feminism' as well as an overview of 'the way gender matters have been dealt with and discussed within stylistics' (p. 346).

PRAGMATIC STYLISTICS

Black, E. (2006), *Pragmatic Stylistics*, Edinburgh University Press.

A thorough introduction to theories of pragmatics, and applications of these theories in the stylistic analysis of narrative fiction.

Chapman, S. and B. Clark (eds) (2019), *Pragmatics and Literature*, Palgrave Macmillan, <https://doi.org/10.1075/lal.35> (last accessed 23 September 2021).

A collection of recent work on the application of pragmatic theories to literary analysis, including implicatures, irony, relevance, (im)politeness, and lexical pragmatics. The introduction to the book presents an overview of pragmatic theories with a focus on shared aims and distinctions, and the way they can be used in understanding communication in literary texts.

COGNITIVE STYLISTICS

Semino, E. and J. Culpeper (eds) (2002), *Cognitive Stylistics: Language and Cognition in Text Analysis*, John Benjamins, <https://doi.org/10.1075/lal.1> (last accessed 23 September 2021).
  A demonstration, in twelve chapters, of ways in which insights from cognitive psychology combine with insights from linguistics in accounting for the way readers construct and negotiate meanings in literary texts.
Stockwell, P. (2002), *Cognitive Poetics: An Introduction*, Routledge.
  The book outlines cognitive poetic approaches to the reading of literature and applies them to literary genres across different historical periods. For example, it applies deictic shift theory to a nineteenth-century novel, scripts and schemas to an old English poem, possible worlds and mental spaces to science fiction, and parable and projection to Middle English allegories.

CORPUS STYLISTICS

McIntyre, D. and B. Walker (2019), *Corpus Stylistics: Theory and Practice*, Edinburgh University Press.
  The book outlines corpus stylistics as a 'systematic approach to the techniques of using corpora in stylistic analysis' and explains 'the theoretical and methodological issues that underlie this practice' (p. 2).
Mahlberg, M. (2013a), 'Corpus analysis of literary texts', in C. A. Chapelle (ed.), *The Encyclopedia of Applied Linguistics*, Wiley-Blackwell, <https://doi.org/10.1002/9781405198431.wbeal0249> (last accessed 23 September 2021).
  An overview of principles and approaches in corpus stylistics.

MULTIMODAL STYLISTICS

Kress, G. and T. van Leeuwen [1996] (2006), *Reading Images: The Grammar of Visual Design*, Routledge.
  The book views images as articulating ideological positions, and develops a descriptive framework for visual communication.
Nørgaard, N. (2019), *Multimodal Stylistics of the Novel: More than Words*, Routledge.
  The book offers a systematic framework for the analysis of multimodal as well as 'visually conventional novels' (p. 3). The book explores the semiotic potential for meaning of a novel's verbal text, typography, layout, photographs, drawings, book-cover design, and physical form.

CRITICAL STYLISTICS

Jeffries, L. (2010), *Critical Stylistics: The Power of English*, Palgrave Macmillan.
  The book integrates critical discourse analysis and mainstream stylistics into critical stylistics. The main contribution of the book is a comprehensive set of textual conceptual functions for the investigation of ideological control in different text types.
Jeffries, L. (2014), 'Critical stylistics', in M. Burke (ed.), *The Routledge Handbook of Stylistics*, Routledge, pp. 408–20.

This book chapter distinguishes critical stylistics from critical discourse analysis, relates the underlying tenets of the approach to SFL, and offers a brief introduction to critical stylistics as 'a framework which places stylistic analysis at the heart of the endeavour to see the power in language' (p. 408).

CONCLUSION

Revisiting stylistics

The journey of stylistics since the turn of the previous century has not been without criticism or controversy. In its early days, stylistics was particularly interested in literary texts. The application of linguistic methods to the study of literature invited fierce criticism from prominent literary critics. The dispute was sparked off by a review by Helen Vendler of Roger Fowler's book *Essays on Style and Language* (1966). Vendler described stylisticians as linguistics who are 'simply under-educated in the reading of poetry' and who lack the 'sense and value' necessary to appreciate literature (Vendler 1966: 460). Vendler's review came out with an editorial postscript by the prominent literary critic F. W. Bateson. Thereafter, Bateson and Fowler exchanged accusations and refutations, which were subsequently gathered and published in Fowler's *The Languages of Literature* (1971). The debate has been 'immortalised in stylistic folklore as the "Fowler–Bateson controversy"' (Simpson [2004] 2014: 148).

In response to Vendler, Fowler affirmed that linguistics is not a machine that puts out interpretive analyses of literary texts. He argued that literature is quintessentially language and as such it is open to formal linguistic analysis. Bateson replied that the proposed 'academic alliance between post-Saussure linguistics and post-I. A. Richards criticism' is not possible because the grammarian 'will divide and subdivide the verbal material' and the literary critic 'will synthesise and amalgamate it' (Bateson 1966, cited in Simpson [2004] 2014: 151). For Bateson, grammar and literary criticism are mutually exclusive as the former is analytic and the latter is synthetic. Fowler rejected the grounds on which linguistics was disqualified and described Bateson's argument as misleading and as emanating from ignorance about the nature and potential of linguistics. Bateson insisted that linguistics is not useful to the appreciation of literary texts and Fowler lined up arguments in defence of the relevance of linguistics to the study of literature. The Fowler–Bateson debate is reprinted in Simpson's *Stylistics: A Resource Book for Students* ([2004] 2014: 148–57).

More than a decade later, the American critic Stanley Fish levelled another attack on stylistics. It was triggered by Halliday's (1971) stylistic analysis of William Golding's novel *The Inheritors*. Halliday carried out an analysis of transitivity choices in the narrative and described the way these patterns encode the mind-styles of the characters. Fish criticised the absence of connection between descriptive and interpretive acts in the works of formalist and functionalist stylisticians. For him, these stylisticians were more concerned with asserting their interpretations rather than with proving them. The heart of Fish's critique of the stylistics of the time was that it sought to 'establish an inventory of fixed significances' and ascribed interpretation to syntactic structures ([1973] 1996: 94). The formal patterns, Fish counter-argued, do not possess the meanings to be 'discovered' by the stylistician in the process of analysis. Instead, these meanings are constructed by the reader, who is given a more active role in negotiating rather than discovering meaning.

In order to close the 'interpretive gaps' opened up by stylisticians, Fish called for an 'affective stylistics' in which 'the focus of attention is shifted from the spatial context of a page and its observable regularities to the temporal context of a mind and its experiences' ([1973] 1996: 109). In this 'new stylistics', the effect of a text does not reside in the text to be extracted but is rather created by the reader. Fish's interest is in the way the reader's expectations and previous experiences are mobilised to create individual responses and enable multiple interpretations of the text. In response to these charges, stylistics broadened its scope to include the contexts of text production and reception, branching out into trends concerned with the investigation of ideologies and the construction of people and processes (e.g. feminist stylistics). The discipline has been developing progressively since then, taking on modes of representation other than the verbal text (e.g. multimodal stylistics) and integrating concepts from cognitive sciences to offer further insights into the processes of reading and interpretation (e.g. cognitive stylistics).

More recently, the French linguist Jean-Jacques Lecercle (1993) published yet another critique of the aims and methods of contemporary stylistics. The attack is 'short' but 'damning' and 'uncompromising' (Simpson [2004] 2014: 2). Lecercle argued that stylistics had always hesitated between the generic (the study of registers and style) and the idiosyncratic (style as individual expression), which made the field difficult to define. In fact, it is the recent movement from the concern with individual style to the general interest in the way the study of language intersects with allied fields such as rhetoric, narratology, and semiotics that is taking stylistics 'away from linguistics as a philosophy of language and its application to the literary texts [. . .] into style as the locus and the medium of the writer's dwelling in language' (Lecercle 1993: 16). Lecercle noted that work in the area was written less from a 'scientific' perspective and more 'from the points of view of deconstruction, Marxism, reader response criticism or cultural materialism' (1993: 16). As a result, the name of the field was 'on the wane' even though the referent was 'doing rather well' (1993: 15).

Lecercle's assertion that the term 'stylistics' was retracting from the titles of books to their subtitles and that few students were eager to carry out research in the area has been proved false by contemporary research and teaching practices.

Stylistics is 'taught and researched in university departments of language, literature and linguistics the world over' (Simpson [2004] 2014: 2). It is making a strong presence in the titles of important publications in the area, including, but not limited to, Wales ([1990] 2011), Mills (1995), Bradford (1997), Semino and Culpeper (2002), Verdonk (2002), Semino and Short (2004), Simpson ([2004] 2014), Black (2006), Gregoriou (2009), Jeffries (2010), Jeffries and McIntyre (2010), Mahlberg (2013b), Burke (2014), Gibbons and Whiteley (2018), McIntyre and Walker (2019), and Ringrow and Pihlaja (2020). Stylistics today is not only 'very much alive and well' (Simpson [2004] 2014: 2) but also 'a progressive discipline' that has the 'explanatory power' to account for the meaning and effect in a wide range of text types (Gibbons and Whiteley 2018: 322).

Limitations of coverage

Stylistics today is a robust field of study. It offers the analyst a wide range of analytical frameworks inspired by theoretical and practical developments in other fields. It is also continually testing and updating these frameworks in light of empirical research that applies these frameworks in the analysis of text types drawn from different discourses and using different modalities. The interaction with other fields and the research-based appraisal of the analytical frameworks has resulted in a plethora of stylistic trends that defies comprehensive presentation within the confines of a single book.

For these reasons, and for reasons that have to do with the characteristics of the intended readership, this textbook has been purposively, and unavoidably, selective in the choice of analytical frameworks and the texts to analyse. The stylistic frameworks selected have an overall functional and pragmatic orientation and are underlined by a concern with language use and analysis. This has two obvious advantages. First, it gives the frameworks an overall coherent outlook in that they draw on concepts and notions from Halliday's systemic functional linguistics (e.g. the notions of choice, register, transitivity, and modality) and from theories of pragmatics (e.g. politeness theory, speech act theory, conversational implicatures, and the cooperative principle). Second, this choice gives the target learners the psychological advantage of moving towards the unfamiliar (the stylistic analysis) from a familiar territory (knowledge of language and familiarity with language analysis). Language learners, especially in foreign language contexts, 'have learned how to analyse sentences grammatically', which makes them 'more consciously aware of linguistic structure and better equipped to analyse it and its relationship to meaning' (Short and Candlin 1989: 183).

Moving forward

In this textbook, I have tried to provide you with the necessary theoretical knowledge and hands-on experience to get you started in your own journey of exploration and research. In Part I of the book, I presented the key terms and concepts which you will find circulating in any discussion of stylistics and which are central to the analytical frameworks introduced in Part II. The nine chapters in this part are practice-oriented. I believe that the best way to learn about stylistics is to carry out stylistic analyses, and to do so with as little support as possible. To enable greater independence, every chapter includes a checklist of analytical categories relevant to the stylistic framework used. The chapters also offer sample stylistic analyses to help you see through the process and guide your own independent analysis of the texts offered for further practice. In the design of the chapters, I have taken care to offer you constant support. This includes, in addition to the checklists, an introduction to the chapter, an outline of the nature of communication in the genre, a sketch of the stylistic framework to be used, definitions of technical terms, and hints to help you navigate through the practice activities.

The chapters in Part II offer formalist and functionalist stylistic analyses of poems, critical linguistic and feminist stylistic analyses of fictional extracts, a pragmatic stylistic analysis of a dramatic dialogue, cognitive stylistic analyses of jokes, multimodal stylistic analyses of print advertisements, a critical stylistic analysis of a political statement, and a corpus stylistic analysis of online journalism. The range of text types is wide, including canonical and non-canonical literature, humorous writing, political documents, online news articles, and multimodal advertisements. The range of frameworks covers traditional trends in stylistics (e.g. formalist stylistics) and more recent trends (e.g. multimodal and corpus stylistics). This wide spectrum of text types and analytical frameworks represents the progressive nature of the discipline. Stylistics is a field that 'prides itself on being a discipline that does not stand still' (Gibbons and Whiteley 2018: 322).

Given the fast-developing nature of the discipline, the historical development offered in Part III is only a synoptic outline. The field has come a long way since the formalist days at the turn of the previous century. It has taken on genres other than literature (e.g. political documents), modes of representation other than the verbal mode (e.g. visual brochures), and analytical frameworks that are less text-centred and more interested in the cognitive processed involved in reading and interpretation. In this part of the book, I took you back to the early days and explored the driving impetus of stylistics. We have seen how stylistics, throughout its hundred-year journey or so, reinvented itself in response to developments in linguistics, literature, and other allied fields, as well as in response to theoretical and research-based developments within the field. The journey is ongoing and the destination is not in sight. Indeed, Lecercle's remark that '*stylistics*, like the Phoenix, is forever reborn' captures the essence of the discipline, even though Lecercle's use of the statement was not meant as favourable (Lecercle 1993: 14; original italics).

Now that you have read this book, you have a good idea of how stylistics started, how it branched out into the many analytical frameworks over the course of the years, and where it stands today. In fact, the unavoidable limitations of coverage, explainable with reference to the aims and target audience of the book, leave you with an increasingly expanding terrain to explore. If you are interested in further exploring the concepts of style, register, and dialect as perspectives of variation in spoken and written texts, you will find Biber and Conrad's *Register, Genre, and Style* (2009) very useful. However, if you would like to start with a textbook on style variation for the non-specialist, Haynes's *Style* (1995) is a good starting point.

It is also my hope that Chapter 11 of this book has sparked your interest in the journey of stylistics and that you would like to read more on it. I would like to assume a yes answer and redirect you to Bradford's *Stylistics* (1997: 2–13). The first two chapters of the book offer 'a simplified history' of modern stylistics (Bradford 1997: 11). This account, short as it may be, offers an interesting perspective on the 'progress of modern stylistics from its origins in classical rhetoric to its function in modern literary studies' (1997: xii). A more detailed account is found in part I of *The Routledge Handbook of Stylistics* (Burke 2014). The first chapter traces the roots of the discipline to Aristotle and the next one anchors the beginnings of modern stylistics in the theories of formalism and later structuralism. The subsequent two chapters focus on functional stylistics and reader response theories, both of which grew as a reaction to the exclusive concern with the words on the page in earlier trends. Other chapters in the handbook offer contemporary perspectives on the interrelation between stylistic trends and key ideas in prominent linguistic and literary theories in the twentieth century and beyond. These include speech acts and im/politeness theory, conversation analysis, the cooperative principle, relevance theory, narratology, schema theory, text world theory, feminism, corpus linguistics, film studies, and neuroscience.

In addition to offering theoretical insights into how stylistics came into contact with these fields, the chapters in the handbook also offer a practical demonstration of how concepts from these fields are used in stylistic analysis. Before delving into research-based publications, however, I would recommend you start by reading on the range of research methods in stylistics and on the use of data in stylistic research. Jeffries and McIntyre's *Stylistics* (2010: 12–21) offers a readable guide to the beginning researcher. When you are ready to move on to more advanced topics, you may start with *Language and Style* (2010). This collection of essays, edited by McIntyre and Busse, offers an application of more recent trends in stylistics to literary works. These include the study of text worlds in poetry, a corpus-based pragmatic stylistic investigation of drama, and analysis of multimodality in fiction.

The range of publications in the area is so broad that any attempt at comprehensive coverage is bound to leave out significant works and/or trigger disagreement. This is a sign of the robustness and vitality of the discipline. I will conclude this section by recommending three more recent books that show you in what direction stylistics is moving. The first is *Contemporary Stylistics: Language, Cognition, Interpretation* (2018) by Gibbons and Whiteley. The focus of the book is on 'contemporary' trends in stylistics. These include reader response methods (such as conceptual metaphors and building and switching text worlds during the reading process), the cognitively informed stylistic frameworks that originated as a result of the 'cognitive turn' in the 1980s and 1990s (such as analysis of figure and ground, schemas and scripts, and cognitive deixis), and corpus stylistics.

If you are interested in exploring corpus stylistics further, McIntyre and Walker's *Corpus Stylistics: Theory and Practice* (2019) is a good reference. The book introduces basic terms in corpus linguistics and guides you through building a corpus, annotating it, and running different statistical tests on corpora. The book also demonstrates how corpus stylistics can support cognitive, pedagogical, and historical stylistic research. The last book to consider here is Nørgaard's *Multimodal Stylistics of the Novel: More than Words* (2019). The first chapter outlines the motivations and challenges of multimodal stylistics and proposes an analytical framework for the stylistic analysis of multimodal meaning-making in the novel. Subsequent chapters offer a set of tools for the analysis of meanings created by different semiotic modes such as wording, typography, layout, images, book-cover design, and the physical form of the novel. The toolkit offered in this book is meant to 'extend the traditional focus in stylistics on wording to include other modes and their multimodal interaction' (2019: 305). Stylistics will, expectedly, continue to thrive and branch out.

Closing statement

In 1958, Roman Jakobson delivered a seminal paper titled 'Closing Statement: Linguistics and Poetics' (referred to here as 'Closing Statement') at a conference in Indiana. The paper was published two years later in Sebeok's collection of essays *Style in Language* (1960: 350–77). Although the title has the modifier 'Closing', Jakobson's paper launched the start of modern stylistics and is considered 'a manifesto for a language-based stylistics' (Zyngier and Fialho 2016: 214).

You have now reached the closing section of this book and I hope that it is a 'closing statement' for you in much the same way Jakobson's 'Closing Statement' was for stylistics. When you finish reading this book or taking the course for which it is prescribed, your journey has just started. The book has equipped you with the key concepts in the study of style in language and the necessary tools to explore meaning-making in a variety of text types on your own. It has also offered a composite picture of the how theory and practice interplay in stylistics. You are now ready to take further steps towards expanding your stylistic perspective and further expanding your analytical toolkit. The resources I have suggested throughout the book will give you a sense of direction, and the two key journals in the area, *Language and Literature* and the *Journal of Literary Semantics*, will keep you abreast of emerging trends and innovative applications to text types that are getting increasingly multimodal and complex.

ANSWER KEY

> Chapter 1, Style and Stylistics

1.1 'I am having a great time. Are you coming? Missing you, teacher.' The friend-to-friend text message is truncated, that is, the subject 'I' and the auxiliary verb 'am' have been deleted. The message contains the texting abbreviations 'gr8', 'r', and 'u'. It also contains the verb 'love' and the address term 'm8', which is another texting abbreviation. The student-to-teacher version provides the missing elements 'I am', replaces the texting abbreviations with 'great', 'are', and 'you', and replaces the verb 'love' with 'missing' and the address term 'm8' with 'teacher', which are more appropriate in the context of the student–teacher relationship. The friend-to-friend text message is also a single run-on sentence with no punctuation. The student-to-teacher version provides the missing punctuation and the single run-on sentence becomes three statements.

1.2
   a) informal – the use of contractions and the choice of words (e.g. finish)
   b) formal – the use of passive and the choice of words (compare with (a) above)
   c) formal – the complex structure and the choice of words (e.g. purchase)
   d) informal – the use of simple and colloquial words (compare with (c) above)
   e) informal – the use of the first person and simple words
   f) formal – the impersonal tone and the word choice (compare with (e) above)
   g) formal – the use of title and surname; the choice of words
   h) informal – the conversational tone, dropping the relative pronoun, and the choice of words (compare with (g) above)
   i) informal – the use of first and second person; the use of the abbreviation ASAP

j) formal – the impersonal tone and the word choice (compare with (i) above)

1.3 Field: style in language
Tenor: formal
Mode: spoken
Rewriting suggestions:
A: Does anyone know what today's class is about?
B: Style in language, right?
A: Yeah. Style, generally, is a specific characteristic of human activity that results from choices, within the accepted norms, of a definite mode or manner of conducting this activity.
B: Are you telling me natural objects like trees have no style?
A: You could say that because their shape and colour are not the result of deliberate choice. But it does not take away from their beauty, of course.
C: What does a person's language choice or style tell us about that person?
B: Well, style is indicative of a speaker's social or ethnic group, and their locatedness in region or time period.
A: Awesome! Can we move on now?

1.4
a) Cockney
b) General American English
c) African American Vernacular English
d) Early Modern English

Rewriting suggestions:
a) 'Someone has been up here,' she said. – 'Yes, it was Mr Cousins,' said Linda. 'I think he was after pinching something from your bag, Sergeant Joe, only I came up and caught him opening it.' – 'He mentioned he was a friend of yours,' said Dolly. 'I wouldn't want him as a friend of mine.' – 'Yes, we thought we'd better see if he'd pinched anything,' said Linda.
b) Now, we're going to be stopping 32 kilometres outside of the preserve to fill the car up with petrol and get drinks and stuff. Keep that in mind, guys. (*Hell's Belle*, 2019, horror movie)
c) He isn't going to do nothing. What's happening? – Are you trying to poach my girls? – Your girls? – Yeah. – Do you think you are still running $20 tricks on Stewart Avenue or something? You haven't answered my question, man. You are a clown. (*Star*, 2016–19, musical series)
d) Cassius: Will you have supper with me tonight, Casca?
Casca: No, I have a previous commitment.

1.5
a) written
b) spoken

The first sentence uses the third person indefinite pronoun 'one', which creates a sense of detachment. The second sentence, on the other hand, uses the second person pronoun 'you', which creates a sense of familiarity. The impersonal pronoun 'one' is common in written, formal

English, while the personal pronoun 'you' is more common in spoken English.

c) cook to cook in a restaurant
d) professional chef to trainees during chef training

The first sentence uses the non-technical terms 'big knife' and the 'small one [knife]', while the second uses chef jargon, namely, 'cleaver' and 'boning knife'.

e) car dealer
f) any other job

The first sentence uses car-dealing jargon, namely, 'silver metallic 1970 Cadillac de Ville convertible', while the second one uses layperson's terms to refer to the same object.

g) The speaker/writer is a supporter of the Palestinian cause.
h) The speaker/writer is a not supporter of the Palestinian cause.

The first speaker/writer uses the ideologically loaded verb 'martyred' (to die for one's beliefs) and these beliefs are encoded in the name given to the fronted object 'freedom fighters'. The second speaker, on the other hand, uses a less loaded verb 'killed' and refers to the object of the verb as 'terrorists'. For the first speaker, the referents have lost their lives in pursuit of a just cause – their freedom; for the second speaker, however, their death is a desirable end because of their violent conduct.

i) formal
j) officialese

The first sentence uses formal but non-technical vocabulary, while the second sentence uses the technical terminology of ornithology (the scientific study of birds).

1.6
- a) The foregrounded element is the word 'break'. It is foregrounded via repetition. It is repeated three times in the first line.
- b) The foregrounded elements are the phrases 'so cool', 'so calm', and 'so bright'. They are foregrounded via parallelism. The three phrases have the same structure, namely, so+adjective.
- c) The foregrounded elements are the phrases 'sang his didn't' and 'danced his did'. They are foregrounded via syntactic deviation. In the structure of the English clause, possessive adjectives, such as 'his', are followed by nouns to form noun phrases, as in 'his house'. In the line above, cummings has used the auxiliary verbs 'didn't' and 'did' after the possessive adjective 'his'. This is a position in which nouns are expected in English syntax.
- d) The foregrounded element is the word 'tumbling'. It is foregrounded via graphological deviation. The -ing part of the word 'tumbles down' into the next line, which serves to symbolically enact tumbling down of the houses, eyes, people, smiles, faces, streets, and steeples.

Note:
Different answers are possible here because cummings's poem deviates from many norms of the English language and of the poetry register. For

example, none of the lines begins with a capital letter, and there is no punctuation whatsoever. Check also how the spelling of the word 'wonderful' is broken down into two lines.

- e) The foregrounded element is the word 'love'. It is foregrounded via semantic deviation. 'Love', the human emotion, is described as 'thick', as though it was an object or a liquid. The words 'love' and 'thick' are not semantically compatible. In the second line, 'love' is described as 'thin'. Again, 'love' and 'thin' do not collocate. These descriptions of 'love' violate the collocational constraints of English semantics.

Note:
Different answers are possible here because the two lines contain a number of deviations. For example, none of the lines begins with a capital letter, and there is no punctuation whatsoever. This is a deviation from graphological rules. Also, the adjectives 'thick' and 'thin' are preceded by the intensifier 'more' and followed by the inflectional comparative marker morpheme '-er' at the same time. This is a deviation from the morphological rules of English. Check also what love is compared to in the two lines.

- f) The foregrounded element is the word 'seafood'. It is foregrounded via semantic deviation. The other words in the line, namely, 'murder', 'lust', 'greed', and 'revenge', are all abstract nouns and have negative connotations. The word 'seafood' is neither abstract nor does it share the negative connotations of the other words. All the others, except 'seafood', collocate with each other.

Chapter 2, Formalist Analysis of Poetry

2.1 The poem describes loneliness and oblivion as the most basic needs or 'wants' of modern man.
- a) The first sentence starts at the beginning of the poem and ends with *the wish to be alone* (line 5), while the second sentence starts with *Beneath it* and ends with *the desire for oblivion runs* (line 10).
- b) The verb in the second sentence is *run*. The absence of a main verb in the first sentence is appropriate to the theme of wishing to be alone in the first stanza, while the verb in the second sentence constructs the desire for death as more dynamic, though an undercurrent.
- c) The normal paradigm is 'the sky is overcast with dark clouds'. Every invitation card is an activity or an occasion we are requested to attend – a social obligation. The use of *the sky grows dark with invitation-cards* suggests an overwhelming number of invitations, and an impatience with social obligations. The speaker wants to be freed from the obligation to socialise and to uphold social commitments.
- d) The word *sex* (line 3) does not occur with its habitual linguistic company. There are no printed directions to sex. The normal paradigm is *printed directions of using a machine*. We need printed directions to be able to

operate sophisticated machines. The use of *sex* in this context constructs it as an automated, mechanical activity. Indeed, the *printed directions* make sex an impersonal activity – an activity whose rules are explicitly laid down and shared. It becomes a social exercise, and it adds to the list of social activities that the speaker seeks to break away from.

e) The use of *tabled fertility rites* echoes the disapproval of the automatic and mechanical nature of sex. To underline disapproval of the social outlook on marriage, the speaker refers to it as *fertility*; and to underline disapproval of marriage parties as yet another social commitment, the speaker refers to them as *rites*, which has primitive overtones. To top off the disapproval of the mechanical nature of the social institution of marriage, the fertility rites are described as *tabled*. The semantic deviation via departure from conventional collocational constraints, just like the other instances of deviation in the poem, is meant to slow down the reading and focus the reader's attention on the textual construction of modern social life.

f) The first and fifth lines (stanza 1) and the sixth and tenth lines (stanza 2) are repeated. The first stanza, and the poem, begins with the wish to depart human company; the second stanza, and the poem, closes with the wish to depart human life. In these lines, the words *wish, alone, desire*, and *oblivion* occur twice each. The repetition serves to remind readers what the poem is about. It invites them to consider these lines as central to any interpretation of the poem.

g) The second line of each stanza (lines 2 and 7) is an expression of the speaker's impatience with the 'most social' activities – gatherings. The third line of each stanza (lines 3 and 8) expresses disapproval of the mechanical nature of the 'most personal' activity – sexual life. The fourth line of the first stanza critiques the mechanical nature of family gatherings, and the fourth line of the second stanza critiques *life insurance* as a *costly aversion of the eyes from death*. The first stanza closes, as it starts, with the speaker's wish to depart companionship, and the second closes, as it starts, with the wish to depart life.

The middle three lines of the first stanza are parallel with one another. They are all sentences with the same structure beginning with *however*. The middle three lines of the second stanza are also parallel structures. They are all noun phrases beginning with *despite*, which is mentioned in the first noun phrase (line 7) and ellipted in subsequent noun phrases.

The parallelism in the two stanzas invites readers to look for meaning connections between the parallel structures. All the activities of modern man, namely, the social gatherings, sexual activity, the family, and life insurance, are artificial aspects of modern life that we engage in out of social necessity. The more natural undercurrent is a wish for loneliness in body and soul. This parallelism, indeed this symmetry, is appropriate to the thematic concerns of the poem. It is symbolic of the technicality of modern social life that this poem is a critique of.

h) The two stanzas have more or less the same punctuation. This graphological choice is appropriate to the representation of the monotony and artificiality of modern life in the poem.
i) The two stanzas also have the same punctuation, the same rhyme scheme (ABCDA), the same number of lines (five each), and the same number of words (forty each). Again, this choice is appropriate to the representation of the monotony and artificiality of modern life that the poem is a critique of.

2.2 The word 'brain' in the poem does not refer to the physical organ in the head. It is used metonymically to refer to the brain's imaginative capacity. The poem is about the power of the human mind.

a) The sky is a physical object that is described as 'wide'. The 'brain' is not. The irreconcilability of the words 'sky' and 'brain' in the company of 'wide' creates a semantic deviation and drives the reader to look for another meaning relation in order for the metaphor to yield a coherent interpretation. By 'wide brain' the speaker refers to the 'width of human imagination'. The imaginative capacity of the human brain is so wide that it can envision even the limitless sky.
b) The speaker extends the container metaphor in 'The one will the other contain'. The human brain's conceiving imagination is so enormous that it can easily 'contain' the sky by way of imagining it. In the frame, the brain is such a wide 'imaginative container' that it can easily imagine such wide objects as the sky, and beyond.
c) Again, the sea is a physical object that is described as 'deep'. The 'brain' is not. The juxtaposition of the words 'brain' and 'deep' creates a semantic deviation. It drives the reader to look for a more consistent and coherent meaning relation. The 'deep brain' indicates the 'breadth of human imagination'. The conceiving power of the human brain is so encompassing that it can easily fathom the deep seas.
d) 'The one will the other absorb' extends the 'brain as container' metaphor. The human brain's imaginative capacity can easily 'absorb' the depth of the seas.
e) This line compares the imaginative power of the brain to that of 'sponges'. The brain can envisage the depth of the seas as easily as sponges suck up water from buckets.
f) God is not a physical object and therefore has no weight. So is the brain. The speaker takes the construction of the brain to the level of God. Just like God, the brain is boundless and, accordingly, weightless.
g) The brain differs from God as 'Syllable from Sound'. God is 'Sound', says the speaker. Existentially, sounds pre-date syllables. They are the raw material and they can stand on their own. Syllables, however, cannot exist independently of sounds.

   There is another side to this argument, which is an extension of the 'brain as container' metaphor. Syllables contain sounds. In this frame, God, the essence, takes shape in the brain's enormous conceiving power.

h) The poem has no punctuation marks like commas and full stops (periods) to mark transitions and sentence ends. It only has dashes throughout. This is characteristic of Emily Dickinson's poetry. She punctuates her poems with dashes. Therefore, while this constitutes a deviation from the graphological norms of language, it is consistent with the internal norms of Emily Dickinson's poetry.

The first dash after 'The Brain' serves to slow down the start of the poem and give the word 'brain' the particular emphasis that suits the thematic concern of the poem. The other dashes in the poem serve to help the reader with the oral reading of the poem.

i) This phonological parallelism serves to enact the parallelism at the level of arguments. The brain is projected as capable of containing the sky (stanza 1), absorbing the sea (stanza 2), and apprehending the essence of God (stanza 3).

Chapter 3, Functionalist Analysis of Poetry

3.1 The poem is a register of the acts of cruelty that human beings inflict upon each other.

a) In addition to the two non-finite verbs 'dying' and 'sitting', the poem has a total of twenty-one processes. Four of these processes are material action, fifteen mental, one relational and one behavioural process. the twenty-one processes break down as follows:

material: misused (×2), cast (×2); mental: look out upon (×2) – perception, see (×7) – perception, hear (×2) – perception, mark (×1) – perception, observe (×3) – perception; relational: am silent (×1); behavioural: (×1) sit; existential: none.

b) All the mental, relational, and behavioural processes are associated with the speaker. None of the material processes, however, are associated with the speaker.

c) In the fifteen mental processes, the speaker assumes the role of sensor; in the two relational and behavioural processes, the speaker is the carrier of attribute and behaver, respectively. The association of the speaker with mental, relational, and behavioural processes throughout the poem signposts an attitude of inaction towards the suffering of the people in the text world of the poem. The speaker 'senses' the cruelty inflicted by people upon each other and remains not only inactive but also silent towards it. The attitude of inactivity is borne out by the absence of material processes associated with the speaker, and the attitude of silence is underscored by the absence of verbalisation processes in the poem.

d) There is only one full stop (period) in the entire poem; it closes the poem. The poem is therefore composed of one sentence. This is an interesting choice. The acts of cruelty in the poem are all done by the same 'subject' (more able human beings), unto the same objects (less able human beings). The collapse of human values in the world of the poems is projected as reiterative, which may be packed to fit into a single sentence.

e) Verbs: see (a) above; nouns/nominal groups: sorrows of the world, oppression, shame, convulsive sobs from young men, anguish, deeds, low life, mother, her children, wife, her husband, treacherous seducer of young women, ranklings of jealousy and unrequited love, these sights on earth, workings of battle, pestilence, tyranny, martyrs, prisoners, a famine at sea, sailors, lots who shall be killed, the lives of the rest, sights, degradations, arrogant persons, laborers, the poor, negroes, the like, meanness, agony, without end; adjectives: remorseful, silent.

Almost all the lexical choices in the poem have negative connotations. Positive adjectives like 'young' are used before 'men' and 'women' to intensify the horrific nature of cruelties, and the positive noun 'love' is preceded by the adjective 'unrequited'. These choices serve to underline the meanness of human beings to each other, and to underscore the indictment of passively looking at all this suffering.

f) There are fifteen mental processes we can change into material processes (see (a) above). For example, *I hear secret convulsive sobs from young men* may be changed into *Young men are sobbing convulsively and secretly*; and *I see, in low life, the mother misused by her children* can become *Children are misusing their mother*. This change in transitivity will shift the focus from the speaker's state of inaction to the actions themselves that are causing the collapse of human values.

3.2 The speaker in the poem used unconventional, indeed empowering, connotations to define her loneliness.

a) Material: rides (×1), aiming (×1), driving (×1), leaving behind (×1), stopped (×1), lived (×1), wake (×1), breathe (×1); mental: wondering (×1), want to ask (×1), knows (×2); relational: I am lonely (×5).

b) Material processes outnumber the other process types in the poem. The processes associated with the speaker are predominantly relational, while those associated with the description of her loneliness are material and mental. This choice helps construct loneliness in terms of action and knowledge.

c) The speaker compares her loneliness to a plane riding across the Rockies. The image of a plane travelling a large distance, unaccompanied and uninterrupted, towards a known destination and guided only by its own radio beam is suggestive of certainty and determination. This construction helps to redefine loneliness by detaching it from the conventional undesirable connotations of depressing solitude and associating it with freedom of movement and clarity of objective.

d) The comparison of loneliness to a 'woman driving across country day after day' sustains the construction of loneliness in terms of freedom, and the use of 'leaving behind . . . little towns she might have stopped and lived and died in' accentuates the assuredness of purpose. Like the plane, the woman is travelling non-stop in a specific direction towards a specific destination. This loneliness is not equivalent to solitude but is constructed in terms of assured single-mindedness that won't get deflected until the goal is achieved.

e) In the third stanza, the speaker compares herself to a lonely person waking up early and when everyone else is still sleeping. This image adds a new dimension to the construction of happiness. Loneliness does not 'happen' to the speaker; she chooses it. The speaker's loneliness is a matter of deliberate choice.

f) The textual construction of loneliness in the poem is enhanced by the comparison to a 'rowboat ice-fast on the shore . . . that knows what it is'. Loneliness is compared to a wooden boat tied to the shore on cold winter nights. Despite the unfavourable conditions, it is the boat that has the 'gift for burning'. It is the source of the warmth needed for life to go on in winter. The loneliness of the speaker is driven by self-awareness and is empowering.

g) Adrienne Rich was female and a feminist.

h) The repetition of the word 'lonely' underscores the centrality of 'loneliness' in the poem, and helps explicitly link the different images in all the stanzas.

i) The speaker in the poem speaks for the addressee. She asks the questions for them (lines 1 and 8). In effect, this leaves us with two interlocutors but only one voice in the poem. This choice underscores the assertiveness of the speaker and her emphatic attitude towards her loneliness and the way it shapes her identity.

j) The choice of 'Song' for the title suggests that the speaker is celebrating loneliness as part of her identity. It is a song to chant.

Chapter 4, Critical Linguistic Analysis of Fiction

4.1 Charles Dickens's *Hard Times* ([1854] 1998)
a) Epistemic —
Perception —
Deontic: you would carpet your room; It wouldn't hurt them; They wouldn't crush and wither; you mustn't fancy; You are never to fancy; You are not . . . to do anything of that kind; You are to be in all things regulated and governed . . . by fact; will force the people to be a people of fact; You must discard the word Fancy; You have nothing to do with it; You are not to have, in any object of use or ornament; you cannot be allowed to walk upon flowers in carpets; you cannot be permitted to paint foreign birds; you must not have quadrupeds represented upon walls; You must use . . .
Boulomaic: We hope to have, before long, a board of fact

b) The narrator is a non-participating character in the narrative, narrating from outside the consciousness of the participating characters. This is a Category B reflector mode.

c) The text is dominated by deontic modality, which makes it positively shaded. The general tone of the discourse is certain and assertive.
d) The narrator reports the speech and speech acts of the characters but makes no attempt to report their thoughts. The conversational turns, and speech, of the gentleman, Sissy, and Gradgrind are reported using direct speech. The inverted commas, along with the other markers of direct speech, denote this mode of speech presentation. The narrator also employs narrative report of speech act in reference to Sissy, as in 'Sissy blushed, and stood up' and 'The girl curtseyed, and sat down.'
e) The narrator's use of direct speech to report the words of the gentleman and Thomas Gradgrind sustains the authorial construction of the two characters. They are rational and exact, espousing a fact-only philosophy and approach to teaching. The narrator's preference for direct speech is line with the profile of the two characters. Their words are reported verbatim in a 'fact-only' way. The narrator makes no attempt to change them. In reporting students like Sissy, on the other hand, the narrator uses direct speech and narrative report of speech act. This includes reporting the way they pose and react.
f) The ideological outlook of the school principal and the government officer is carried by modality and shading. The predominance of deontic modality and positive shading in the extract is appropriate for the assertive approach of the two gentlemen who are attempting to impose on the schoolchildren a fact-only teaching philosophy.

4.2 William Golding's *Lord of the Flies* ([1954] 1999)
a) Epistemic: Who knows we're here?; They knew at the airport; Nobody knows where we are; Perhaps they knew where we was going to; and perhaps not; But they don't know where we are; Nobody knows where we are; We may be here a long time; So we may be here a long time
Perception: Jack ... looked uncertainly at Ralph
Deontic: We'll have rules
Boulomaic —
b) The narrator is a non-participating character in the narrative, narrating from outside the consciousness of the participating characters. This is a Category B reflector mode.
c) The dominant modality type in the extract is epistemic modality, which makes the text negatively shaded. This choice gives the narrative a general tone of uncertainty.
d) The narrator uses two modes of speech presentation, namely, direct speech, as in 'Nobody knows where we are', and narrative report of speech acts, as in *He grinned suddenly*.
e) The narrator describes the way characters look at each other and even the way they breathe, but does not attempt to report their thoughts.
f) The narrator's use of direct speech takes the reader closer to the children's growing uneasiness at the prospect of being stranded on the island indefinitely. The reader experiences it 'first-hand', without narratorial mediation. The narrator's report of speech acts, as in 'He

gaped at them' and 'He gazed at their intent faces', adds descriptive commentary to the interaction. The use of these two modes of speech presentation enables the narrator to comment on the children's moods and reactions without affecting the faithfulness of the representation of the children's concern and fears.

g) The negative shading of the text is appropriate for the mood of the children, who are uncertain about connection with their families and apprehensive about life on the island. Piggy's frequent use of epistemic modality markers constructs him as easily alarmed and lacking in self-assurance.

h) Ralph uses non-modalised language at the end of the extract in order to comfort the children and help them overcome anxiety. It works. Fear subsides and the children become more welcoming of the new environment.

i) To represent the children as assured and confident, you may choose to shift from epistemic modality to either deontic modality or even non-modalised expressions.

Chapter 5, Feminist Analysis of Fiction

5.1 Margaret Atwood's *The Handmaid's Tale* (2011)

a) The narrator, Offred, is a participating character in the narrative. She makes three nominal references to Ofglen (twice as 'a shape' and once as a 'nondescript woman') and three pronominal references all of which are in the indefinite pronoun (once as 'the right one' and twice as 'this one').

b) **Ofglen**

Verbal element	Transitivity pattern	Semantic role
comes along	Material process	(affected = none)
reaches me	Material process	(affected = none)
is the right one	Relational process	Attribute = right one
says to me	Verbalisation process	Sayer = Ofglen
is my spy	Relational process	Attribute = my spy
is a little plumper	Relational process	Attribute = plumper
Her eyes are brown.	Relational process	Attribute = brown eyes
Her name is Ofglen.	Relational process	Equivalence
walks demurely	Material process	(affected = none)
has never said	Verbalisation process	(negated)
may be a ... believer	Relational process	Attribute = a ... believer

Offred

answer	Verbalisation process	Sayer = Offred
am her spy	Relational process	Attribute = her spy
know about her	Mental process	Sensor (Offred)
have not said	Verbalisation process	(negated)
can't take the risk	Material process	(negated)

Both characters

peer at each other's faces	Material process	(affected = none)
turn	Material process	(affected = none)
walk together	Material process	(affected = none)
aren't allowed to go	Material process	(affected = maids)
are ... well protected	Material process	(affected = maids)

c) In addition to referring to Ofglen as a 'shape', the narrator describes her as 'a little plumper than I am'. She describes her eyes as 'brown', her walking as demure, and her hands as 'red-gloved' and 'clasped' in form. The narrator also compares Ofglen's 'little steps' to 'a trained pig's, on its hind legs'.

d) Ofglen is described as a 'shape' and referred to using indefinite pronouns. This 'impersonal' construction of Ofglen is enhanced by the fragmentation of her body. The narrator describes her figure as plump, her eyes as 'brown', her walk as demure, her hands as 'red-gloved' and her 'short little steps' as resembling a pig's hind legs. The types of processes and semantic roles in which the two female characters appear bear out the construction. The two women appear in nine material processes in which they either affect nobody or are themselves affected. The other processes in which the two women appear are relational (7), verbalisation (4), and mental (1). In short, the extract constructs women as undefined, impersonal, and fragmentable.

5.2 Charlotte Brontë's *Jane Eyre* ([1846] 2003) and Charles Dickens's *Hard Times* ([1854] 1998)

a) Blanche's body parts (in order of appearance): shoulders, neck, complexion, eyes, hair, curls, breast, knee; Bounderby's body parts (in order of appearance): head, forehead, veins in the temple, skin to the face, eyes, eyebrows.

b) Blanche's body parts are described in detail. We are told that her shoulders look *tall*, *fine*, and *sloping*, and that her complexion is *olive*, *dark*, and *clear*. The narrator uses evaluative adjectives to describe Blanche's neck, which is *long* and *graceful*, her eyes, which are *large*, *black*, and *brilliant*, and her hair, which is *fine*, *raven-black*, *arranged*, *longest*, and *glossiest*. The description is suggestive, and fragments Blanche's body for the male gaze. Bounderby's body parts, on the other hand, are described in less detail. In fact, the narrator describes only Bounderby's head parts. His head and forehead are qualified as *great* and *puffed*, the vein in his temple as *swelled*, and the skin to his face as *strained*. The body parts are not fragmented, and the description of head parts does not construct the male body as an object for the female gaze.

c) The description of the body parts of Blanche and Bounderby perpetuates a stereotypical construction of men and women. Men are described in less detail whereas women's bodies are fragmented for the male gaze.

The description of men's bodies focuses on physical strength, whereas the description of female bodies highlights sexual attractiveness and employs evaluative, even suggestive, vocabulary.

d) Answers may vary. What details are considered appropriate for inclusion in the culture to which the target children belong? What details are you leaving out? Why? Does the gender of the children affect your choices?

Chapter 6, Pragmatic Analysis of Drama

6.1

a) Kent starts by addressing King Lear as 'Royal Lear' and describes him as 'my king', 'my father', 'my master', and 'my great patron'. By using these endearment terms, Kent is appealing to King Lear's empathy and attempting to make Lear change his mind. When Lear turns Kent down, Kent soon strips Lear of his royal title and calls him by his first name (turns 2 and 4). He also describes him as 'mad', foolish and rash, and addresses him as 'old man'. The change in the terms of address corresponds to a change in power relations. Kent stands up in defiance of King Lear, which ultimately leads to his banishment from the kingdom.

b) There are three participants in this dramatic dialogue. King Lear has six turns, Kent seven turns and Cornwall just one turn. Although Kent has one turn more than Lear, no character can be said to be dominating in terms of the number of turns. In terms of turn length, however, Kent's turns run into thirty-four lines combined, compared with Lear's nineteen lines overall. Obviously, Kent holds the floor longer than King Lear. Lear interrupts Kent at the start of the extract, but from then onwards Kent is more dominant. He interrupts Lear midway through the dialogue, declines to carry out Lear's orders, and defies the king.

c) Analysis of speech acts underlines Kent's challenge of King Lear's authority. Lear makes at least six directive speech acts, unmitigated with any markers of politeness. Three of these are speech acts of order: 'Out of my sight' (line 21), 'turn thy hated back [u]pon our kingdom' (lines 43–4), and 'Away!' (line 46); the other three are speech acts of threat: 'make from the shaft' (line 5), 'on thy life, no more' (line 17), 'if, on the tenth day following [t]hy banish'd trunk be found in our dominions, [t]he moment is thy death' (lines 44–6). Kent is the recipient of all these speech acts but acts only upon the last two directives in lines 44–6.

Kent, on the other hand, makes three direct speech acts whose recipient is King Lear: 'Reverse thy doom' (line 11), 'check [t]his hideous rashness' (lines 12–13), and 'Revoke thy doom' (line 31). Because of the absence of any markers of politeness, these speech acts constitute a threat to King Lear's positive face. The face-threatening nature of these directive speech acts provokes King Lear into banishing Kent from the kingdom.

d) Both King Lear and Kent have a high involvement style. They both have a fast-paced speaking style with no pauses or hesitations. They also both interrupt each other in their competition for the floor.

6.2

a) There are four participants in this dramatic dialogue. Professor Higgins has eight turns, Liza six turns, Mrs Pearce one turn and Mr Pickering one turn. Higgins's turns are also longer than Liza's. Not only does Higgins hold the floor longer, he also controls it. He hands it over to Liza when he wants and takes it back (by way of interrupting Liza) when he wants.

b) There are five speech acts in this dialogue. The speech acts are all made bald on record with no use of markers of politeness. They are face-threatening. Three of these direct speech acts are made by Higgins: 'Hold your tongue', 'Somebody is going to touch you, with a broomstick, if you don't stop snivelling', and 'Sit down'. The other two direct speech acts are made by Mrs Pearce: 'Don't cry, you silly girl', and 'Sit down.' The recipient of all five speech acts is Liza. Liza's compliance with all the speech acts reflects the social power difference between her and the other participants in the dialogue. She is dominated by Professor Higgins and also by Mrs Pearce, who makes two directive speech acts in the only conversational turn she has in the dialogue.

c) Professor Higgins has a high involvement style. His speaking style is a fast-paced style with no pauses or hesitations. He holds the floor for a long time, and hands it over and takes it back from Liza at will. Liza's style, by contrast, is high considerateness. There is a long gap between her turns, and she neither interrupts nor overlaps the other characters. These styles sustain the power difference between the two characters.

d) If Liza and Professor Higgins had equal social power, they would have a more or less equal number of turns and turns of a similar length. Higgins would also mitigate his bald-on-record speech acts in order to lessen the threat to Liza's face. Liza would be making mitigated speech acts as well. The two speakers would compete for the floor and their speech styles would be high-considerate. (The rewritten conversations may vary.)

Chapter 7, Cognitive Analysis of Linguistic Humour

7.1

1) **TEACHER:** The Mississippi River flows in which state?
STUDENT: Liquid.
Set-up The Mississippi River flows in which state?
Punchline Liquid

Linguistic element in the set-up that creates ambiguity   The polysemous noun 'state'.
Interpretation (1a)   The Mississippi River flows in which US state?
Interpretation (1b)   The Mississippi River flows in which state of matter?
Which interpretation yields positive cognitive effects? How is this achieved?   Interpretation (1a) yields positive cognitive effects because it easily interacts with cognitive assumptions about US geography and rivers.
Which interpretation is obtained for the minimum justifiable processing effort? How is this achieved?   Interpretation (1a) is obtained for the minimum processing effort. The use of 'Mississippi river' alongside 'flow' and 'state' makes the processing effort required to derive (1a) minimal.
Which interpretation is revealed to be intended in the punchline?   Interpretation (1b).
Is the intended interpretation consistent with the principle of relevance?   No it is not. It takes unjustifiably extra processing effort to derive (1b).

2) **TEACHER:** How can you prevent diseases caused by biting insects?
JOSE: Don't bite any.
Set-up   How can you prevent diseases caused by biting insects?
Punchline   Don't bite any.
Linguistic element in the set-up that creates ambiguity   The syntactic category of the word 'biting'. It may be an adjective qualifying the noun 'insects' and making up an NP; it may also be a verb whose object is 'insects' and subject unrevealed.
Interpretation (2a)   How can you prevent diseases caused by biting (adjective) insects (noun)? 'Biting insects' is a noun phrase here.
Interpretation (2b)   How can you prevent diseases caused by biting (verb) insects (object of verb)? 'Biting insects' is a verb phrase here.
Which interpretation yields positive cognitive effects? How is this achieved?   Interpretation (2a). There is an easily accessible context in which (2a) has a manifestly adequate range of contextual effects. This interpretation easily interacts with cognitive assumptions about insects.
Which interpretation is obtained for the minimum justifiable processing effort? How is this achieved?   Interpretation (2a) is obtained for minimal processing effort because of the use of the word 'disease' alongside 'insects'.
Which interpretation is revealed to be intended in the punchline?   Interpretation (2b).
Is the intended interpretation consistent with the principle of relevance?   No it is not. The reader/listener requires extra processing effort to search for relevance in (2b).

3) **A:** How do you make a turtle fast?
B: Take away his food.
Set-up   How do you make a turtle fast?
Punchline   Take away his food.

Linguistic element in the set-up that creates ambiguity The word 'fast' may be an adjective meaning 'quick' or a verb meaning 'to eat no food for a particular period of time'.
Interpretation (3a) How do you make a turtle quick?
Interpretation (3b) How do you make a turtle not eat food for a particular period of time?
Which interpretation yields positive cognitive effects? How is this achieved? Interpretation (3a) yields positive cognitive effects. It easily interacts with cognitive assumptions about turtles being slow.
Which interpretation is obtained for the minimum justifiable processing effort? How is this achieved? Interpretation (3a) is obtained for the minimum processing effort. The use of 'turtle' alongside 'fast' minimises the processing effort required to derive (3a).
Which interpretation is revealed to be intended in the punchline? Interpretation (3b).
Is the intended interpretation consistent with the principle of relevance? No it is not. Extra processing effort is required in order to work out the relevance in (3b).

4) **POSTMASTER:** Here is your five-cent stamp.
   SHOPPER: Do I have to stick it on myself?
   POSTMASTER: No, sir. On the envelope, please.
   Set-up Do I have to stick it on myself?
   Punchline No, sir. On the envelope, please.
   Linguistic element in the set-up that creates ambiguity The preposition 'on' may be a particle for the verb 'stick' or the head preposition in the prepositional phrase 'on myself'.
   Interpretation (4a) Do I have to stick on the stamp myself? (Do I have to do it myself?)
   Interpretation (4b) Do I have to stick the stamp on myself? (Do I have to stick it on me?)
   Which interpretation yields positive cognitive effects? How is this achieved? Interpretation (4a) yields positive cognitive effects because it easily interacts with cognitive assumptions the use of stamps at the post office.
   Which interpretation is obtained for the minimum justifiable processing effort? How is this achieved? Interpretation (4a) is obtained for the minimum processing effort. The fact that the phrase 'five-cent stamp' is uttered by a postmaster makes the processing effort required to derive (4a) minimal.
   Which interpretation is revealed to be intended in the punchline? Interpretation (4b).
   Is the intended interpretation consistent with the principle of relevance? No it is not. The reader/listener requires extra processing effort to search for relevance in (2b).

5) **TEACHER:** Where was the Declaration of Independence signed?
   STUDENT: At the bottom of the page.

Set-up Where was the Declaration of Independence signed?
Punchline At the bottom of the page.
Linguistic element in the set-up that creates ambiguity The question word 'where'.
Interpretation (5a) In which building/city/state was the Declaration of Independence signed?
Interpretation (5b) On which part of the page was the Declaration of Independence signed?
Which interpretation yields positive cognitive effects? How is this achieved? Interpretation (5a) yields positive cognitive effects. It easily interacts with cognitive assumptions about the importance of time and location when signing historic documents.
Which interpretation is obtained for the minimum justifiable processing effort? How is this achieved? Interpretation (5a) is obtained for the minimum processing effort. The use of 'Declaration of Independence' alongside 'signed' minimises the processing effort required to derive (5a).
Which interpretation is revealed to be intended in the punchline? Interpretation (5b).
Is the intended interpretation consistent with the principle of relevance? No it is not. Extra processing effort is required in order to work out the relevance in (5b).

Chapter 8, Multimodal Analysis of Advertisements

8.1
1) The Advil advert
   a) The use of 'clogged nose' restricts the scope of addressee to people with clogged noses who wish to have them cleared. The use of a question posits this target audience in the position of answerer. The likely answer is 'yes'. This creates a 'virtual' conversational exchange that ends with the advice in the second part of the advert's verbal text.
   b) The use of an elliptical question creates an effect of familiarity. The advertiser is constructed as familiar with the intended audience's health issue and, therefore, in a good position to suggest medical advice.
   c) The advice is 'Get Advil'. This is a directive speech act unmitigated with any markers of politeness. The choice of a directive with no politeness markers makes the command sound more beneficial to the target audience than to the advertising company, as in 'grab a free pizza before we run out'.
   d) The visual contains an action process. Plunging the clogged nose forms the vector in the advert. The young man's hand pulling the plunger is the actor and the clogged nose is the goal.
   e) It is a close shot. The use of a close-up shot creates a feeling of 'closeness'. Nasal blockage is not unlikely and could happen to anyone in the audience.

f) It is a formally stylised photograph. The colours are articulated. Red is used for the verbal text and the plunger head, which serves to link them to the red packet of Advil. The saturation of the red colour in all these places serves to heighten the suggestion of strength of the pain reliever.

g) The young man with the clogged nose is positioned in the lower left-hand side of the photograph, thereby constructed as real and given. The Advil product is positioned in the lower right-hand side of the photograph, thereby constructed as real and new. It is a new solution to a common health issue.

h) The elliptical verbal question and the close-up shot construct the advertiser as though they were familiar with the health issue of the target audience. The saturation of the red colour in the verbal and visual texts underscores the strength of the pain killer. The vector and the directive speech act call upon the intended audience to buy the product and get relief from nasal blockage.

2) The United Way Movement advert

a) The verbal texts in this advert and in advert 2 in the chapter are identical. The analysis of the verbal text in advert 2 in the chapter is, therefore, applicable here.

b) Suggested verbal text: When it gets cold, they need you. Donate now! (Answers may vary.)

c) There is an action process in the visual. The vector is realised by the extended hand forming a horizontal line across the photograph. The actor is the heavy rain and the goal is the homeless young person sleeping on the street.

d) It is a long shot. Long shots position the viewer as socially distant.

e) It is a frontal angle that invites audience involvement.

f) It is a non-modalised expression of the dangers of living on the streets.

g) The stretched hand is positioned in the upper half of the photograph, thereby constructed as ideal, while the homeless young person sleeping on the street is positioned in the lower half of the photograph, thereby constructed as real. The suffering of the homeless is real and the intervention to protect them is an ideal to attain.

h) The non-modalised photograph presents an authentic account of the dangerous life of the homeless. The long shot suggests that the audience is distant from the suffering of the homeless. The frontal angle, along with the big-sized capitalised verbal text, urge the audience to get actively involved.

Chapter 9, Critical Stylistic Analysis of Political Discourse

9.1 The relationship between the United States and Libya under Qaddafi was always turbulent, with harsh rhetoric used against each other. In fact, Obama took action (economic sanctions) on Libya before releasing the statement on 25 February 2011.

a) Qaddafi is mentioned twice in the statement, 'Muammar el-Qaddafi' and 'Qaddafi'. He is mentioned by name and stripped of his presidential title. In both appearances, reference is to his government rather than to him as president.
b) Obama's verbal assault on the Libyan government is all packaged inside NPs and passed more as assumed information than questionable propositions. The government's 'continued violation of human rights, brutalisation of its people, and outrageous threats' are presented as given knowledge which is not contestable. So is the 'strong and broad' condemnation of these repressive practices by the international community. Obama also takes the liberty of describing the reaction of the international community, which is qualified as 'rightly' drawn. These assumed violations and the assumed international consensus serve to legitimise the planned intervention in Libya, which had already been in motion at the time of this statement.
c) Obama's inclination to use action is borne out by the patterns of causality in the statement. Material action verbs (MAI and MAE processes), and the concomitant choice of semantic roles, constitute the predominant transitivity and agency choice in the statement, which reflects the US attitude towards the embattled regime. In these processes, the Libyan government is projected as agent of violation of human rights, of international norms, and of common decency. It is also agent of brutalisation, outrageous threats, and the denial of human dignity. The United States is agent of coordinated action against the Libyan government and of support of the Libyan people. Neither the Libyan government, the Libyan people, nor the US are structured in any verbalisation, mental, or relational processes. It is action throughout.
d) The statement does not have a complex web of subordination, which reflects clarity of ideological priorities. The first sentence, using noun phrase modification, prioritises the brutality and inhumanity of the Libyan government; the second prioritises the government's violation of international norms and common decency; the third prioritises the action taken against this government; the fourth prioritises coordination towards more action; the fifth prioritises solidarity with the Libyan people; and the last sentence uses passive transformation to prioritise the human dignity of the Libyan people. This choice carries forward Obama's ideological outlook on Qaddafi and intention to intervene militarily.
e) Other linguistic choices extend this ideological outlook. The phrase 'continue to closely coordinate' logically presupposes existing close coordination between the US and the international community. The participants in this community are enumerated by Obama: 'our friends and allies, and the United Nations'. The protestors against this regime are not identified as people with socio-economic grievances but equated with all the Libyan people, which serves to heighten the regime's isolation. And modality completes the picture. Except for two modal verbs,

the statement's message is communicated in non-modalised assertions. The two modalised propositions use a high-value deontic modal of obligation 'must' and a median-value epistemic modal of certainty 'will'. The overall tone of the statement reflects a strong degree of assertive and committed attitude, which is consistent with our remarks in answer to the previous questions.

f) Use the Libyan statement to guide your rewriting of the Tunisian statement.

Chapter 10, Corpus Analysis of Online Journalism

10.1 The top twenty collocates of *Islamic* in the English Web 2018 (enTenTen18) and Arabic Web 2012 (arTenTen12, Stanford Tagger) corpora can be found in Figures 10.1 and 10.2, respectively, and therefore will not be repeated. Below is a discussion of collocates 11 to 20 in English Web 2018 (enTenTen18).

- The word *Iraq* is the next strongest collocate on the list. It has a logDice value higher than that of five other collocates in the top ten list. If you click on the three dots after logDice and choose *only this* to generate the concordance lines, you will find that the word *Iraq* is used consistently in the concordance lines in reference to the Islamic State.
- In addition to *Iraq*, six other collocates on this list are associated with militancy and armed aggression against individuals and modern states. These collocates are, in a descending order of logDice value, *radical, extremism, front, movement, ISIS,* and *caliphate*. A closer look at the concordance lines confirms this finding.
- The remaining three collocates, namely, *scholar, Sharia,* and *jurisprudence,* relate to Islamic teachings and Muslim scholars.
- The semantic field of violence still dominates the list of collocations but words related to Islamic law and scholarship find their way into the list.

Below is a discussion of collocates 11 to 20 in Arabic Web 2012 (arTenTen12).

- The word معتدل (*moderate*) is the next strongest collocate on the list, with a logDice value of 1.038.
- The next word is مصرف, which is a synonym of بنك (*bank*) that had already appeared in the sixth position on the list of top ten collocates.
- Two of the remaining eight collocates have negative connotations. These are no. 14 متطرف (*extremist*) and no. 19 متشدد (*hard-line*).
- The other six collocates relate to either national or international concerns (i.e. collocates 16, 17, and 20) or to religious or secular concerns (i.e. collocates 13, 15, and 15).
- Overall, the semantic fields, here and earlier, relate to religious, socio-economic, and political themes. Extremism and violence make a presence in the data but a presence that is marginal and negligible.

	Lemma	Cooccurrences	Candidates	T-score	MI	LogDice ↓
1	State	78,695	3,951,692	280.14	9.51	9.11
2	Republic	22,631	756,814	150.30	10.09	8.99
3	Jihad	8,684	41,609	93.18	12.90	8.57
4	extremist	8,559	159,515	92.47	10.94	8.34
5	fundamentalist	6,800	89,552	82.43	11.44	8.13
6	militant	7,040	212,274	83.84	10.24	7.97
7	fundamentalism	5,229	36,050	72.30	12.37	7.85
8	terrorist	9,758	754,244	98.57	8.89	7.77
9	terrorism	7,613	467,466	87.11	9.22	7.73
10	radical	8,466	673,743	91.81	8.84	7.65
11	extremism	4,479	72,093	66.90	11.15	7.56
12	scholar	7,287	1,019,085	85.04	8.03	7.11
13	revolution	6,297	855,853	79.06	8.07	7.05
14	jurisprudence	2,895	63,179	53.77	10.71	6.95
15	republic	3,188	172,203	56.38	9.40	6.89
16	Movement	3,165	187,534	56.17	9.27	6.86
17	caliphate	2,547	36,313	50.45	11.32	6.81
18	Studies	4,454	611,193	66.49	8.06	6.79
19	Revolutionary	2,436	106,318	49.30	9.71	6.62
20	Maghreb	2,044	9,846	45.20	12.89	6.55

FIGURE 10AK.1 Collocational behaviour of *Islamic* (range −1 to 1) in English Web 2018 (enTenTen18)

If we change the default range to −1 to 1, we get the list shown in Figure 10AK.1 in English Web 2018 (enTenTen18).

As Figure 10AK.1 indicates, the collocates are almost identical and the change in the KWIC range does not change the semantic fields associated with *Islamic* in the corpus in any significant way. (Islamic) *State, Republic, Jihad, extremist, extremism, militant, terrorist,* and *terrorism* are still high up on the

"terrorist" and/or ...		
Islamic	2,579	8.79
Islamic terrorist		
foreign	5,153	8.31
foreign terrorist		
suspected	1,068	8.29
suspected terrorist		
Islamist	780	8.23
Islamist terrorist groups		
Palestinian	1,260	8.05
Palestinian terrorist		
criminal	2,363	7.96
criminal and terrorist		
extremist	695	7.92
terrorist and extremist		
deadly	787	7.59
deadly terrorist attack		
Hamas	483	7.53
the Hamas terrorist organization		
insurgent	484	7.53
terrorist and insurgent		
alleged	710	7.29
alleged terrorist		
counter	442	7.27
counter terrorist financing		

FIGURE 10AK.2 Word Sketch of *terrorist* in English Web 2018 (enTen Ten18)

list of strong collocates. Iran disappears from the list, but *Republic, revolution,* and *revolutionary* bring it back on closer examination of the concordance lines.

10.2 Analysis of the collocation behaviour of *terrorist* in English Web 2018 (enTenTen18).
- The search word *terrorist* (as an adjective) returns 398,610 hits or occurrences in English Web 2018 (enTenTen18).
- The strongest collocate of *terrorist* in the corpus is *Islamic* with a logDice of 8.79.
- The second strongest collocate is *foreign*, with a logDice of 8.31. It is the collocate with the highest number of hits or occurrences in the corpus.
- The list of top ten collocates includes two words related to the religion of Islam, namely, *Islamic* and *Islamist*.

nouns and verbs modified by "good"		
faith	8.8	4.6
interest	8.1	4.7
practice	8.6	5.8
deal	9.3	7.2
example	8.9	7.2
reason	8.9	7.3
thing	6.6	8.5
job	6.7	8.9
idea	7.3	9.8
news	4.9	8.2
morning	–	8.4
boy	–	8.7

FIGURE 10AK.3 Comparison of the collocational behaviour of *good* in the written academic and spoken transcripts subcorpora of the British National Corpus (BNC)

- The list also includes two words related to an Arab country, namely, *Palestinian* and *Hamas*.
- No other faith or country appears in the list.

10.3 Comparison of the collocational behaviour of *good* in the written academic and spoken transcripts subcorpora of the British National Corpus (BNC).
- The collocates of the adjective *good* in written and spoken English are expectedly different. The difference results from the register variation (see Chapter 1 for more on register). This information is useful in writing dictionary entries and in the construction of dictionaries of collocation. The same search procedure may also be useful in comparing the collocational behaviour of a word in two different subcorpora. You could try comparing the collocational behaviour of *terrorist* in two subcorpora of English Web 2018 (enTenTen18). To do this, select the corpus and click *Word Sketch Difference* on the left-side panel on the main menu screen. Click on 'Advanced' and change the default option from 'lemmas' to 'subcorpora'. Type *terrorist* under 'lemma', select 'UK domain' as subcorpus number 1, select 'cnn.com' as subcorpus number 2, and select 'adjective' as the part of speech. Keep all other options unchanged and click 'go' to compare the collocational behaviour of the search word in the two subcorpora.

Chapter 11, The Story of Stylistics

11.1 Let's repeat e. e. cummings's lines for ease of reference.

Pity this busy monster, manunkind,
not. Progress is a comfortable disease

Readers are familiar with the word 'mankind'. It is a noun composed of two nouns 'man' and 'kind' and is used to refer to 'humanity'. This automatised conception of 'mankind' is challenged by cummings's use of the prefix 'un-' before the second word 'kind'. According to word formation rules in English, adjectives, adverbs, and verbs can take the prefix 'un-'; nouns normally do not. Our expectations of the morphological structure of 'mankind' is defeated, making us rethink not only the syntactic category of 'kind' in the compound 'mankind' but the meaning of this part of the compound. By defamiliarising the automatised conception of the morphological structure of 'mankind', cummings defamiliarises the automatised conception of the meanings of component nouns, or at least the second one.

11.2
- a) It was inspired by formalism. *Practical criticism and new criticism*
- b) It attempted to offer a less 'impressionistic' model of literary studies. *Practical criticism and new criticism*
- c) It started in Britain. *Practical criticism*
- d) It started in America. *New criticism*
- e) It started in the 1920s. *Practical criticism*
- f) It started in the 1940s. *New criticism*
- g) It focused on the text. *Practical criticism and new criticism*

11.3
- a) It was popular in the 1960s in the USA. *Formalist stylistics*
- b) It was popular in the 1980s in Britain. *Functionalist stylistics*
- c) It was influenced by Chomsky's view of language as a mental phenomenon.
  Formalist stylistics
- d) It was influenced by Halliday's view of language as a social phenomenon.
  Functionalist stylistics
- e) It viewed style as deviation from an underlying form. *Formalist stylistics*
- f) It viewed style as choice from available options. *Functionalist stylistics*
- g) It showed an interest in analysis of language in context. *Functionalist stylistics*
- h) It mostly analysed poetry and prose. *Formalist stylistics*
- i) It analysed poetry, prose, and drama. *Functionalist stylistics*
- j) It was criticised for assigning meanings to forms. *Formalist stylistics (Fish criticised both for this)*
- k) It asserted that only linguistic forms with functional significance are relevant to interpretation. *Functionalist stylistics*

11.4
- a) It draws on theories of the human mind. *Cognitive stylistics*
- b) It draws on systemic functional linguistics. *Critical and pragmatic stylistics*

c) It is computer-aided.   *Corpus stylistics*
d) It focuses more on readers than on texts.   *Cognitive stylistics*
e) It investigates authorial ideologies and power relations in texts.   *Critical stylistics (also pragmatic and corpus stylistics)*
f) It focuses on dramatic conversation.   *Pragmatic stylistics (all other three, too)*
g) Analysis is qualitative and quantitative.   *Corpus stylistics*
h) It analyses large collections of texts.   *Corpus stylistics*

11.5 The use of images would be well received by the (student) readers, who find pictures everywhere they go, physically and online. It is a welcome visual stimulus that would enhance the reader-friendliness of the chapter layout. The overall appeal of the chapter would certainly improve if pictures were added. So would the level of engagement with the content of the chapter, especially if the pictures were selected with care so that all the stylisticians in the pictures were gazing either at the reader or at the text to be read, thus inviting engagement with the scholars and their contribution to the field. The effect of the pictures would be enhanced if they were close-ups, which would create an intimate connection with the scholars and, if they were not disconnected by frames, would enhance the sense of engagement with the story of stylistics.

GLOSSARY[1]

affective stylistics
a reaction to narrow text-oriented literary criticism. Advocated by Stanley Fish in the 1970s, affective stylistics, aka reader response stylistics, foregrounds the mental operations involved in the process of 'making', not discovering, meaning, by the reader.

alliteration
a stylistic device that involves the repetition of the same initial consonant sounds in two or more nearby words. Alliteration is employed for foregrounding effect, serving to highlight concepts by phonologically linking the words representing them. For example, *The fair breeze blew, the white foam flew.*

assonance
a stylistic device that involves the repetition of the same vowel sounds, usually in stressed syllables, in two or more nearby words. Assonance is employed for foregrounding effect, serving to highlight concepts by phonologically linking the words representing them. For example, *The early bird catches the worm.*

bald on record
a speech act that is bald on record is direct and makes no effort to lessen the impact of the threat to the recipient's face.

clause
a grammatical stretch of words with a subject and a finite verb. A clause may be independent forming part of a sentence, as in *Jim is studying English because he wants to become an English teacher*, and may be dependent forming a sentence on its own, as in *Jim is studying English.*

close reading
a technique of text analysis, popularised by practical critics in Britain and adopted by new critics in America, that involves careful and sustained

---

[1] Wales, K. [1990] (2011), *A Dictionary of Stylistics*, 3rd edn, Pearson, offers a comprehensive glossary of key terms.

reading of text only, with little regard to authorial intentions or reader psychology.

cognitive poetics
a branch of stylistics that draws on cognitive theories to account for the conceptual processes involved in reading literary texts.

cognitive stylistics
a stylistic trend that adopts cognitive linguistic theories to investigate how readers construct textual meanings.

cohesion of foregrounding
refers to the way the foregrounded features identified in isolation are brought together in the interpretation of the whole text.

collocation
the habitual co-occurrence of words. For example, the verb *deliver* tends to occur with *lecture* but not with *operation*. We say that *deliver* and *lecture* collocate.

complex sentence
a sentence which contains an independent clause and one or more dependent clauses, as in *Because the weather was good, Mary went out and took the children to a park*.

compound sentence
a sentence which contains two or more coordinated independent clauses, as in *Mary is poor but she is generous*.

computational linguistics
the use of computational models to model the production and comprehension of natural languages.

conceptual blending
a theoretical framework within cognitive stylistics whose concern is with the description of the cognitive processes involved in meaning creation. The idea is that two or more input spaces, or conceptual frames, seemingly unrelated, are brought together or integrated, resulting in a new conceptual structure. This new emergent meaning is a blend. For example, in *The smart phone has knocked out the feature phone* there are two input spaces, one relating to phones and the other to boxing. Relevant features from each input space are selected and integrated into a new blended space in which the phones are seen as boxers fighting to win a match. The conceptual blending theory also goes by the names blending theory and integration theory.

conceptual metaphor theory
views metaphors as a property of concepts rather than words. According to the theory, a particular concept (also called a target domain) is mapped onto a different concept (called a source domain). For example, in *John attacked my claims and won the debate* the terminology of war (the source domain) is mapped onto the target domain of argument, thereby creating a conceptual metaphor of argument as war.

conversational implicatures
extra meanings that result from the non-observance by an utterance of the maxims of conversation in certain contexts.

cooperative principle
a principle of conversation that was proposed by H. P. Grice in 1975. It

says that speakers structure their utterances in such a way that the hearers understand them. They give enough information (quantity), tell the truth (quality), are relevant to the context (relation), and are clear (manner).

corpus
a very large collection of samples of (spoken and written) texts compiled to represent a particular language, dialect, or genre, and stored in electronic form.

corpus linguistics
a branch of computational linguistics which is concerned with the investigation of language patterning and use in huge, electronically stored, collections of naturally occurring language, both spoken and written.

corpus stylistics
a stylistic trend that adopts corpus linguistic methods in the study of style in literary and non-literary texts.

critical discourse analysis
a development from critical linguistics popularised in the 1980s by Norman Fairclough. It investigates the way(s) texts encode and reproduce dominance and social power, and it aims at promoting resistance to social inequality.

critical linguistics
refers to the work of Roger Fowler and other colleagues in the late 1970s, who draw on analytical concepts and methods from M. A. K. Halliday's systemic functional linguistics in order to examine the relationship between language and social meanings, and the linguistic construction of ideological meanings.

critical stylistics
a later development in stylistics introduced by Lesley Jeffries (2010), which expands the analytical tools of critical linguistics and critical discourse analysis into a more comprehensive set of tools for the investigation of the power of texts (written and spoken) to pass on implicit ideologies and manipulate the ideological outlooks of the audience.

defamiliarisation
the effect a work of art has on readers, namely, presenting a familiar thing or concept as if it were new. This is achieved via deviation, parallelism, and repetition (see **foregrounding**).

deixis
refers to words or phrases (such as *this*, *that*, *now*, *then*, and *here*) that are understood only with reference to the time, place, or context of speaking or writing.

deviation
the breaking of normal rules of linguistic structure at the different levels of the language system.

dialect
a variety of a language used in one part of a country (regional dialect), or by the people of a particular social class (social dialect) or ethnicity (ethnic dialect), whose words, grammar, and/or pronunciation varies from other forms of the same language.

discourse
refers to stretches of language larger than a sentence, such as paragraphs, conversations, articles, interviews, and so on.

discourse stylistics
a term popularised in the late 1980s to denote a trend in stylistic scholarship characterised by a move away from formalist towards contextualised stylistic analysis. The trend includes critical and pragmatic stylistics.

existential presupposition
refers to the assumption of the existence of the entities named or described by the speaker. Existential presuppositions are triggered by definite noun phrases, as in *The school principal is tall*, and by possessive constructions, as in *My daughter is sick*.

face
is one of the concepts associated with the politeness theory according to which every language user has basic wants. The first is the need to feel appreciated, which is called *positive face*; the second is the need to have one's actions unimpeded by others, which is known as *negative face*.

feminist stylistics
a stylistic trend that adopts Halliday's functional grammar for the investigation of the representation, and ideological evaluation, of women in male-authored texts.

field
the topic of the conversation or text that influences the choice of language, such as the field of politics, advertising, chemistry, aviation, and so on.

foregrounding
a textual strategy by means of which a part of a text is made more prominent against the background of the norms of ordinary language.

formalist stylistics
a stylistic trend whose roots are traceable to the Russian formalists (see **Russian formalism**). Like Russian theoreticians, formalist stylisticians were interested in the linguistic structure (or form) of literary texts, especially poetry, and in the differences between literary and non-literary language, principally the effect of defamiliarisation, which is linguistically achieved through deviation, repetition, and parallelism.

functionalist stylistics
a stylistic trend that is based on Halliday's functional grammar and views stylistic variation in texts as a result of authorial choices that are ideologically motivated.

generative grammar
a linguistic theory advanced by Noam Chomsky in the 1950s. It considers grammar a mental phenomenon, consisting of a set of rules that generates an infinite number of sentences.

generative stylistics
a stylistic trend that adopts Noam Chomsky's theory of generative grammar, and views stylistic variation in texts (or surface structures) as a result of the application of transformational rules to underlying (or deep) structures.

genre
a discourse type that has distinctive patterns of organisation and communicative functions (e.g. business reporting has patterns of textual organisation and communicative functions different than those of the poetry genre).

graphology
: refers to the writing system of a language and the rules that govern handwriting and typography, such as punctuation, font size, capitalisation, and so on.

high considerateness style
: a conversational style in interpersonal communication that is characterised by a relatively slower pace, longer pauses between turns and little or no overlap and interruption. A character that uses this style is often regarded as hesitant, reserved, or even incompetent.

high involvement style
: a conversational style in interpersonal communication that is characterised by a faster pace, little to no pauses between the turns, and some overlap or even completion of others' turns. A character that uses this style is often regarded as assertive, dominant, or even pushy.

ideology
: a particular point of view concerning the ideas, beliefs, and values in a particular culture or society.

implicature
: a meaning that is not explicitly stated but is inferred from an utterance. For example, the speaker in *Mary is married but unhappy* implies that happiness is an expected consequence of marriage. This implicature is drawn from the use of *but* in the utterance, but is not literally stated in the sentence.

lexical semantics
: the study of meaning (or sense) relations between words and sentences.

literariness
: the creative use of language that is marked by deviations, parallelisms, and repetitions. Some scholars argue that this is a property of only literary texts such as poetry, and some argue it is present in all text types. Guy Cook ([1992] 2001) suggests that the literariness of a text is not based on its linguistic features but on its potential to defamiliarise reality.

linguistic stylistics
: refers to research work in stylistics which aims at testing or refining linguistic theory rather than describing the aesthetic effects of literary texts.

logical presupposition
: refers to the speaker's assumption of something being true or being part of shared knowledge between the speaker and hearer. Logical presuppositions may be triggered by factive verbs, as in *I did not know that John came*, iterative word, as in *Mary is late again*, or change-of-state verbs, as in *Jim's boss has become very demanding*. The first sentence presupposes that John came, the second presupposes that Mary was late before, and the third sentence presupposes that Jim's boss was not as demanding in the past.

maxims of conversation
: four principles of cooperation, proposed by H. P. Grice, that govern everyday communication. These are the maxims of quality (make a contribution that is true), quantity (make your contribution as informative as required), relation (make a relevant contribution), and manner (make an ambiguity-free contribution).

metre
   refers to the regular patterning of stressed and unstressed syllables in poetry, and even in conventional forms of communication such as advertisements, riddles, songs, and (political) slogans.

modality
   refers to the use of auxiliary verbs (e.g. should), nouns (e.g. possibility), verbs (e.g. doubt), adjectives (e.g. likely), and adverbs (e.g. definitely) which indicate the attitude of the speaker or writer towards the proposition expressed.

mode
   the medium in which language is used and which influences the choice of vocabulary and structures, such as spoken and written language.

morpheme
   the smallest unit in language that has meaning or grammatical function and that cannot be divided further.

morphology
   the study of the internal patterning of words: the way roots and affixes combine to make words. For example, the word *unhappiness* is formed from the noun-forming suffix *-ness* and the negative prefix *-un* attaching to the root *happy*.

multimodal stylistics
   a stylistic trend that adopts Gunther Kress and Theo van Leeuwen's visual grammar, which is based on M. A. K. Halliday's systemic functional linguistics. It describes the way visual semiotic modes such as page layout, typography, colours, and images interact with each other and with language to create meaning and effect.

musicology
   a multidisciplinary academic approach to the study of music. It views music as action in relation to society, culture, history, media, and gender.

neologism
   a new word, phrase, or expression invented by users of a language in response to advances in science and technology (e.g. 'e-commerce') or in response to contextual demands in literature (e.g. 'manunkind' by e. e. cummings). The first set of neologisms often finds its way into dictionaries; the second does not.

New Criticism
   a literary critical approach to literary text interpretation that was popularised in America by Cleanth Brooks and Robert Warren in the 1940s. The approach builds on Practical Criticism and shares its theoretical arguments, but it de-emphasises concern with readers' emotional and psychological reactions.

nominalisation
   a process of word formation whereby a suffix is added to a verb in order to derive a noun, as in *expansion* from *expand*.

pedagogical stylistics
   a stylistic trend that uses stylistic analysis as a teaching tool in language and literature classrooms for native and non-native speakers of English.

phrase
   a grammatical stretch of words, without a finite verb, which is classified after its head word. A noun phrase, for example, is headed by a noun (e.g. *the blue car*).

politeness
refers to the use of language to signal closeness or intimacy between speaker and hearer (positive politeness) or to show awareness of the listener's right to freedom of action (negative politeness). Markers of positive politeness include, among others, the use of compliments (*Lovely cap. Can I try it on?*), and claiming common ground (*It has been a long day and we must be hungry. Let us go eat.*) Markers of negative politeness, on the other hand, include the use of hedging expressions to minimise the threat of the imposition (*I wonder if you could help me move this desk.*) and acknowledging the imposition and apologising for it (*I am sorry I am calling at this time but I need to talk to you.*).

politeness theory
a pragmatic theory of communication proposed by Penelope Brown and Stephen C. Levinson. Central to the theory are the concepts of positive face (the need to feel appreciated) and negative face (the need to have freedom to act). When we make any request, we compromise the hearer's negative face. Our speech act is face-threatening, which may be mitigated with politeness markers in order to save the hearer's face, or left unmitigated, depending on, among other factors, the social power difference between the hearer and speaker.

Practical Criticism
a literary critical approach to literary text interpretation that was popularised in Britain by I. A. Richards in the 1920s. Based on the formalist literary theory, the approach argues that meaning is a property of the text (not author) and describes the way readers' interaction with the text reflects on their emotions and thoughts.

pragmatic stylistics
a stylistic trend that uses pragmatic theories in investigating speaker meaning in dramatic texts/conversations.

Prague linguistic circle
a group of linguists and literary critics who met in Prague in the 1920s in order to develop a new method of literary analysis informed by structural linguistics. The group includes, among others, the Russian formalist Roman Jakobson and Czech literary scholars Jan Mukařovský and Viktor Shklovsky. The circle has a significant and continuing influence on linguistics, and is credited with the influential notion of foregrounding.

principle of relevance
a principle developed by Dan Sperber and Deirdre Wilson as part of the theoretical framework for utterance interpretation known as relevance theory. According to the principle, an utterance is optimally relevant if it yields enough positive cognitive effects (i.e. if it combines with, strengthens, or contradicts existing schemata) for the least processing effort by the recipient.

reader response stylistics
see **affective stylistics**.

register
a variety of language defined according to the situation.

relevance theory
    a pragmatic and cognitive theory for understanding human communication according to which a communicator provides evidence of their intended meaning, which is inferred by their audience on the basis of the linguistic evidence provided.

rhyme
    refers to the repetition of an identical, or similar, sound or sequence of sounds in the final stressed syllable of two words, especially at the end of lines in poems.

rhythm
    the regular patterns of stressed and unstressed syllables. It is often a feature of poetry but it is also found in non-literary works such as advertisements, jokes, and proverbs.

Russian formalism
    refers to a school of literary criticism in the early twentieth century in Russia whose main focus was on literariness, that is, the qualities that distinguish literary language from ordinary language. Russian formalists also sought to make literary analysis less vague and less impressionistic by basing it on the exact categories of linguistics.

schema theory
    a cognitive theory underlined by the idea that meaning is not a property of texts but is instead built up by the reader by way of accommodating incoming knowledge within existing conceptual knowledge and mental pictures of the world. Knowledge of the world is stored in the human mind in terms of packages, or schemata, which are continually enriched, or even challenged, in response to incoming knowledge in the act of reading.

semantics
    the study of meaning in language.

semiotics
    the study of the different signs used in communication (also known as semiotic systems). Semiotic systems may be linguistic (e.g. human language), visual (e.g. colour and page or screen layout), audio (e.g. voice loudness, pitch, and rhythm), gestural (e.g. facial gestures and body movement), or spatial (e.g. the positioning of the viewer vis-à-vis the participants in the text or image).

simple sentence
    a sentence which contains only one clause, such as *Mary is smart*.

slang
    refers to a subset of the vocabulary, and grammar, of a language used, often in speaking, by a particular group of people in restricted contexts.

sociolect
    refers to a variety of language associated with a particular demographic group such as different social classes, or women vs men (Biber 1995).

speech act
    refers to the use of language to perform 'acts'. For example, if someone says *Turn down that TV immediately*, they have performed the speech act of ordering. Other speech acts include offering *Would you like a cup of coffee?*, requesting *Can*

you pass the salad?, recommending *Style 101 is the right course for you at this stage*, apologising *I am sorry I couldn't come*, accusing *You stole my wallet*, prohibiting *No overtaking!*, thanking *Thank you*, greeting *Good morning*, leave-taking *Good night!*, congratulating *Congratulations on the promotion!*, promising *I will buy you a car when you graduate!*, condoling *I was sorry to hear about your loss*, and so on.

speech act theory
a theory of language use, associated with J. L. Austin, which is concerned with the pragmatic effect of utterances. According to the theory, an utterance such as *It is very hot in here!* gives information about temperature but could have the 'force' of an indirect request to turn on the air conditioner. The 'effect' of the utterance is the result of the indirect speech act.

speech community
refers to a group of people who share a variety of language as well as the conventions and expectations about its use.

speech situation
the non-linguistic context of interaction. The elements of a speech situation include the participants and their social roles, the setting (time and place), the topic and purpose of interaction, and the mode in which the interaction is delivered. Our choice of language is affected by the elements of the speech situation.

stanza
a group of lines in a poem that forms a unit and is often set off from the other units by a blank line.

style
variation in a language user's speech or writing in response to user-specific factors such as age or gender, and situation-specific factors such as the topic, relationship between speaker and hearer, or the medium of interaction.

stylistics
the study of style in language.

systemic functional linguistics
a linguistic theory by M. A. K. Halliday in the 1970s. It views language as a network of systems, with options available to the language user at every point of each system.

syntax
concerns the way words, phrases, and clauses are ordered and grouped to form sentences in a language, and the rules which govern the formation of these sentences.

tenor
refers to the relationship between the participants in the discourse, which influences the choice of vocabulary and structures.

text world theory
a cognitive linguistic approach to discourse analysis according to which the reader is 'transported' into the text world, rather than looking on as an outsider. A discourse is processed through mental world creation. It constructs text worlds, or mental images, in the reader's mind, including images of the discourse world (the most immediate situation that includes the text, its sender,

and its receiver) and the text world (the mental image of the communicative event constructed by the discourse recipient).

transitivity
refers to the choices made by the speaker or writer to represent world-views. These choices include three elements in the clause: processes (choosing a verb of action, event, or state), participants (placing people in relation to the process), and circumstances (expressions of time, place, or manner). These choices are often linked to the author's ideological outlook on the world.

turn management
refers to the order of turns in (dramatic) conversation. Turn-taking is generally smooth, with the turn-holder giving the floor to the next participant when their turn is over. There may be conflict at turn changeover, however. The turn-holder may wish to keep the floor longer and deny others their turns; they may also get interrupted. Turn-taking strategies and conflict for the floor contribute to understanding the dramatic situation and the relation between characters.

typography
refers to the visual representation of the printed text on the page or screen. There is a growing interest in the meanings created by the use of upper-case letters, italics, boldface, and other typographic features.

vector
a spatial line that represents the process of interaction between two objects in a visual.

REFERENCES

Accent Bias Britain (n.d.), 'Accents in Britains', <https://accentbiasbritain.org/accents-in-britain/> (last accessed 4 October 2021).

Alaghbary, G. S. (2014), 'The United States' reaction to the Arab Spring: A critical stylistic analysis', *Journal of Language Aggression and Conflict*, 2(1), 151–75, <https://doi.org/10.1075/jlac.2.1.06ala> (last accessed 23 September 2021).

Alaghbary, G. S. (2019), 'Ideological positioning in conflict: The United States and Egypt's domestic political trajectory', in M. Evans, L. Jeffries and J. O'Driscoll (eds), *The Routledge Handbook of Language in Conflict*, Routledge, pp. 83–102.

Alonso-Almeida, F. and M. I. González-Cruz (2012), 'Exploring male and female voices through epistemic modality and evidentiality in some modern English travel texts on the Canaries', *Research in Language*, 10(3), 323–43, <https://doi.org/10.2478/v10015-011-0031-z> (last accessed 23 September 2021).

Atwood, M. (2011), *The Handmaid's Tale*, Penguin Random House UK.

Austin, J. (1962), *How to Do Things with Words*, Harvard University Press.

Biber, D. (1995), *Dimensions of Register Variation: A Cross-Linguistic Comparison*, Cambridge University Press.

Biber, D. and S. Conrad (2009), *Register, Genre, and Style*, Cambridge University Press.

Biber, D., S. Johansson, G. Leech, S. Conrad and E. Finegan (1999), *Longman Grammar of Spoken and Written English*, Pearson Education.

Black, E. (2006), *Pragmatic Stylistics*, Edinburgh University Press.

Borgogni, D. (2016), '"The thick and black clouds of Obloquie": Modality and point of view in Abiezer Coppe's "A Remonstrance"', *Open Linguistics*, 2(1), <https://doi.org/10.1515/opli-2016-0035> (last accessed 23 September 2021).

Bradford, R. (1997), *Stylistics*, Routledge.

Brontë, C. [1846] (2003), *Jane Eyre*, Penguin Classics.

Brooks, C. and R. Warren (1938), *Understanding Poetry*, Holt, Rinehart and Winston.

Brooks, J. (2009), 'The growing absurdity of the South African apartheid: Transitivity in Christopher Van Wyk's "In Detention"', *Innervate*, 2, 26–34.

Brown, P. and S. Levinson (1987), *Politeness: Some Universals in Language Use*, Cambridge University Press.

Brumfit, C. and R. Carter (eds) (1986), *Literature and Language Teaching*, Oxford University Press.
Burke, M. (ed.) (2014), *The Routledge Handbook of Stylistics*, Routledge.
Burton, D. (1982), 'Through glass darkly: Through dark glasses', in R. Carter (ed.), *Language and Literature: An Introductory Reader in Stylistics*, George Allen & Unwin, pp. 195–214.
Carter, R. (1986), 'Linguistic models, language, and literariness: Study strategies in the teaching of literature to foreign students', in C. Brumfit and R. Carter (eds), *Literature and Language Teaching*, Oxford University Press, pp. 110–32.
Carter, R. (1989), 'What is stylistics and why can we teach it in different ways?', in M. Short (ed.), *Reading, Analysing and Teaching Literature*, Longman, pp. 161–77.
Carter, R. and P. Stockwell (2008), 'Retrospect and prospect', in R. Carter and P. Stockwell (eds), *The Language and Literature Reader*, Routledge, pp. 291–302.
Chang, W. M. and M. Haugh (2011), 'Strategic embarrassment and face threatening in business interactions', *Journal of Pragmatics*, 43(12), 2948–63, <https://doi.org/10.1016/j.pragma.2011.05.009> (last accessed 23 September 2021).
Chapman, S. and B. Clark (eds) (2019), *Pragmatics and Literature*, Palgrave Macmillan, <https://doi.org/10.1075/lal.35> (last accessed 23 September 2021).
Chomsky, N. (1957), *Syntactic Structures*, Mouton.
Clark, B. (1996), 'Stylistic analysis and relevance theory', *Language and Literature*, 5(3), 163–78, <https://doi.org/10.1177/096394709600500302> (last accessed 23 September 2021).
Clark, B. (2013), *Relevance Theory*, Cambridge University Press, <https://doi.org/10.1017/CBO9781139034104> (last accessed 23 September 2021).
Clark, U. and S. Zyngier (2003), 'Towards a pedagogical stylistics', *Language and Literature*, 12(4), 339–51, <https://doi.org/10.1177/09639470030124003> (last accessed 23 September 2021).
Coffey, L. (2013), *Innocent Until Proven Filthy: A Corpus-Based Critical Stylistic Analysis of Representations of Men in Women's Magazines*, doctoral dissertation, University of Huddersfield.
Collie, J. and S. Slater (1987), *Literature in the Language Classroom: A Resource Book of Ideas and Activities*, Cambridge University Press.
Cook, G. [1992] (2001), *The Discourse of Advertising*, Routledge.
Craig, H. (2004), 'Stylistic analysis and authorship studies', in S. Schreibman, R. Siemens and J. Unsworth (eds), *A Companion to Digital Humanities*, Blackwell Publishing, pp. 273–88.
Culpeper, J. (2002), 'A cognitive stylistic approach to characterization', in E. Semino and J. Culpeper (eds), *Cognitive Stylistics: Language and Cognition in Text Analysis*, John Benjamins, pp. 251–77.
Culpeper, J., M. Short and P. Verdonk (eds) (1998), *Exploring the Language of Drama: From Text to Context*, Routledge.
Dancygier, B. (2006), 'What can blending do for you?', *Language and Literature*, 15(1), pp. 515, <https://doi.org/10.1177/0963947006060549>.
Dickens, C. [1854] (1998), *Hard Times*, Penguin Group.
Dickinson, E. (1998), 'The Brain is Wider than the Sky', in *The Poems of Emily Dickinson: Variorum Edition*, ed. R. W. Franklin, The Belknap Press of Harvard University Press, p. 269.

Enkvist, N. E. (1964), 'On defining style', in N. E. Enkvist, J. Spencer and M. J. Gregory, *Linguistics and Style*, Oxford University Press, pp. 3–56.

Evans, M. (2018), 'Style and chronology: A stylometric investigation of Aphra Behn's dramatic style and the dating of *The Young King*', *Language and Literature*, 27(2), 103–32, <https://doi.org/10.1177/0963947018772505> (last accessed 23 September 2021).

Fish, S. (1970), 'Literature in the reader: Affective stylistics', *New Literary History*, 2(1), 123–62, <https://doi.org/10.2307/468593> (last accessed 23 September 2021).

Fish, S. (1980), *Is There a Text in this Class? The Authority of Interpretative Communities*, Harvard University Press.

Fish, S. (1996), 'What is stylistics and why are they saying such terrible things about it?' [1973], in J. J. Weber (ed.), *The Stylistics Reader from Roman Jakobson to the Present*, Arnold, pp. 94–116.

Forceville, C., E. El Refaie and G. Meesters (2014), 'Stylistics and comics', in M. Burke (ed.), *The Routledge Handbook of Stylistics*, Routledge, pp. 485–99.

Fowler, R. (ed.) (1966), *Essays on Style and Language*, Routledge and Kegan Paul.

Fowler, R. (1971), *The Languages of Literature*, Routledge and Kegan Paul.

Fowler, R. (1991), *Language in the News: Discourse and Ideology in the Press*, Routledge.

Fowler, R., B. Hodge, G. Kress and T. Trew (eds) [1979] (2019), *Language and Control*, Routledge.

Gibbons, A. (2013), 'Multimodal metaphors in contemporary experimental literature', *Metaphor in the Social World*, 3(2), 180–98, <https://doi.org/10.1075/msw.3.2.04gib> (last accessed 23 September 2021).

Gibbons, A. and S. Whiteley (2018), *Contemporary Stylistics: Language, Cognition, Interpretation*, Edinburgh University Press.

Goddard, A. (1998), *The Language of Advertising*, Routledge.

Golding, W. [1954] (1999), *Lord of the Flies*, Penguin Books.

Gregoriou, C. (2009), *English Literary Stylistics*, Palgrave Macmillan.

Grice, H. (1975), 'Logic and conversation', in P. Cole and J. Morgan (eds), *Syntax and Semantics, vol. 3: Speech Acts*, Academic Press, pp. 41–58, <https://doi.org/10.1163/9789004368811_003> (last accessed 23 September 2021).

Hakemulder, J. (2007), 'Tracing foregrounding in responses to film', *Language and Literature*, 16(2), 125–39, <https://doi.org/10.1177/0963947007075980> (last accessed 23 September 2021).

Halliday, M. A. K. (1971), 'Linguistic function and literary style: An inquiry into the language of William Golding's *The Inheritors*', in S. Chatman (ed.), *Literary Style: A Symposium*, Oxford University Press, pp. 330–68.

Halliday, M. A. K. (1985), *Introduction to Functional Grammar*, Edward Arnold.

Halliday, M. A. K. (2003), 'Introduction: On the "architecture" of human language', in J. Webster (ed.), *On Language and Linguistics*, Continuum, pp. 1–29.

Harrison, C. and P. Stockwell (2014), 'Cognitive poetics', in J. Littlemore and J. R. Taylor (eds), *The Bloomsbury Companion to Cognitive Linguistics*, Bloomsbury, pp. 218–33.

Haynes, J. (1995), *Style*, Routledge.

Herman, V. (1998), 'Turn management in drama', in J. Culpepper, M. Short and P. Vedonk (eds), *Exploring the Language of Drama: From Text to Context*, Routledge, pp. 19–33.

Hogan, P. (2014), 'Stylistics, emotion and neuroscience', in M. Burke (ed.), *The Routledge Handbook of Stylistics*, Routledge, pp. 516–30.

Hoover, D. L. (2007), 'Corpus stylistics, stylometry, and the styles of Henry James', *Style*, 41(2), 174–204.

Hoover, D. L., J. Culpeper and K. O'Halloran (2014), *Digital Literary Studies: Corpus Approaches to Poetry, Prose and Drama*, Routledge.

Ibrahim, M. (2018), *The Construction of the Speaker and Fictional World in The Small Mirrors: Critical Stylistic Analysis*, unpublished doctoral dissertation, University of Huddersfield.

Iwamoto, N. (1998), 'Modality and point of view: A contrastive analysis of Japanese wartime and peace time newspaper discourse', in B. Parkinson (ed.), *Edinburgh Working Papers in Applied Linguistics*, University of Edinburgh, pp. 17–41.

Jacobs, G. (1999), *Preformulating the News*, John Benjamins, <https://doi.org/10.1075/pbns.60> (last accessed 23 September 2021).

Jakobson, R. (1960), 'Closing statement: Linguistics and poetics', in T. A. Sebeok (ed.), *Style in Language*, MIT Press, pp. 350–77.

Jeffries, L. (2010), *Critical Stylistics: The Power of English*, Palgrave Macmillan.

Jeffries, L. (2014), 'Critical stylistics', in M. Burke (ed.), *The Routledge Handbook of Stylistics*, Routledge, pp. 408–20.

Jeffries, L. and D. McIntyre (2010), *Stylistics*, Cambridge University Press.

Jeffries, L. and B. Walker (2018), *Keywords in the Press: The New Labour Years*, Bloomsbury.

Jensen, M., K. Lottrup and S. Nordentoft (2018), 'Floral foregrounding: Corpus-assisted, cognitive stylistic study of the foregrounding of flowers in *Mrs Dalloway*', *Globe: A Journal of Language, Culture and Communication*, 7, 34–56.

Kamalu, I. and K. Fasasi (2018), 'Impoliteness and face-threatening acts as conversational strategies among undergraduates of state universities in Southwest Nigeria', *Language Matters: Studies in the Languages of Africa*, 49(2), 23–38, <https://doi.org/10.1080/10228195.2018.1467478> (last accessed 23 September 2021).

Kedveš, A. (2013), 'Face threatening acts and politeness strategies in summer school application calls', *Jezikoslovlje*, 14(2), 431–44.

Kennedy, J. (1982), 'Metaphor in pictures', *Perception*, 11(5), 589–605, <https://doi.org/10.1068/p110589> (last accessed 23 September 2021).

Kilgarriff, A., V. Baisa, J. Bušta, M. Jakubíček, V. Kovář, J. Michelfeit, P. Rychlý and V. Suchomel (2014), 'The Sketch Engine: Ten years on', *Lexicography*, 1, 7–36 <https://doi.org/10.1007/s40607-014-0009-9> (last accessed 23 September 2021).

Kress, G. and T. van Leeuwen [1996] (2006), *Reading Images: The Grammar of Visual Design*, Routledge.

Kumar, S. K. (1974), 'Indian Women', in *Cobwebs in the Sun*, Tata McGraw-Hill, p. 4.

Larkin, P. (2003), 'Wants', in *Collected Poems*, ed. A. Thwaite, Faber and Faber.

Lazar, G. (1993), *Literature and Language Teaching: A Guide for Teachers and Trainers*, Cambridge University Press.

Lecercle, J. J. (1993), 'Briefings, 3: The current state of stylistics', *The European English Messenger*, 2(1), 14–18.

Leech, G. (1983), *Principles of Pragmatics*, Longman.

Leech, G. (1992), 'Pragmatic principles in Shaw's *You Never Can Tell*', in M. Toolan (ed.), *Language, Text and Context*, Routledge, pp. 259–78.

Leech, G. N. [1969] (2007), *A Linguistic Guide to English Poetry*, Longman.

Leech, G. (2008), *Language in Literature: Style and Foregrounding*, Routledge.

Leech, G. and M. Short [1981] (2007), *Style in Fiction*, 2nd edn, Routledge.

Levin, H. J. (1971), *The Invisible Resource*, RFF Press.

Levin, S. R. (1965), 'Internal and external deviation in poetry', *Word*, 21(2), 225–37, <https://doi.org/10.1080/00437956.1965.11435425> (last accessed 23 September 2021).

Lin, B. (2016), 'Functional stylistics', in V. Sotirova (ed.), *The Bloomsbury Companion to Stylistics*, Bloomsbury Academic, pp. 57–77.

Louw, W. (1997), 'The role of corpora in critical literary appreciation', in A. Wichman, S. Fligelstone, T. McEnery and G. Knowles (eds), *Teaching and Language Corpora*, Addison Wesley Longman, pp. 240–51.

Love, H. and J. F. F. Burrows (1998), 'The role of stylistics in attribution: Thomas Shadwell and "The Giants' War"', *Eighteenth Century Life*, 22(1), 18–30.

McIntyre, D. (2008), 'Integrating multimodal analysis and the stylistics of drama: A multimodal perspective on Ian McKellen's *Richard III*', *Language and Literature*, 17(4), 309–34, <https://doi.org/10.1177/0963947008095961> (last accessed 23 September 2021).

McIntyre, D. (2010), 'Dialogue and characterisation in Quentin Tarantino's *Reservoir Dogs*: A corpus stylistic analysis', in D. McIntyre and B. Busse (eds), *Language and Style: Essays in Honour of Mick Short*, Palgrave Macmillan, pp. 162–83.

McIntyre, D. and B. Busse (eds) (2010), *Language and Style: Essays in Honour of Mick Short*, Palgrave Macmillan.

McIntyre, D. and B. Walker (2019), *Corpus Stylistics: Theory and Practice*, Edinburgh University Press.

Mahlberg, M. (2007), 'Corpus stylistics: Bridging the gap between linguistic and literary studies', in M. Hoey, M. Mahlberg, M. Stubbs and W. Teubert (eds), *Text, Discourse and Corpora*, Continuum, pp. 219–46.

Mahlberg, M. (2009), 'Patterns in news stories: A corpus approach to teaching discourse analysis', in L. Lombardo (ed.), *Using Corpora to Learn about Language and Discourse*, Peter Lang, pp. 99–132.

Mahlberg, M. (2010), 'Corpus linguistics and the study of nineteenth-century fiction', *Journal of Victorian Culture*, 15(2), 292–8, <https://doi.org/10.1080/13555502.2010.491667> (last accessed 23 September 2021).

Mahlberg, M. (2013a), 'Corpus analysis of literary texts', in C. A. Chapelle (ed.), *The Encyclopedia of Applied Linguistics*, Wiley-Blackwell, <https://doi.org/10.1002/9781405198431.wbeal0249> (last accessed 23 September 2021).

Mahlberg, M. (2013b), *Corpus Stylistics and Dickens's Fiction*, Routledge.

Mahlberg, M. (2014), 'Corpus stylistics', in M. Burke (ed.), *The Routledge Handbook of Stylistics*, Routledge, pp. 378–92.

Miall, D. S. and D. Kuiken (1994), 'Foregrounding, defamiliarization, and affect: Response to literary stories', *Poetics*, 22(5), 389–407, <https://doi.org/10.1016/0304-422X(94)00011-5>.

Milic, L. (1967), *Style and Stylistics*, Free Press.

Mills, S. (1995), *Feminist Stylistics*, Routledge.

Montoro, R. (2012), *Chick Lit: The Stylistics of Cappuccino Fiction*, Continuum.

Montoro, R. (2014), 'Feminist stylistics', in M. Burke (ed.), *The Routledge Handbook of Stylistics*, Routledge, pp. 346–61.

Moya Guijarro, A. J. and M. J. Pinar Sanz (2008), 'Compositional, interpersonal and representational meanings in a children's narrative: A multimodal discourse analysis', *Journal of Pragmatics*, 40(9), 1601–19, <https://doi.org/10.1016/j.pragma.2008.04.019> (last accessed 23 September 2021).

Murphy, S. (2015), '*I will proclaim myself what I am*: Corpus stylistics and the language of Shakespeare's soliloquies', *Language and Literature*, 24(4), 338–54, <https://doi.org/10.1177/0963947015598183> (last accessed 23 September 2021).

Newmark, P. (1988), *A Textbook of Translation*, Prentice-Hall International.

Nørgaard, N. (2003), *Systemic Functional Linguistics and Literary Analysis: A Hallidayan Approach to Joyce – A Joycean Approach to Halliday*, University Press of Southern Denmark.

Nørgaard, N. (2009), 'The semiotics of typography in literary texts: A multimodal approach', *Orbis Litterarum*, 64(2), 141–60, <https://doi.org/10.1111/j.1600-0730.2008.00949.x> (last accessed 23 September 2021).

Nørgaard, N. (2010), 'Multimodality and the literary text: Making sense of Jonathan Safran Foer's *Extremely Loud and Incredibly Close*', in R. Page (ed.), *New Perspectives on Narrative and Multimodality*, Routledge, pp. 115–26.

Nørgaard, N. (2014), 'Multimodality and stylistics', in M. Burke (ed.), *The Routledge Companion to Stylistics*, Routledge, pp. 471–84.

Nørgaard, N. (2019), *Multimodal Stylistics of the Novel: More than Words*, Routledge.

Nørgaard, N., R. Monotor and B. Busse (2010), *Key Terms in Stylistics*, Continuum.

O'Connor, M. (1976), *Reef Poems*, University of Queensland Press.

O'Halloran, K. (2007), 'The subconscious in James Joyce's "Eveline": A corpus stylistic analysis that chews on the "Fish hook"', *Language and Literature*, 16(3), 227–44, <https://doi.org/10.1177/0963947007072847> (last accessed 23 September 2021).

Ohmann, R. (1964), 'Generative grammars and the concept of literary style', *WORD*, 20(3), 423–39, <https://doi.org/10.1080/00437956.1964.11659831> (last accessed 23 September 2021).

Ohmann, R. (1966), 'Literature as sentences', *College English*, 27(4), 261–7.

Pearce, M. (2008), 'Investigating the collocational behaviour of MAN and WOMAN in the BNC using Sketch Engine', *Corpora*, 3(1), 1–29. <https://doi.org/10.3366/E174950320800004X> (last accessed 23 September 2021).

Peck, J. and M. Coyle (1995), *Practical Criticism: How to Write a Critical Appreciation*, Palgrave Macmillan.

Pop, A. (2010), 'Implicatures derived through maxim flouting in print advertising: A contrastive empirical approach', *Toronto Working Papers in Linguistics*, 33(1).

Radzi, N. S. M. and M. Musa (2017), 'Beauty ideals, myths and sexisms: A feminist stylistic analysis of female representations in cosmetic names', *GEMA Online® Journal of Language Studies*, 17(1), 21–38, <http://doi.org/10.17576/gema-2017-1701-02> (last accessed 23 September 2021).

Rich, A. (2003), 'Song', in *Collected Poems 1950–2012*, intro. C. Rankine, W. W. Norton, pp. 369–70.

Richards, I. A. (1929), *Practical Criticism: A Study of Literary Judgment*, Harcourt Brace Jovanovich.

Ringrow, H. and S. Pihlaja (2020), *Contemporary Media Stylistics: Contemporary Studies in Linguistics*, Bloomsbury Academic.

Ross, G. (1998), *The Language of Humour*, Routledge.

Searle, J. (1969), *Speech Acts*, Cambridge University Press.

Semino, E. and J. Culpeper (eds) (2002), *Cognitive Stylistics: Language and Cognition in Text Analysis*, John Benjamins, <https://doi.org/10.1075/lal.1> (last accessed 23 September 2021).

Semino, E. and M. Short (2004), *Corpus Stylistics: Speech, Writing, and Thought Presentation in a Corpus of English Writing*, Routledge.

Seo, S. (2013), 'Hallidayean transitivity analysis: The Battle for Tripoli in the contrasting headlines of two national newspapers', *Discourse and Society*, 24(6), 774–91, <https://doi.org/10.1177/0957926513503267> (last accessed 23 September 2021).

Shakespeare, W. [1605] (2004), *King Lear*, Simon & Schuster.

Shaw, B. [1916] (2004), *Pygmalion and Three Other Plays*, intro. and notes J. A. Bertolini, Barnes & Noble Classics.

Shklovsky, V. [1917] (1965), 'Art as technique', in *Russian Formalist Criticism: Four Essays*, trans. and intro. L. T. Lemon and M. J. Reis, University of Nebraska Press, pp. 5–24.

Shklovsky, V. [1925] (1991), *Theory of Prose*, trans. B. Sher, Dalkey Archive Press.

Short, M. (ed.) (1989), *Reading, Analysing and Teaching Literature*, Longman.

Short, M. [1996] (2014), *Exploring the Language of Poems, Plays and Prose*, 2nd edn, Routledge.

Short, M. and Candlin, C. (1989), 'Teaching study skills for English literature', in M. Short (ed.), *Reading, Analysing and Teaching Literature*, Longman, pp. 178–203.

Simpson, P. (1988), 'The transitivity model', *Critical Studies in Mass Communication*, 5(2), 166–72, <https://doi.org/10.1080/15295038809366696> (last accessed 23 September 2021).

Simpson, P. (1993), *Language, Ideology and Point of View*, Routledge.

Simpson, P. [2004] (2014), *Stylistics: A Resource Book for Students*, 2nd edn, Routledge.

Sopčák, P. (2007), 'Creation from nothing: A foregrounding study of James Joyce's drafts for Ulysses', *Language and Literature*, 16(2), 183–96, <https://doi.org/10.1177/0963947007075984>.

Sperber, D. and D. Wilson (1986), *Relevance*, Harvard University Press.

Sperber, D. and D. Wilson (1995), *Relevance: Communication and Cognition*, 2nd edn, Blackwell.

Starcke, B. (2006), 'The phraseology of Jane Austen's *Persuasion*: Phraseological units as carriers of meaning', *ICAME Journal*, 30, 87–104.

Steen, G. (1994), *Understanding Metaphor in Literature: An Empirical Approach*, Longman.

Stockwell, P. (2002), *Cognitive Poetics: An Introduction*, Routledge.

Stockwell, P. (2015), 'Cognitive stylistics', in R. Jones (ed.), *The Routledge Handbook of Language and Creativity*, Routledge.

Stubbs, M. (1996), *Text and Corpus Analysis: Computer-Assisted Studies of Language and Culture*, Blackwell.

Stubbs, M. (2005), 'Conrad in the computer: Examples of quantitative stylistic methods', *Language and Literature*, 14(1), 5–24, <https://doi.org/10.1177/0963947005048873> (last accessed 23 September 2021).

Sunderland, J. (2011), *Language, Gender and Children's Fiction*, Continuum.

Taguchi, N. (2002), 'An application of relevance theory to the analysis of L2 interpretation processes: The comprehension of indirect replies', *International Review of Applied Linguistics in Language Teaching*, 40(2), 151–76, <https://doi.org/10.1515/iral.2002.006> (last accessed 23 September 2021).

The White House, Office of the Press Secretary (2011a), 'Statement by the President on events in Tunisia', press release, 14 January, <https://obamawhitehouse.archives.

gov/the-press-office/2011/01/14/statement-president-events-tunisia> (last accessed 23 September 2021).
The White House, Office of the Press Secretary (2011b), 'Statement by the President on Libya sanctions', press release, 25 February, <https://obamawhitehouse.archives.gov/the-press-office/2011/02/25/statement-president-libya-sanctions> (last accessed 23 September 2021).
Thorne, C. (1965), *Ideology and Power*, Collier-Macmillan.
Thorne, J. P. (1970), 'Generative grammar and syntactic analysis', in J. Lyons (ed.), *New Horizons in Linguistics*, vol. 1, Penguin Books, pp. 185–97.
Toolan, M. (2014), 'Stylistics and film', in M. Burke (ed.), *The Routledge Handbook of Stylistics*, Routledge, pp. 455–70.
Torday, P. (2011), *Salmon Fishing in the Yemen*, Orion Publishing Group.
Trimarco, P. (2014), *Digital Textuality*, Palgrave Macmillan.
Tsur, R. [1992] (2008), *Toward a Theory of Cognitive Poetics*, 2nd edn, Sussex Academic Press.
van Peer, W. (2007), 'Introduction to foregrounding: A state of the art', *Language and Literature*, 16(2), 99–104, <https://doi.org/10.1177/0963947007075978> (last accessed 23 September 2021).
van Peer, W. and J. Hakemulder (2006), 'Foregrounding', in K. Brown (ed.), *Encyclopedia of Language and Linguistics*, vol. 4, 2nd edn, Elsevier, pp. 546–50.
Vendler, H. (1966), 'Review of *Essays on Style and Language* by Roger Fowler', *Essays in Criticism*, 16, 458–60.
Verdonk, P. (2002), *Stylistics*, Oxford University Press.
Wales, K. [1990] (2011), *A Dictionary of Stylistics*, 3rd edn, Pearson.
Walker, B. (2011), 'Character and characterisation in Julian Barnes's *Talking It Over*: A corpus stylistic analysis', unpublished doctoral dissertation, Lancaster University.
Weber, J. J. (ed.) (1996a), *The Stylistics Reader from Roman Jakobson to the Present*, Arnold.
Weber, J. J. (1996b), 'Towards contextualized stylistics: An overview', in J. J. Weber (ed.), *The Stylistics Reader from Roman Jakobson to the Present*, Arnold, pp. 1–8.
Werth, P. (1999), *Text World: Representing Conceptual Space in Discourse*, Longman.
Whitman, W. (1995), 'I Sit and Look Out', in *The Complete Works of Walt Whitman*, intro. and notes S. Matterson, Wordsworth Editions, p. 205.
Widdowson, H. G. (1975), *Stylistics and the Teaching of Literature*, Longman.
Widdowson, H. G. (1983), 'The deviant language of poetry', in C. J. Brumfit (ed.), *Teaching Literature Overseas: Language-Based Approaches*, Pergamon Press, pp. 7–16.
Widdowson, H. G. (1992), *Practical Stylistics*, Oxford University Press.
Wilson, D. (2018), 'Relevance theory and literary interpretation', in T. Cave and D. Wilson (eds), *Reading Beyond the Code: Literature and Relevance Theory*, Oxford University Press, pp. 185–204.
Wilson, D. and D. Sperber (1994), 'Outline of relevance theory', *Links & Letters*, 1, 85–106, <https://doi.org/10.7146/hjlcb.v3i5.21436> (last accessed 23 September 2021).
Wilson, D. and D. Sperber (2004), 'Relevance theory', in L. R. Horn and G. Ward (eds), *The Handbook of Pragmatics*, Blackwell, pp. 607–32.
Wynne, M. (2006), 'Stylistics: Corpus approaches', in K. Brown (ed.), *Encyclopedia of Language and Linguistics*, vol. 12, 2nd edn, Elsevier, pp. 223–6.

Yus, F. (2003), 'Humor and the search for relevance', *Journal of Pragmatics*, 35, 1295–331, <https://doi.org/10.1016/S0378-2166(02)00179-0> (last accessed 23 September 2021).

Yus, F. (2016), 'Relevance theory and contextual sources-centred analysis of irony: Current research and compatibility', in M. P. Cruz (ed.), *Relevance Theory: Recent Developments, Current Challenges and Future Directions*, John Benjamins Publishing, pp. 147–71, <https://doi.org/10.1075/pbns.268> (last accessed 23 September 2021).

Yus Ramos, F. (1998), 'Relevance theory and media discourse: A verbal-visual model of communication', *Poetics*, 25(5), 293–309, <https://doi.org/10.1016/S0304-422X(97)00020-X> (last accessed 23 September 2021).

Zyngier, S. and O. Fialho (2016), 'Pedagogical stylistics: Charting outcomes', in V. Sotirova (ed.), *The Bloomsbury Companion to Stylistics*, Bloomsbury Academic, pp. 208–30.

INDEX

advertisements, 87–8, 90–8
affective stylistics, 132, 148, 178
alliteration, 178
AntConc, 113, 119
assonance, 178

checklist
   corpus stylistic, 113
   critical linguistic, 44
   critical stylistic, 102–3
   feminist stylistic, 55
   formalist stylistic, 27
   functionalist stylistic, 36–7
   multimodal stylistic, 89–90
   pragmatic stylistic, 65
   relevance theoretic, 78
clause, 15, 178
close reading, 128–9, 178–9
cognitive linguistics, 136
cognitive poetics, 77, 179
cognitive stylistics, 77–8, 136–7, 179
cohesion of foregrounding, 19, 179
collocation, 16, 114–18, 179
compositional meaning, 89–90, 92, 95
computational linguistics, 137, 179
conceptual blending, 179
conceptual metaphor theory, 179
conversational implicatures, 64, 179
cooperative principle, 136, 179–80
corpus, 112, 114, 119–20, 137–8, 180
   Arabic Web 2012 (arTenTen12), 113–14, 119
   British National Corpus (BNC), 112, 119, 137–8
   Brown Corpus, 137

COBUILD, 137
Corpus of Contemporary American English (COCA), 112, 120
English Web 2018 (enTenTen18), 113–14, 119
Lancaster, Oslo, and Bergen (LOB) Corpus, 137
Survey of English Usage Corpus, 137
corpus linguistics, 111–12, 137–8, 180
corpus software
   Antconc, 113, 119
   Sketch Engine, 112–19, 120
   WordSmith, 113, 120, 138
corpus stylistics, 111–21, 138, 180
critical discourse analysis, 101, 135, 140, 180
critical linguistics, 42–52, 134–5
critical stylistics, 100–9, 140–1, 180

defamiliarisation, 26–7, 125–6, 180
deixis, 107, 180
deviation, 13–18, 26–7, 180
   discoursal, 17–18, 29–30
   graphological, 17, 130
   morphological, 14–15, 130
   phonological, 130
   semantic, 15–16, 28–9, 130
   syntactic, 15–16, 29, 130
dialect, 5–7, 180
   ethnic, 6–7
   regional, 6
   social, 6
   temporal, 7
discoursal deviation, 17–18, 29–30
discourse, 17, 180
discourse stylistics, 136, 181

equating and contrasting, 101–2, 107
ethnic dialect, 6–7
   African American Verancular English (AAVE), 6, 11
   General American English (GAE), 6, 11
exemplifying and enumerating, 102
existential presupposition, 103, 181

face, 64–5, 181
   negative, 64–5
   positive, 65
feminist stylistics, 53–61, 135, 181
field, 7–8, 10, 181
floor, 64, 68
foregrounding, 18, 26–7, 181
formalist stylistics, 25–33, 125–6, 148, 181
functionalist stylistics, 35–41, 133–4, 148, 181

generative grammar, 130, 181
generative stylistics, 130–1, 181
genre, 181
   advertising, 87–8
   drama, 63–4
   fiction, 42–3, 53–4
   linguistic humour, 76–7
   online journalism, 111–12
   poetry, 25–6
   political discourse, 100–1
graphological deviation, 17, 130
graphology, 17, 181

hypothesising, 102, 107

ideology, 36, 53, 100–1, 134–5, 140–1, 182
implicature, 64, 182
   conversational implicatures, 64, 179
implying and assuming, 102, 107
interactive meaning, 88–9, 91–2, 95

lexical semantics, 16, 182
linguistic stylistics, 131, 182
literariness, 26, 126, 182
literary criticism, 127–8, 147
logical presupposition, 103, 182

maxims of conversation, 64, 70–1, 182
metre, 183
modality, 43–4, 46–8, 183
mode, 8–10, 183
morpheme, 14–15, 183
morphological deviation, 14–15, 130
morphology, 14–15, 183
multimodal stylistics, 87–98, 139–40, 183
musicology, 183

naming and describing, 101, 104
negating, 102
neologism, 14, 183
new criticism, 128–9, 183
nominalisation, 101, 104, 183

parallelism, 13–14, 18, 27, 130
pedagogical stylistics, 132, 183
phonological deviation, 130
phrase, 15, 183
politeness, 64, 184
politeness markers, 4
practical criticism, 128–9, 184
pragmatic stylistics, 63–75, 136, 184
Prague school structuralists, 18, 125–6, 184
presentation of speech, 44, 102
presentation of thought, 44, 102
presupposition, 182
   existential presupposition, 103, 181
   logical presupposition, 103, 182
principle of relevance, 77–8, 136, 184
prioritising, 102, 106

reader response stylistics, 132, 184
regional dialect, 6
   American English, 6
   British English, 6
register, 5, 7–10, 184
relevance theory, 76–86, 136–7, 185
repetition, 13–14, 27
representational meaning, 88–9, 91, 94–5
representing actions/events/states, 101, 105–6
representing time/space/society, 102, 107
rhyme, 185
rhythm, 185
Russian formalism, 18, 125–6, 129–30, 185

schema theory, 136, 185
semantic deviation, 15–16, 28–9, 130
semantics, 16, 185
semiotics, 185
sentence, 15
   complex, 15, 179
   compound, 15, 179
   simple, 15, 185
sketch engine, 112–19, 120
slang, 185
social dialect, 6
   Cockney, 6
   British Standard English (BrSE), 6, 11
sociolect, 6, 185
speech act theory, 135, 186
speech acts, 69–70, 185–6
   bald on record, 70, 178

speech community, 186
speech situation, 186
stanza, 186
style, 3–5, 125, 186
    as choice, 12–13
    as deviation, 13–19
    as social meaning, 11
    high-considerateness, 71, 182
    high-involvement, 71, 182
stylistics, 3–5, 127, 129–41, 147–52, 186
    cognitive, 77–8, 137, 179
    corpus, 111–21, 138, 180
    critical, 100–9, 140–1, 180
    feminist, 53–61, 135, 181
    formalist, 25–33, 125–6, 148, 181
    functionalist, 35–41, 133–4, 148, 181
    multimodal, 87–98, 139–40, 183
    pragmatic, 63–75, 136, 184

syntactic deviation, 15–16, 29, 130
syntax, 15, 186
systemic functional linguistics, 35, 133, 139, 141, 149, 186

temporal dialect, 7
    Early Modern English, 7
    Modern English, 7
tenor, 8, 10, 186
text world theory, 186–7
transformational generative grammar, 131
transitivity, 36, 38, 40–1, 134–5, 187
turn-management, 64, 68–9, 187
typography, 187

vector, 187
visual grammar, 88–90, 139

WordSmith, 113, 120, 138

EU representative:
Easy Access System Europe
Mustamäe tee 50, 10621 Tallinn, Estonia
Gpsr.requests@easproject.com

www.ingramcontent.com/pod-product-compliance
Lightning Source LLC
Chambersburg PA
CBHW080548230426
43663CB00015B/2759